100 YEARS
OF BENTLEY

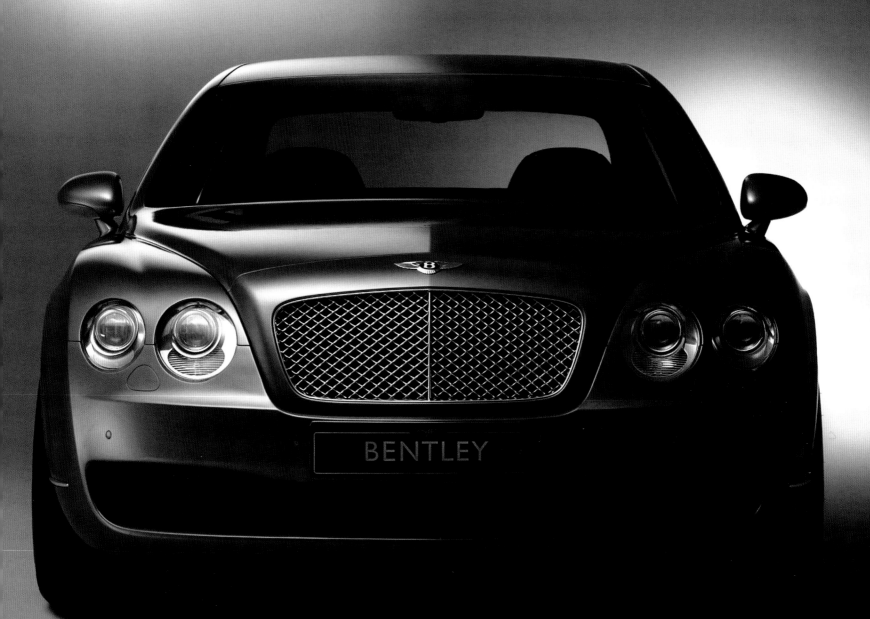

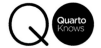

Brimming with creative inspiration, how-to projects and useful information to enrich your everyday life, Quarto Knows is a favourite destination for those pursuing their interests and passions. Visit our site and dig deeper with our books into your area of interest: Quarto Creates, Quarto Cooks, Quarto Homes, Quarto Lives, Quarto Drives, Quarto Explores, Quarto Gifts, or Quarto Kids.

First published in 2019 by White Lion Publishing,
an imprint of The Quarto Group.
The Old Brewery, 6 Blundell Street,
London, N7 9BH,
United Kingdom
T (0)20 7700 6700
www.QuartoKnows.com

A catalogue record for this book is available from the British Library.

ISBN 978 1 78131 915 4
Ebook ISBN 978 1 78131 954 3

10 9 8 7 6 5 4 3 2 1

Edited by Nick Freeth
Designed by Paul Turner and Sue Pressley, Stonecastle Graphics Ltd

Printed in China

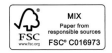

MIX
Paper from
responsible sources
FSC   FSC® C016973
www.fsc.org

100 YEARS OF BENTLEY

Andrew Noakes

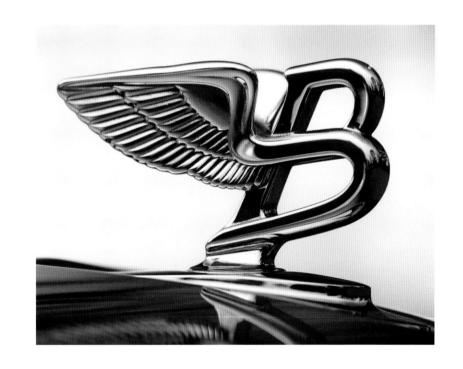

WHITE
LION
PUBLISHING

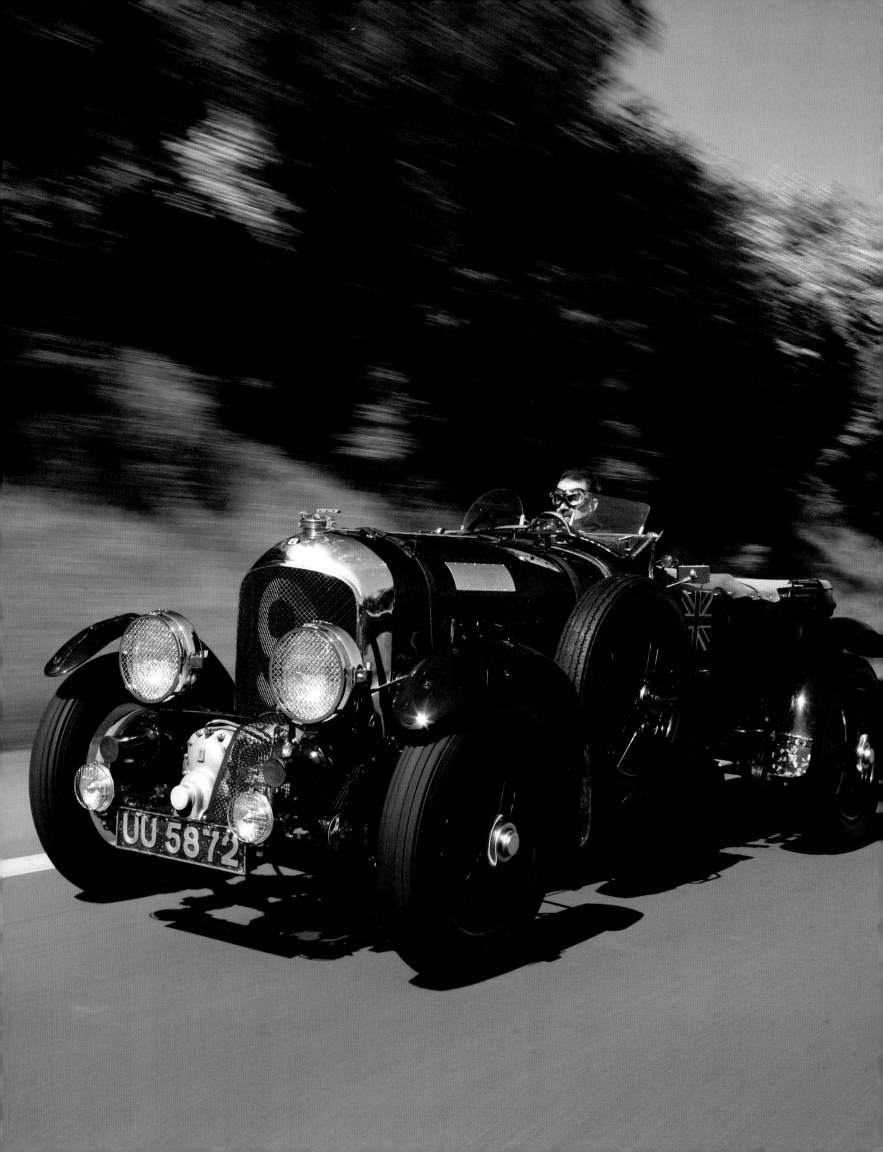

CONTENTS

FOREWORD

This book provides a remarkable insight into the motivation and achievements of a man who made a unique contribution to the development of internal combustion engines and elegant, high-performance cars. W.O. Bentley lived a roller-coaster of a life: even during his early apprenticeship with the Great Northern Railway in Doncaster, he was already deeply involved in the world of motorcycles as an owner, rider, competitor, and innovator who used every trick in the book (and some of his own!) to extract maximum speed and performance from his machines. He then began to apply his growing expertise to motor cars, and, after working on aero engines in the First World War – an aspect of his career that is often overlooked, though he himself regarded it as crucial – set up Bentley Motors in 1919. The company's superlative vehicles with their iconic 'Winged B' mascots, and the fame and publicity attracted by the 'Bentley Boys' – most notably at the gruelling Le Mans 24-hour race in the 1920s – have ensured the immortality of the Bentley name; however, W.O.'s bold commercial venture fell into financial difficulties that were largely beyond his control, and by the mid-1930s, his personal involvement with it had ceased.

But what a testament it is to the engineering quality of his cars that, of the 3,023 of them produced between 1919 and 1931, more than half still exist. Over 60% of these survivors belong to members of our Bentley Drivers Club, who can be found in 46 countries; while our associated charity, the W.O. Bentley Memorial Foundation, is privileged to be the custodian of W.O.'s heritage. It looks after a huge volume of historical documents and artefacts at its headquarters and museum at Wroxton, near Banbury in Oxfordshire. Holding records of every chassis ever built by Bentley in its extensive library, plus an enormous range of original parts, designs and drawings, it is able to deal with enquiries not only from the Club's members, but from anyone researching the history of the marque or seeking information about specific cars, old and new.

For, of course, the Bentley story certainly didn't end with W.O.'s departure – or even with his death in 1971. BDC members also possess a wide range of later models, including those produced by Rolls-Royce, and, over the past twenty years, by Bentley Motors Ltd under the stewardship of the Volkswagen Audi Group. W.O. himself, always the most modest of men, is known to have expressed amazement that cars bearing his name were still being made, and were so treasured by their owners; and we feel sure that he would have been as delighted and thrilled as we are by these more recent Bentleys' extraordinary technical advances.

So what of the next 100 years? In its closing pages, Andrew's book mentions the challenges that all motor car designers and manufacturers are now facing, as the world demands cleaner, quieter, more energy-efficient and, imminently, self-driving ('autonomous') vehicles. It's now some 250 years since the first steam-powered car was developed by French inventor Nicolas Cugnot, nearly 190 years since the creation, by Scotsman Robert Anderson, of the first, crude electric vehicle, and almost 150 years since the first internal combustion engine was built...and we seem to be witnessing the beginning of the end for petrol- and diesel-powered vehicles, despite their high levels of efficiency and practicality. Will the Bentleys being sold in fifty years' time stimulate as much passion among owners and spectators as those that we're currently still able to drive on our public roads? Or will today's fossil-fuel-powered beasts go the way of the steam engines that first fired the young W.O.'s imagination, and will children born in the 2020s be denied the thrill of flooring the accelerator pedal on a piece of mechanical art and hearing the roar of a 'real' engine? Who can say? But whatever may be in store, clubs like ours, and books like this one, have a major role to play in preserving the Bentley legacy, and making sure that the attainments, excitements and innovations of the petrol-engine era are kept alive for future generations.

Ron Warmington   Ken Lea

Chairman   Chairman
Bentleys Drivers Club   W.O. Bentley Memorial Foundation

INTRODUCTION

Bentley is one of Britain's greatest motoring marques. The winged B badge is internationally famous: it adorns some of the world's finest and fastest cars, steeped in more than 100 years of history.

W.O. Bentley trained as a railway engineer, but was excited by the potential of the motor car as it gradually gained acceptance immediately before the First World War. After racing and improving French DFP cars, and his wartime work on aero engines, he set up a company bearing his own name in Cricklewood in 1919. The cars he built were fast, innovative and impeccably made, and they became extraordinarily successful in the early years of the Le Mans 24-hour race – despite W.O.'s misgivings about entering such a gruelling event. They succeeded because they were both fast and strong: Ettore Bugatti, who built delicate, lightweight sports cars, famously called Bentleys the world's fastest lorries.

The design of the first 3 Litre car was refined and adapted to produce the 6½ Litre, 4½ Litre, the famous supercharged 4½ Litre 'Blower' and the 8 Litre – a vast limousine that was a serious rival for the best that Rolls-Royce could offer. But despite the on-track successes of the 'Bentley Boys', and the quality of the cars Bentley built for the road, the company struggled to make a profit. Gentleman racer Woolf Barnato propped up Bentley Motors for a few years, but when his patience wore thin Bentley was taken over by one of its biggest rivals – Rolls-Royce.

The Cricklewood factory was shut down and Rolls-Royce created a new range of Bentleys in Derby. Then after the Second World War Rolls-Royce and Bentley car production was relocated to a former Spitfire engine factory in Crewe. There the company built a string of rapid and refined cars, including the iconic R-type Continental, but gradually Bentleys lost their individuality and became little more than Rolls-Royces with different radiator grilles. Production dwindled to almost nothing.

Bentley's resurgence began in 1982 with the introduction of the Mulsanne Turbo, and then the Turbo R. Sales rose as Bentleys became more distinct from Rolls-Royces, and there were new models like the Continental R and Azure that had no Rolls-Royce equivalents.

After a messy battle for control, BMW acquired the rights to Rolls-Royce, and Volkswagen took over Bentley and the Crewe factory. The new Continental GT, powered by an intriguing W12 engine, became the brand's most successful car and spawned a convertible and a four-door saloon, the Flying Spur, together with the even faster Speed and Supersports models and a host of special editions. There was also a grand new-generation Mulsanne, and Bentley returned to Le Mans with a three-year programme which ended in an emotional victory.

As the company celebrates its centenary it has introduced a new Continental GT and the controversial Bentayga SUV – and a new era of electrified cars that will be capable of outperforming their petrol-engined predecessors is on the horizon. It will be fascinating to see how Crewe blends the technology of tomorrow with the tradition, craftsmanship and character that Bentley is famous for.

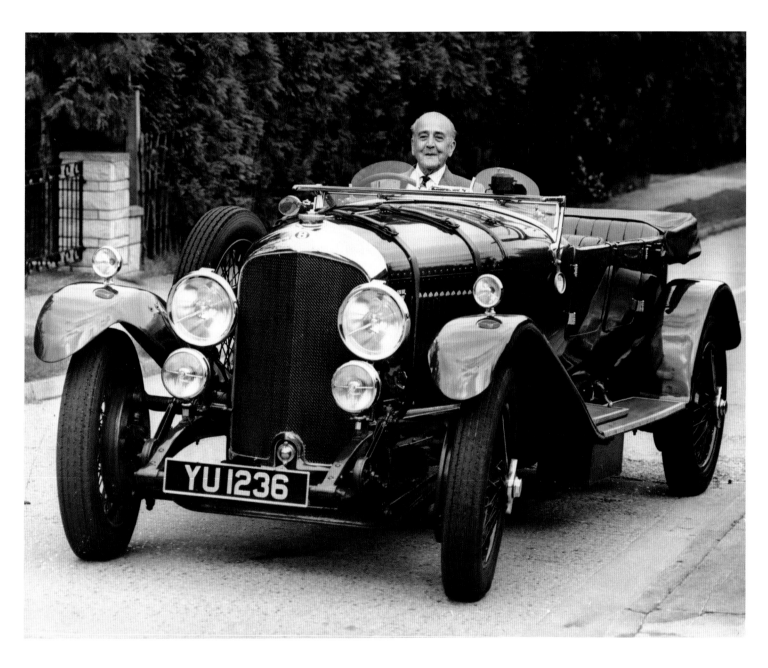

Above: W.O. Bentley in the 1960s at the wheel of one of the many iconic, elegantly powerful cars that bears his name – a 1927 4½ Litre.

BENTLEY TIMELINE

1888	W.O. Bentley born
1912	W.O. joins DFP distributor Lecoq and Fernie
1919	Bentley Motors founded and first car built
1920	First Bentley 3 Litre tested by *Autocar*
1921	First Bentley customer chassis delivered
1923	John Duff enters 3 Litre into the first Le Mans 24-hour race
1924	3 Litre wins Le Mans 24-hours
1925	6½ Litre launched
1926	Woolf Barnato takes over ownership of Bentley Motors
1927	3 Litre wins Le Mans 24-hours; 4½ Litre introduced
1928	Supercharged 4½ Litre 'Blower' unveiled
1929	Speed Six wins Le Mans 24-hours
1930	Barnato beats Blue Train across France in a Bentley Speed Six; Speed Six wins Le Mans 24-hours
1930	8 Litre and 4 Litre developed
1931	Bentley Motors taken over by Rolls-Royce
1933	3½ Litre introduced
1935	W.O. Bentley leaves Bentley Motors for Lagonda
1936	4¼ Litre introduced
1938	'Embiricos' Bentley built
1939	MkV announced
1946	Bentley moves to Crewe and introduces MkVI
1952	Continental and R-type introduced
1955	S-type introduced
1957	Flying Spur introduced
1959	S2 with V8 engine unveiled
1962	S3 introduced
1965	T-type announced
1971	Rolls-Royce and Bentley car company separated from Rolls-Royce aero engine company

Above: 1938 'Embiricos' Bentley

1975	Camargue introduced – only two Bentleys made
1977	T2 introduced
1979	Vickers takes over Rolls-Royce and Bentley
1980	Mulsanne replaces T2
1982	Mulsanne Turbo introduced
1983	Mulsanne Turbo R and Eight introduced
1984	Corniche renamed Continental
1985	Project 90 displayed at Geneva Motor Show
1991	Continental R unveiled
1992	Brooklands replaces Eight and Mulsanne
1994	Java concept unveiled
1995	Azure replaces Continental
1996	Continental T unveiled
1997	Vickers announces Rolls-Royce and Bentley are for sale
1998	Arnage introduced; Volkswagen buys Bentley
1999	Hunaudières concept unveiled; Bentley racing programme started
2000	Arnage Red Label re-introduces Bentley V8 engine
2002	State Limousine presented to HM The Queen; Continental GT introduced
2003	Speed 8 wins Le Mans 24-hours
2005	Flying Spur introduced
2006	Second-generation Azure and Continental GTC introduced; Continental GTZ project begins
2009	Mulsanne unveiled
2011	Second-generation Continental GT introduced
2012	V8 engine added to Continental GT; GT3 and EXP 9F concepts unveiled
2015	Bentayga introduced
2016	EXP 10 Speed 6 concept unveiled
2017	Third-generation Continental GT introduced; diesel engine added to Bentayga range
2018	New-generation Continental GT3 makes race debut; Bentayga hybrid introduced

Above: 2018 Continental GT

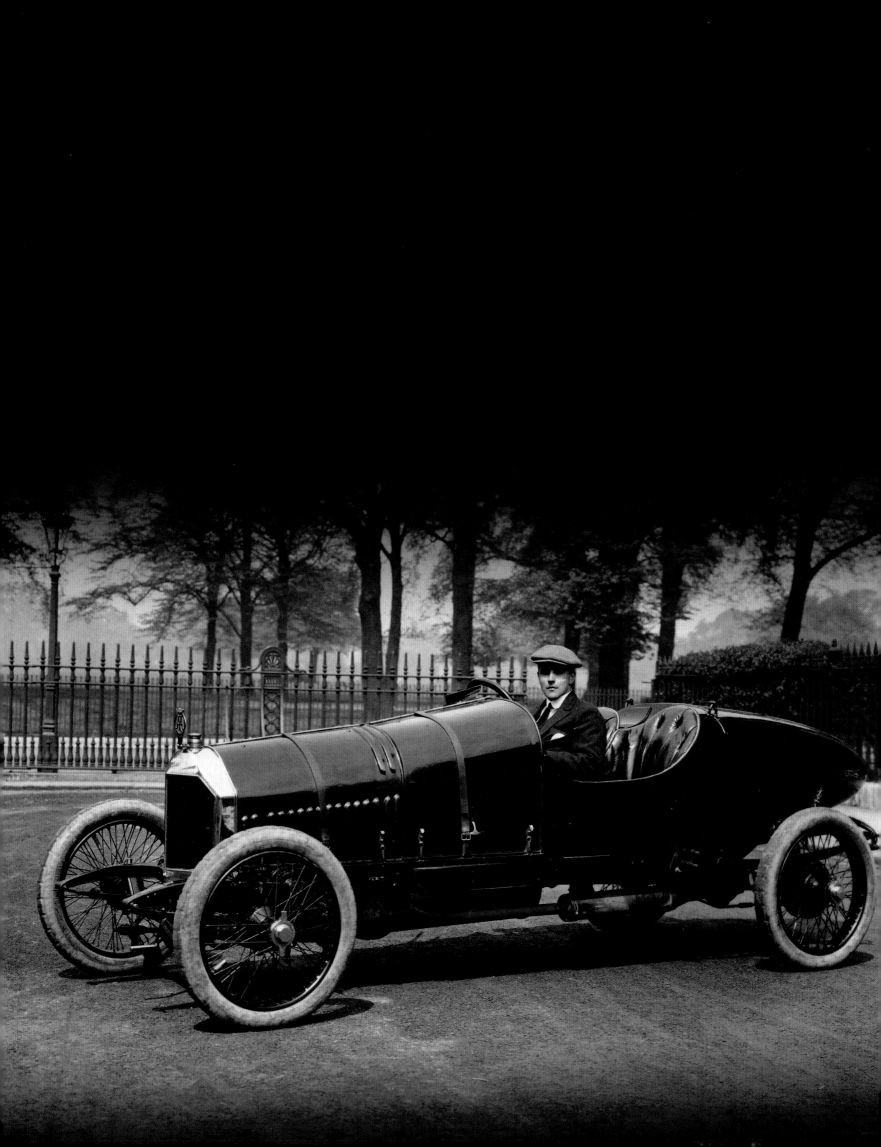

Chapter 1

W.O. BENTLEY

He never liked the name Walter. The boy who grew up to be the founder of the Bentley motor car company was born on 16 September 1888 and was given the names Walter Owen by his parents, but as soon as he had the choice he discarded both names in favour of the initials. Everyone knew him simply as W.O.

The family was a wealthy one. W.O.'s grandfather had built up a successful business dealing in silks and woollens in his native Yorkshire, and had come to London just before the birth of his son, Alfred. In due course Alfred entered the family business, and in 1874 he married Emily Waterhouse. Emily's father Thomas also hailed from Yorkshire, and had moved to Australia to make a fortune in mining and banking before retiring to England.

W.O. was the youngest of Alfred and Emily's nine surviving children (Emily Maud, born in 1879, died when she was four months old), and was a shy boy, nicknamed 'the Bun' on account of his round face and dark, currant-like eyes. He was obsessed with steam engines: when he wasn't playing with his own stationary engine or his clockwork train set, he was agitating to be taken from the Bentley family home in north London to the station at South Hampstead to watch the London and North Western Railway express trains roar in and out of Euston. This early obsession with mechanical things would go on to shape his future career.

Young W.O.'s early education was at Lambrook School near Ascot, and later Clifton College in Bristol, where he was most comfortable with science subjects. He excelled at cricket, proving to be a fine opening batsman and slip fielder, and in his spare time he became interested in photography, acquiring an early Kodak Brownie camera. In 1905, at the age of 16, W.O. moved from Clifton College to King's College in London for a course in engineering theory, and from there headed north to Doncaster to take up a premium apprenticeship with the Great Northern Railway, which cost the Bentley family £75.

Apprentices had a tough time at the Doncaster works. They were expected to be on duty for five and a half days a week, starting at 6 a.m. each day and working a sixty-hour week. At first the tasks given to W.O. and his fellow first-year apprentices were laborious and relatively unskilled jobs such as finishing connecting rods for the steam locomotives, which meant hours of shaping and polishing using only hand tools. After a period of dirty, dangerous work in the foundry where locomotive cylinders and other parts were cast from molten iron, W.O. moved on to the erecting shop where engines were assembled; this finally gave him the chance to work on the steam locomotives he had admired for so long. In the erecting shop, jobs ranged from the precise and relatively clean work of fitting those hand-finished connecting rods to the wheels of a locomotive to dirty, difficult maintenance tasks like removing an engine blast pipe, which inevitably meant ending up covered in soot. It was often tough, grimy work, but Bentley seems to have appreciated the necessity of it and approached it with a certain stoicism.

The final part of W.O.'s apprenticeship would for him have been the most exciting, as he was required to gain experience on the footplate of a railway locomotive. For this he left Doncaster in 1909 to return to London. Based at King's Cross, his first duty was to act as second fireman on

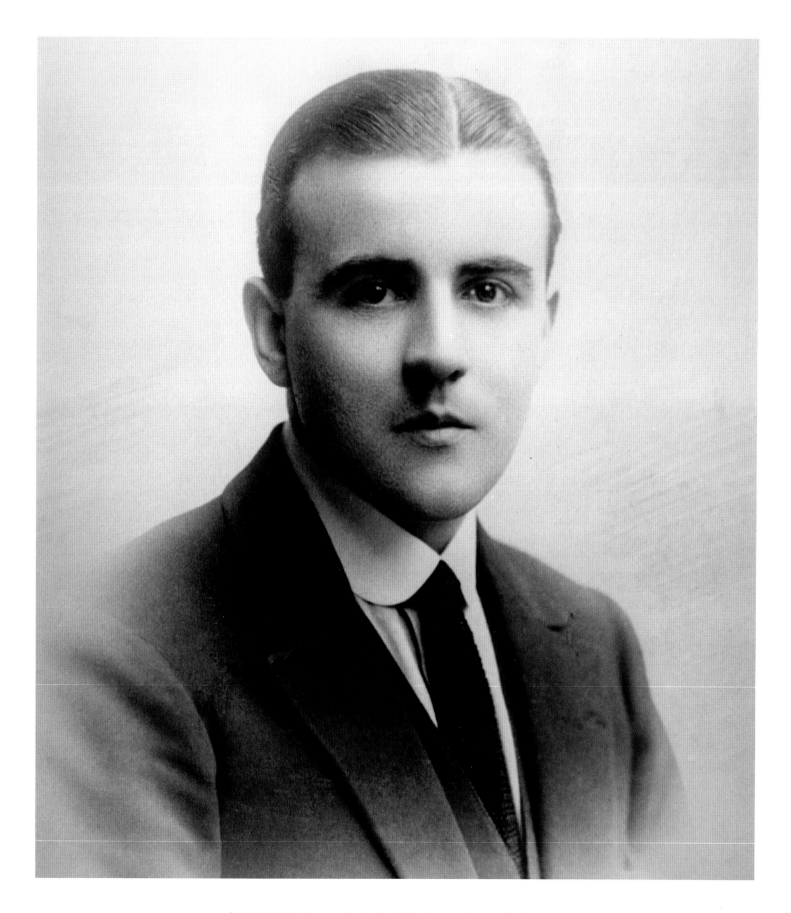

Above: W.O. Bentley was fascinated with steam engines and trains as a child, and had his first taste of engineering when he became an apprentice at the Great Northern Railway's works in Doncaster.

local goods trains, and then on local passenger trains. With these under his belt he was given the opportunity to work on express passenger trains operating between London and Leeds. His longest trip was a 400-mile return journey to Leeds in a day, which involved shovelling more than seven tons of coal.

By now W.O.'s personal transport had been upgraded from a bicycle to a motorcycle. Encouraged by other apprentices' interest in powered two-wheelers he had devoured *The Motor Cycle* magazine, and then visited E.T. Morris's motorcycle shop in London's Finchley Road to do further research on the makes, models and possibilities. After absorbing all the information, and putting in a good deal of thought, he bought a well-used 3hp Quadrant from Morris's, and took it back to Doncaster by train. It made his journeys to the works quicker and less arduous, and he even used it to ride home to London at weekends. The journey from Yorkshire down the dusty Great North Road was a ride of more than 150 miles, and took the best part of eight hours. That he even attempted it says a lot about W.O.'s determined character and also the enthusiasm he was acquiring for motor vehicles, at a time when they were still a rarity. W.O.'s motorcycle was the first powered vehicle the Bentley family had ever owned, though he soon persuaded two of his elder brothers to buy motorcycles of their own. One of them, Arthur, bought a 3½hp Triumph and promptly announced he would attempt to beat the 'End to End' record, from John o'Groats in the northeast of Scotland to Land's End in the southwest of England. Despite lacking proper lighting and having no mechanical expertise, he beat the record.

In May 1907 Arthur and W.O. both entered the London to Edinburgh Trial, which was to be W.O.'s first taste of competitive motorsport. W.O. started off at a good pace but soon found he could barely keep to the required schedule, just managing to check in on time at the control points on the route. In Northumberland he suffered a rear tyre puncture, but a fellow competitor helped him to fix it. North of the border and almost within sight of the finish, W.O. suffered another setback when the Quadrant's engine died. Because W.O. had spent many hours stripping and rebuilding the engine he knew it intimately and was quickly able to diagnose and repair a broken ignition wire. The Quadrant made it to the finish with just minutes to spare, earning W.O. a gold medal for his trouble.

Spurred on by this success, W.O. bought a faster machine, a 3½hp Bell-Quadrant, with which he won a silver medal in the Motor Cycling Club's Sharpenhoe Hill Climb in September 1907. He retired from the 1908 London-Edinburgh trial, though his brother H.M. finished and won a gold medal. W.O. was back in competition the following year, this time riding a much more serious motorcycle: a Coventry-built 5hp twin-cylinder Rex. He entered the London to Land's End Trial alongside H.M., but both had problems with their machines. Just a few days later W.O. entered the Rex in the twenty-four-hour London-Plymouth-London trial and came away with a silver medal.

By now the 5hp Rex wasn't fast enough for him, and he bought a lighter single-cylinder 3½hp Rex Speed King which he entered for races at Brooklands. The world's first purpose-built motor racing track had opened near Weybridge in Surrey, just a few miles to the south of the

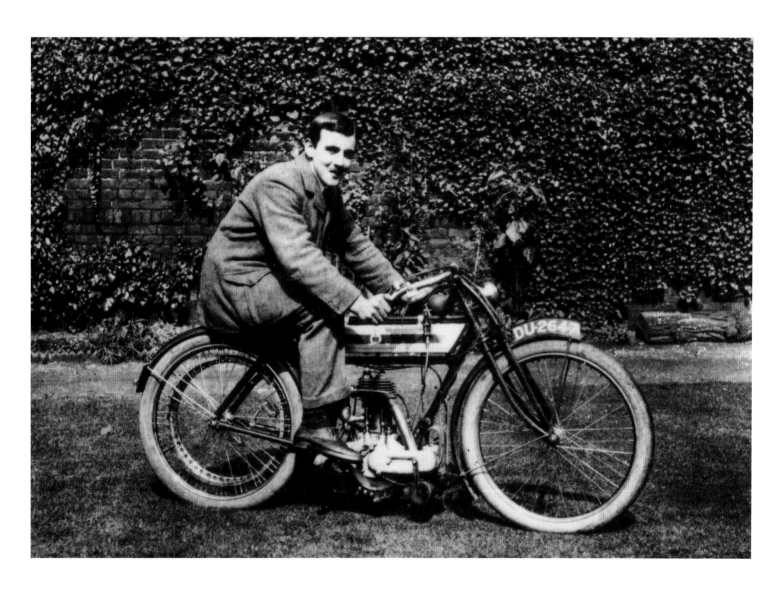

Above: Bentley, like his brothers, was enthusiastic about motor cycles
– which were still an unusual sight in early twentieth-century Britain.
He owned a string of them, and took part in competitions and trials
up and down the country.

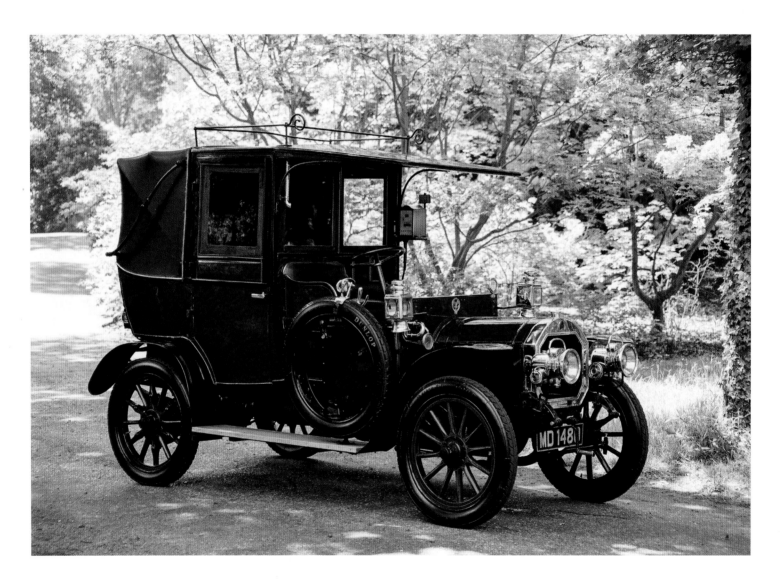

Above: While working at the National Cab Company in West London, W.O. Bentley was responsible for the upkeep of its expanding fleet of Unic taxis like this one. He also found ways to prevent drivers from fiddling their meters.

Bentley family home, in 1907. Those early races provided W.O. with little success, but undeterred, he entered the Isle of Man Tourist Trophy in September 1909.

Car racing had started on the Isle of Man in 1904, and the first bike race had taken place the following year. The Tourist Trophy, for machines with full touring equipment like mudguards and silencers, began in 1907 and quickly became one of the most prestigious events in the UK. It was not a race in the conventional sense, but a time trial, with competitors starting at intervals and riding against the clock rather than directly against each other.

W.O. made meticulous preparations for the event. The single-cylinder Rex engine had a reputation for seizing under sustained hard use, and to avoid this W.O. made a modification to the oil system to introduce more lubricant to the cylinder walls. It proved to be so successful Rex adopted it for their production engines. Bentley also arrived a week before the race to learn the 37-mile course, but crashed while practising. He managed to repair the Rex in time for the race, but another crash put W.O. out of the competition before the first lap was over. Fortunately he was not badly injured.

Later in 1909 W.O. entered two more Brooklands races with the Rex, but by the end of the year he had upgraded to an even faster machine. Unlike the British-built Quadrant and Rex, this was an American bike – a 638cc V-twin Indian of the latest type – and he entered the new machine for trials and races in 1910. Again he competed in the Tourist Trophy and this time completed the first circuit, though not without a scare when the Indian took off over a humpback bridge and landed heavily. But on the second lap the rear

tyre exploded, putting W.O. out of the TT for the second year running.

By the end of 1910 W.O.'s apprenticeship with the Great Northern Railway was at its end. He had entered into it with the ambition of becoming a locomotive designer, but could now see that there would be years of menial work at low pay before he could reach the heights he aspired to. Instead his motorcycle experience had given him the feeling that the motor industry would provide better opportunities.

At the age of 22 he was offered a job with the National Motor Cab Company based in Hammersmith. The company ran a growing fleet of 250 French twin-cylinder Unic taxis, and it was W.O.'s job to look after their maintenance and repair. He was also tasked with investigating the ways the cabbies fiddled the meters so they could carry passengers and pocket the fares, and his tenacious investigations ultimately stamped out the problem. As the fleet grew steadily to 500 cabs, W.O. came up with innovative maintenance methods which minimised the time each one spent off the road.

It was around this time that W.O. bought a car of his own, a secondhand 9hp V-twin Riley. In comfort and versatility it was a step up from a motorcycle, but it had tricky handling and the open bodywork offered little more weather protection than a two-wheeler. It soon made way for a single-cylinder Sizaire-Naudin, then a four-cylinder car of the same make.

An opportunity for W.O. to move on from the National Motor Cab Company came in 1912 when the London based partnership of Lecoq and Fernie advertised for a new investor. Amongst other business interests, Lecoq and

Fernie were the British concessionaires for three French car companies, but when W.O.'s older brother H.M. visited the company he found the partners had little expertise and only a passing interest in cars. With virtually no promotion, what few sales there were relied entirely on word of mouth. Yet one of the brands they represented, DFP, was successful on the continent, and H.M. could see it had plenty of potential if it was properly marketed.

Though H.M. was keen to take the opportunity, there was some feeling within the Bentley family that it would be a better position for W.O., as he had experience of engineering and motor cars that H.M. lacked. W.O. was keen, but felt duty-bound to allow H.M., as the elder brother, to take the chance if he wanted it. Eventually it was decided that the two brothers would decide which of them would go for it based on a simple toss of a coin. W.O. won.

There was then the small matter of raising the £2,000 (equivalent to £1 million or more today) investment that Lecoq and Fernie were asking for, but W.O. arranged for this to be advanced from a trust fund he would one day inherit. Installed inside the company, he made a detailed study of the DFP cars, and took over a 2.0-litre, four-cylinder 12/15hp model from stock for his own use.

Auguste Doriot and Ludovic Flandrin had founded their car company in Courbevoie, a couple of miles outside Paris, in 1906. Doriot had worked for Peugeot and the pair met at Clément-Bayard, which exported cars to Britain under the brand name Talbot. The first Doriot-Flandrin product was a small car with a 1.1-litre, single-cylinder engine supplied by the nearby firm of Chapuis-Dornier. In 1908 they were joined by brothers Alexandre and Jules-René Parant and the

company became Doriot, Flandrin & Parant or DFP. Bigger cars with four-cylinder engines followed, and DFP gained a reputation for solid engineering and good reliability.

W.O. was impressed by the solidity of the DFPs and quickly concluded that the potential his brother H.M. had seen in the cars was very real. What held them back were the inept business practices of Lecoq and Fernie, but after protracted negotiations H.M. was able to buy them out, and a new company called Bentley & Bentley was formed to carry the DFP concession forward. H.M., an accountant by profession, was set up in the firm's existing premises at Hanover Court in Mayfair to look after the business side, while W.O. rented a workshop at New Street Mews, just off Baker Street in neighbouring Marylebone, from the coachbuilder J.H. Easter. There he could concentrate on service and engineering, assisted by 'a little wizard' called Leroux, who had been brought over from DFP in France.

Three DFP models were available, all with four-cylinder engines: a 1.6-litre 10/12hp small car; a 2.0-litre 12/15hp like the one W.O. was running; and a 3.0-litre 16/22hp. W.O. liked the two smaller machines but felt the 3.0-litre was a 'heavy, sluggish car' that had plenty of accomplished competitors at its chassis-only price of £350. In the 1910s it was normal for a buyer to select the chassis they wanted and then order the bodywork from a specialist coachbuilder, and the DFPs supplied by Bentley & Bentley were no exception. J.H. Easter was the usual supplier of coachwork for the DFPs.

W.O. spent a lot of time talking to motor dealers to encourage them to sell DFP cars, aided by his intimate knowledge of the engineering of the vehicles he was

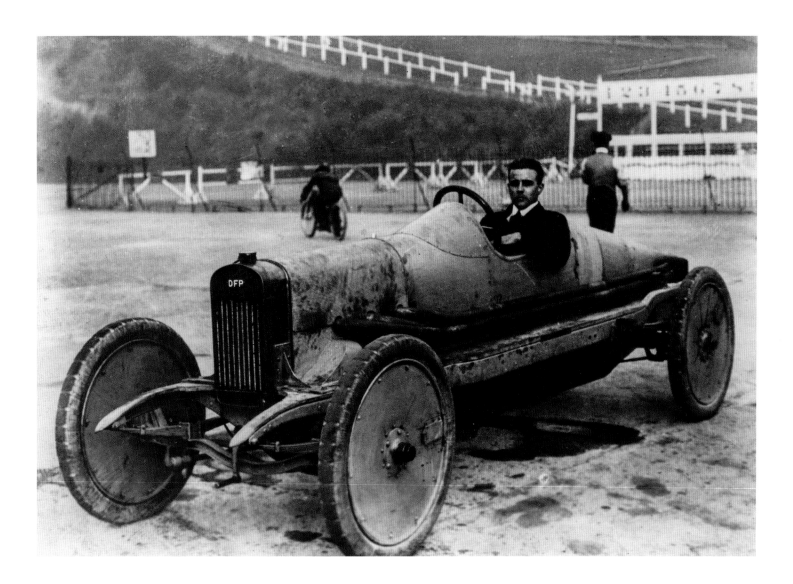

Above: W.O. Bentley at the wheel of a single-seater DFP vehicle at the Brooklands racing circuit in Surrey. The cars were imported from France, and W.O. – in partnership with his brother H.M. – set up a company to handle their marketing and servicing.

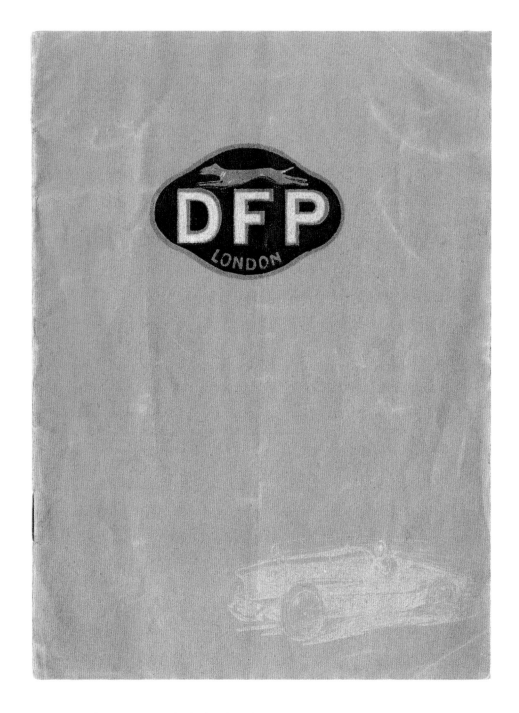

Above: An original sales brochure for the DFP – note the subtle
inclusion of a speeding race car at the bottom of the page.

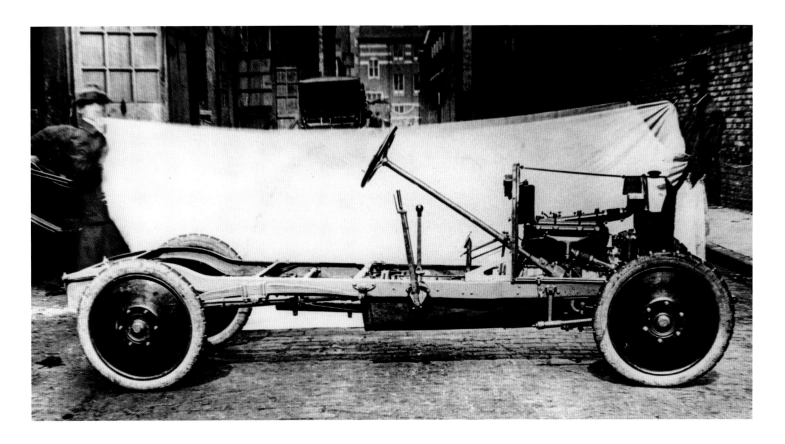

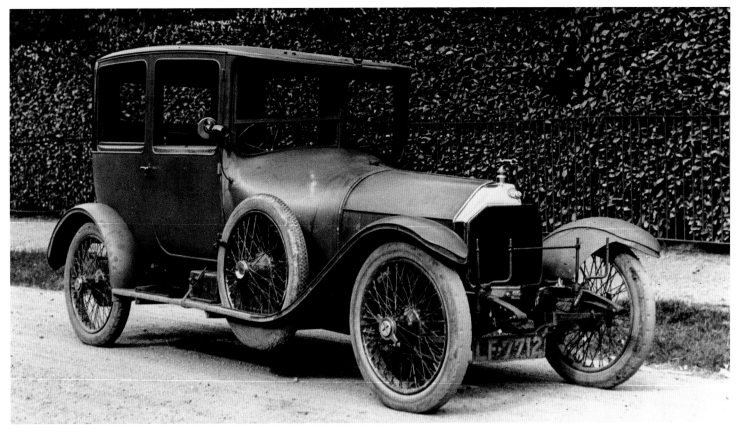

Top: Bentley workers hold up a white background cloth so a DFP chassis can be photographed for catalogues and adverts.

Above: The DFP cars were solid and reliable. Bentley's work made them faster and more exciting.

selling. He was also keen to promote DFP cars by racing them – partly because he had already been bitten by the bug thanks to his motorcycling exploits a few years earlier, but also because motor racing was in vogue, and was a good way to raise awareness of the DFP brand. Leroux prepared the 12/15hp car for competition by extracting the most from the engine, and in June 1912 W.O. entered it for the Aston Clinton Hill Climb, where cars and drivers tackled Aston Hill against the clock. It was a prestigious event, with entries including famous marques like Hispano-Suiza, Austro-Daimler, Talbot and Vauxhall, alongside less common machines like Hurtus, Vinots and Le Guis. W.O.'s biggest rival in the 2.0-litre class was a Humber driven by the company's test driver W.G. Tuck.

Though W.O. had tackled hill climbs on motorcycles, this was his first competitive event in a car. He planned his attack on the course as he watched other competitors sprinting away from the start line, deciding a fast change to second gear at the maximum possible engine speed was the best way to counteract the steep climb that made up the first part of the course. When the flag dropped W.O. gunned the DFP hard, changed up without using the clutch, and kept the DFP in second until the gradient eased off.

To W.O.'s surprise the time he had recorded in the DFP was not just the fastest of the day – it also set a new record in the 2.0-litre class. Tuck's Humber, meanwhile, was disqualified because it was fitted with a non-standard two-seater body with no dashboard and narrow mudguards. W.O. and DFP were an instant success, which Bentley & Bentley capitalised upon with advertisements in the following week's motoring papers. For a while W.O.'s 12/15

took pride of place in the showroom at Hanover Court.

To make the DFP even faster, W.O. wanted to fit a streamlined racing body, a job entrusted to Harrisons in Stanhope Street, on the other side of Regent's Park from the Bentley workshop in New Street Mews. Harrisons produced a narrow two-seater body in aluminium and the car was fitted with low-drag wheel discs and a higher-compression engine. In this form the DFP aimed to topple Tuck's record for the 10-lap Brooklands speed trial, but by then the record speed had been raised by an Arrol-Johnston. The DFP went to Brooklands in November and recorded a rousing 66.78mph average, comfortably besting the previous record and further cementing the reputations of both DFP and W.O.

Bentley & Bentley joined the Society of Motor Manufacturers and Traders and exhibited at the 1912 London Motor Show, which raised their profile and brought in lots of new orders for DFPs. Early in 1913 W.O. was again successful at Aston Clinton and followed this up with a win at another hill climb, Shelsley Walsh, before turning his attention to the Brooklands Whitsun Handicap meeting. But over the longer distances of the Brooklands races the DFP could not keep up with Tuck's rapid works Humber.

W.O. was keen to explore ways to get more power out of the DFP engine, and went to Courbevoie to meet with Auguste Doriot of DFP. Doriot was surprised at the level of interest in making his cars go faster, but was very supportive of Bentley's efforts. He sanctioned modifications to the

Opposite: A DFP saloon parked in the street near the Bentley showroom in Mayfair. Curiously, it's fitted with front tyres that don't match.

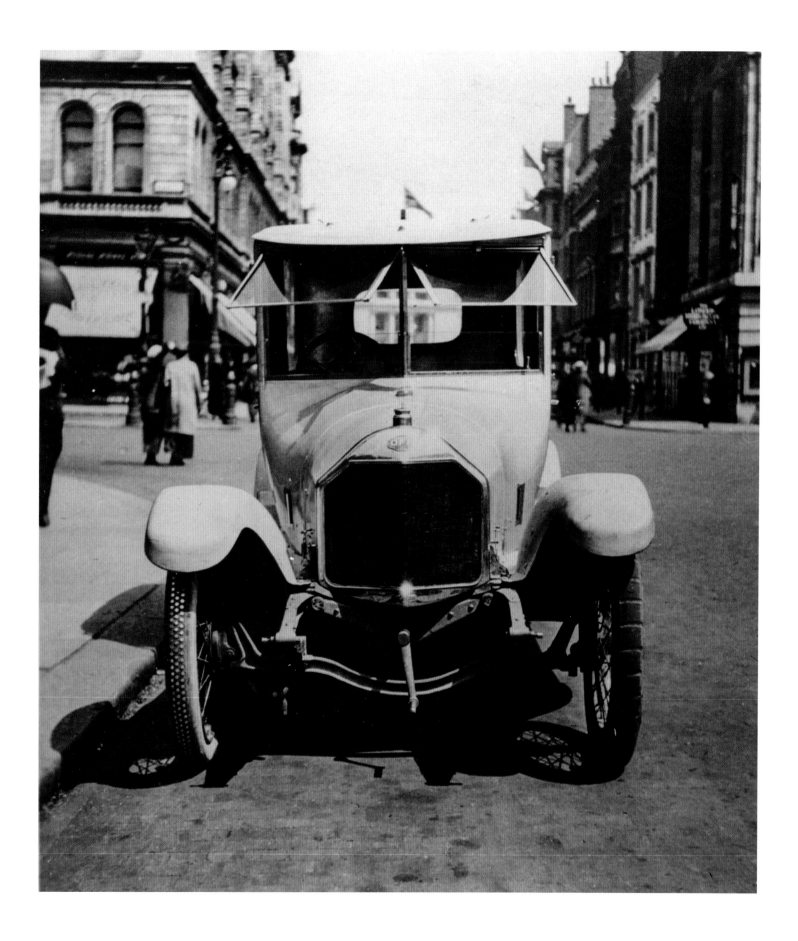

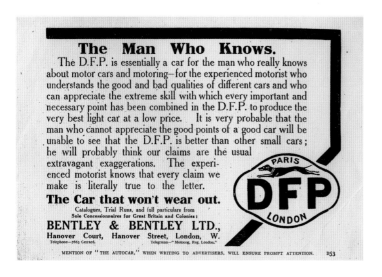

The Man Who Knows.

The D.F.P. is essentially a car for the man who really knows about motor cars and motoring—for the experienced motorist who understands the good and bad qualities of different cars and who can appreciate the extreme skill with which every important and necessary point has been combined in the D.F.P. to produce the very best light car at a low price. It is very probable that the man who cannot appreciate the good points of a good car will be unable to see that the D.F.P. is better than other small cars; he will probably think our claims are the usual extravagant exaggerations. The experienced motorist knows that every claim we make is literally true to the letter.

The Car that won't wear out.

Catalogues, Trial Runs, and full particulars from
Sole Concessionnaires for Great Britain and Colonies:

BENTLEY & BENTLEY LTD.,
Hanover Court, Hanover Street, London, W.
Telephone—7865 Gerrard.   Telegrams—"Motocog, Reg. London."

MENTION OF "THE AUTOCAR," WHEN WRITING TO ADVERTISERS, WILL ENSURE PROMPT ATTENTION.   B53

Above: A Bentley & Bentley advertisement for DFP cars, dating from just before the First World War. It appeared in *The Autocar* magazine.

DFP production cars to improve their performance, raising the compression ratio and improving the intake system. Another problem which Bentley had experienced was that under hard use the cast iron pistons would crack, but at the meeting with Doriot, Bentley would find inspiration for a solution to the problem – from an unlikely source.

Bentley noticed a model of a piston being used as a paperweight on Doriot's desk. It had been presented to Doriot by the Corbin foundry, which was one of DFP's suppliers, and was clearly made from an aluminium alloy. W.O. started to wonder if an aluminium alloy could be devised which could be used to make pistons for the DFP engine. Aluminium alloy pistons would conduct heat better, so the piston crown would run cooler and cracking would be less likely. And alloy pistons would be lighter than cast

iron, allowing higher engine speeds – which would mean the potential for more power. But Doriot was concerned that alloy pistons simply wouldn't be strong enough to cope with the stresses of a running engine. Nevertheless he agreed to put Bentley in touch with Corbin, and it turned out that the foundry already made aluminium pistons for other French car makers. Corbin advised that an alloy of 88 per cent aluminium and 12 per cent copper would do the job, and a batch of experimental pistons made from this alloy was delivered to Bentley's workshops a few weeks later.

The early results were promising. The alloy pistons stood up to normal use without any problems, and the engine clearly delivered more power than before. Buoyed by this success, W.O. made modifications to the pistons to lighten them, and increased the engine's compression ratio. Even then the pistons caused no problems, except for a tendency to make a noise, when started from cold, which became known as 'piston slap'. This came about because the alloy pistons expanded more than the iron cylinder bores as the engine warmed up, so they had to be given large clearances when cold to avoid seizing up when hot. It was a small price to pay for the greatly improved performance and reliability of the engine.

In August 1913 the alloy pistons proved their worth at Brooklands, where W.O. beat Tuck's Humber on handicap and averaged 77.927mph over ten laps to set some new class records, despite being slowed by heavy rain. A few days later the DFP returned to Brooklands and set new records for the flying-start half mile, kilometre and mile at over 80mph. At the Brooklands autumn meeting Tuck's improved Humber set new records for 50 miles, 100 miles

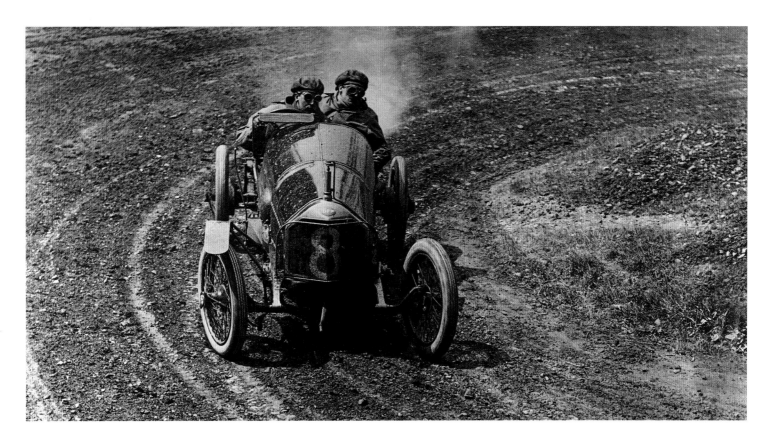

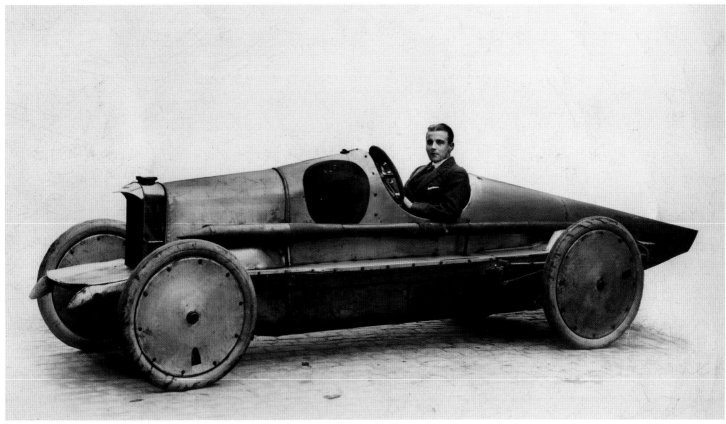

Top: A specially-prepared DFP made it to the finish of the 1914 Isle of Man TT – a creditable performance.

Above: W.O. Bentley poses with the single-seater DFP he used to break records at Brooklands early in 1914.

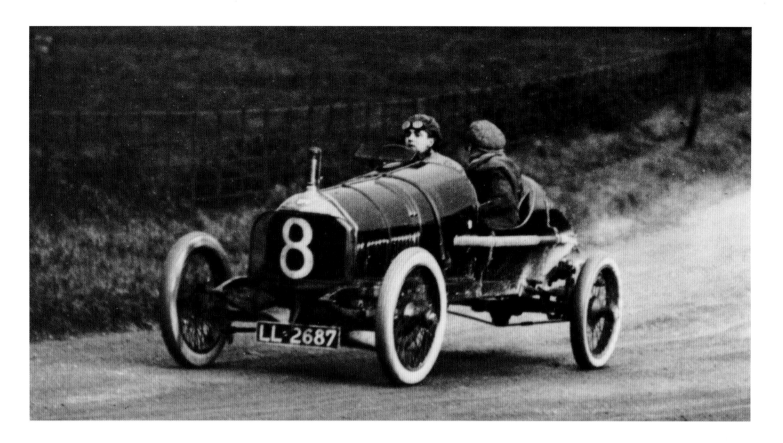

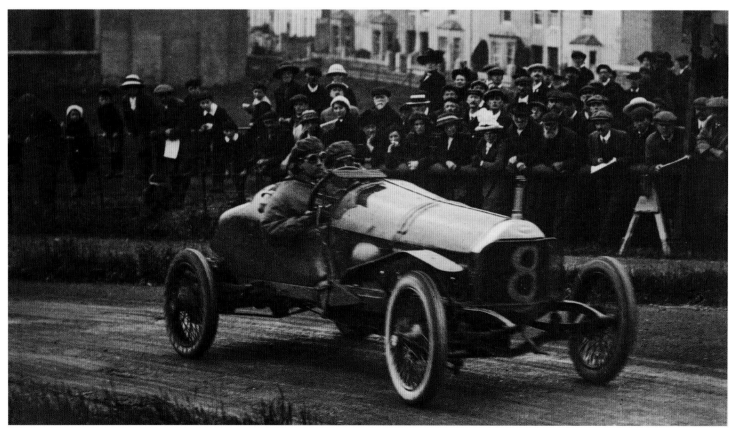

Top : W.O. Bentley competing in the 1914 Tourist Trophy.

His riding mechanic is the 'French wizard', Leroux.

Above: W.O. and Leroux speeding past the Isle of Man TT crowd

in their DFP. They made it to the finish – unlike many rivals.

and one hour – but W.O. then took them for ten laps, 50km, 50 miles and 150km, missing out on the 100-mile record when the DFP ran out of fuel.

Bentley persuaded Doriot to fit aluminium pistons in a new DFP production car, the 12/40 Speed model, which was ready for the London Motor Show later that year. Neither Bentley nor DFP revealed the secret that gave the new car more power than the existing 12/15. Meanwhile there was further work on W.O.'s race car, with a series of modifications aimed at improving its performance still further in preparation for the 1914 season. The engine was given twin spark plugs run from a Bosch dual magneto, and the compression ratio was raised once again. There were changes to the transmission, with an open driveshaft replacing the torque tube and a solid axle replacing the differential, and holes were drilled in the chassis rails to reduce weight.

On New Year's Day 1914 cars and racing took a back seat in W.O.'s life, for once. On that day W.O. married Léonie Gore, two years his senior, and stepsister of a friend from his motorcycle racing days, Jack Withers. Léonie had been W.O.'s intrepid passenger on that first Aston Clinton hill climb in the DFP, and it was in another DFP that the couple spent their honeymoon, touring the West Country. In February W.O. was back at Brooklands attempting more speed records in a 12/40 with a very narrow single-seater body. Running in the 'wrong' direction to get the best of the wind – something nobody had ever thought to do before – W.O. took the flying half mile record at an impressive 89.70mph together with the kilometre, mile and 10-mile class records.

There was another impressive performance at the Isle of Man Tourist Trophy race in June. Though W.O.'s specially prepared DFP was the last of the six finishers, it did at least get to the end of the race, unlike another fifteen competitors (including Tuck's Humber). But the publicity generated by the TT performance was quickly overtaken by developments in the wider world, as Europe descended into 'the war to end all wars'.

While H.M. Bentley signed up for active duty, W.O. felt his best contribution to the war effort would be to get aluminium alloy pistons adopted in engines for Britain's fighting aircraft. The Royal Air Force had not yet been formed, and engine development for Navy aircraft was being directed by the Royal Naval Air Service, controlled by the Admiralty. After a meeting there, W.O.'s ideas were enthusiastically adopted, and he was commissioned into the Royal Navy Volunteer Reserve as a lieutenant. He soon began working with engine manufacturers to introduce alloy pistons, visiting Derby to persuade Rolls-Royce engineer Ernest Hives to use them in the company's first aero engine, the Eagle. He then went to Wolverhampton to explain the advantages of alloy pistons to Louis Coatalen at Sunbeam, and Coatalen adopted them for all Sunbeam's aero engines.

W.O. was then sent to Gwynnes in London, which was building air-cooled rotary engines under licence from the French firm Clerget. Bentley suggested a number of improvements to the design, which had a poor reliability record, but Gwynnes were too busy with engine manufacturing to devote much time to development.. In the end the Admiralty moved Bentley to Humber in Coventry –

his old rivals on the racetrack – where he could complete a new engine design of his own. Bentley's design was a rotary engine like the Clerget, where the crankshaft remained stationary and the whole engine rotated around it. Bentley

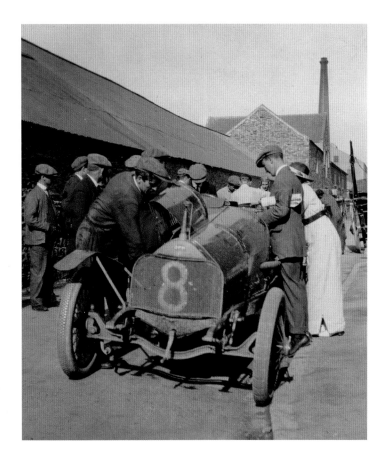

Above: W.O.'s racing DFP gets checked over after a practice run. Note the lack of front-wheel brakes.

Opposite: Bentley's BR2 rotary engine, one of several aero engine projects he was involved in during the war.

had identified that the Clerget's reliability problems were due to uneven cooling of the cylinders: the front of each cylinder was cooled by the airflow much more than the rear. Bentley made a number of changes, including the use of an aluminium cylinder which conducted heat more effectively, fitted with an iron liner. Only the valve gear was carried over from the Clerget design, in order to speed up the development process. The engine was in production by the autumn of 1916, and it proved to be both more reliable than the Clerget – and significantly more powerful, at 154bhp compared to the Clerget's 122bhp. It had slightly greater capacity – 17.3-litres compared to 16.3-litres – but weighed only five pounds more. Fitted with the Bentley engine, the Sopwith Camel fighter plane became a safer aircraft which also had more speed and a higher altitude ceiling, and the engines spent more time in operation and less in maintenance. The Bentley Rotary 1 or BR.1, as it became known, was followed by a larger BR.2 developing 238bhp from 24.9-litres. This was available by the end of the war and powered Sopwith Snipe and Salamander aircraft, among others.

For Bentley the war had been four years of hard work – travelling around Britain to visit engine manufacturers and help develop existing aero engines, and then creating the two new power plants at Humber. W.O. had also been further afield to see at first hand how engines were used and maintained in service and to rectify engine problems, and by the end of the war had been commissioned into the newly formed RAF as a captain. He could now return to the home in Hampstead he shared with Léonie, and consider where his next challenge might lie.

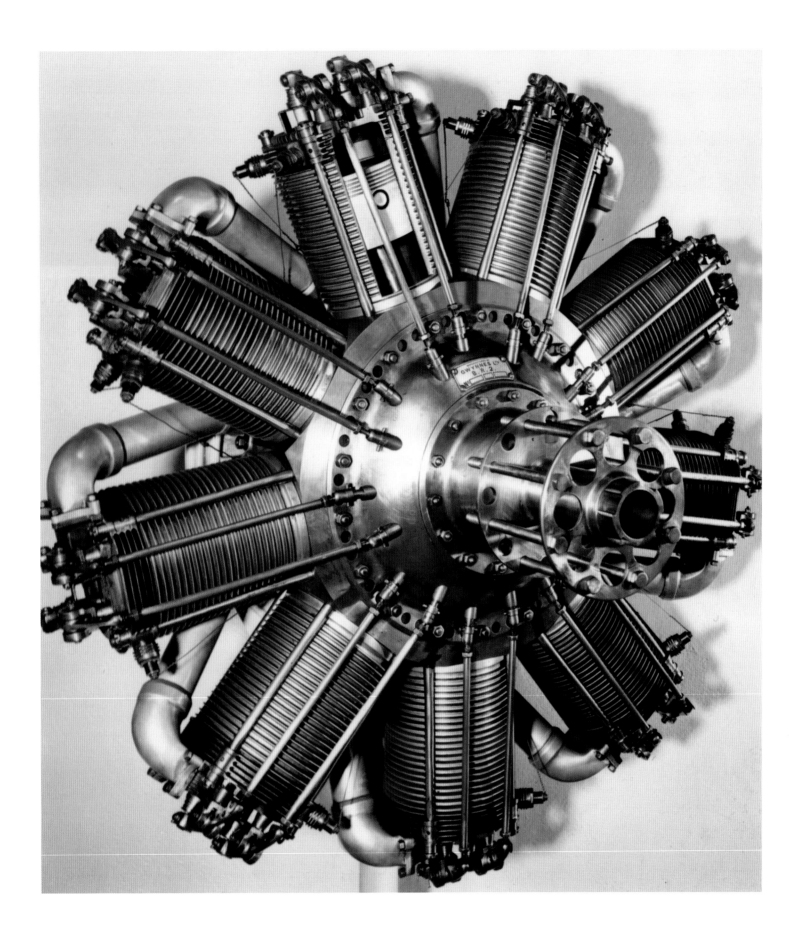

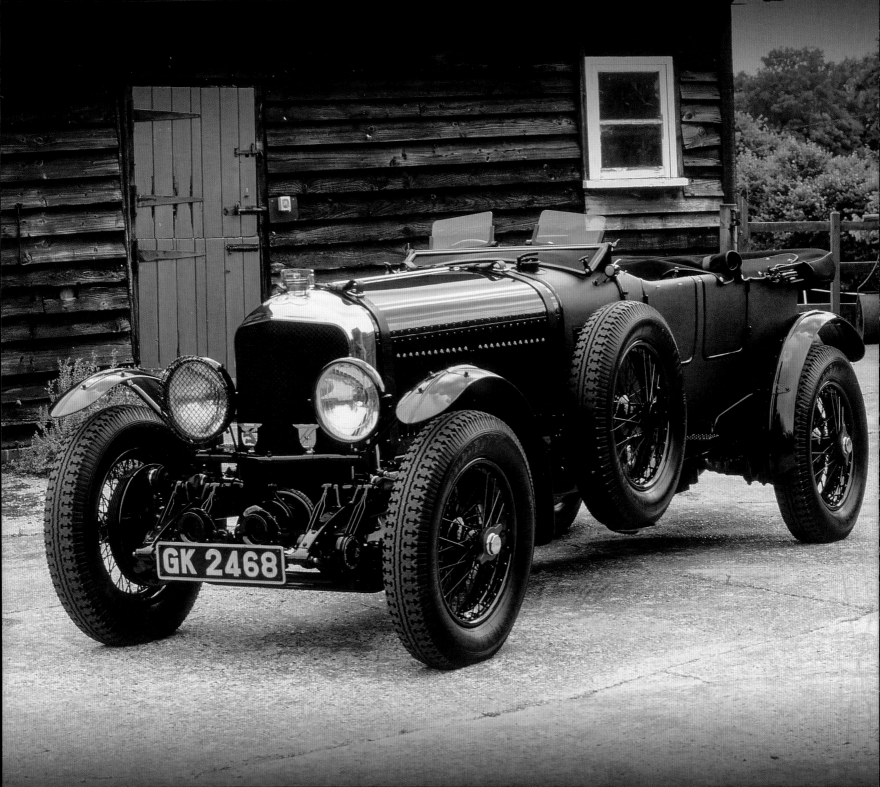

Chapter 2

THE GLORY YEARS

Still only 30, W.O. Bentley had acquired experience in engineering which ranged from steam locomotives to motorcycles, from taxicabs to racing cars to aero engines. He was an accomplished driver and a versatile mechanic, and he had a proven ability to relate to all sorts of people from company owners and senior military figures downwards. His career could have gone in any number of directions, but it was the motor car business which still held the greatest attraction for him.

With the end of the First World War the demand for private cars increased rapidly, and Bentley & Bentley did plenty of trade in secondhand vehicles until new DFP chassis were available again in 1919. But the quality of the cars was not what it had been pre-war, and in any case W.O.'s ambitions in the motor industry lay far beyond a resumption of the Bentley & Bentley company's pre-war activities with DFP: he wanted to build a car of his own.

W.O. felt sure that motoring would become affordable to far more people as time went on, but that there would still be a demand for a high-quality car with good performance along the lines of the Belgian Minerva, the French Bugatti, or the Spanish Hispano-Suiza. It would not be a racing car, although lessons learned from motor racing would certainly be built into its design and construction, but would be a strong, fast touring car capable of high average speeds whatever the road conditions. At Humber, W.O. explored some of his ideas in long discussions with F.T. Burgess, the company's chief designer, and by the end of the war he had a firm idea of the kind of car he wanted to build. It's a measure of Bentley's conviction, and the high esteem in which he was held as an engineer, that by 1919

Burgess had left his comfortable position at Humber to join W.O. in his new venture. Bentley also brought in Harry Varley, an accomplished designer and capable theoretician.

Work began on 20 January 1919 in an office at 16 Conduit Street, a short walk from the Bentley & Bentley showroom in Hanover Square, and by October the first engine had been built upstairs at New Street Mews. The story goes that a nursing home stood adjacent to the Bentley workshop, and that shortly after the engine was fired up for the first time on a test bed a matron appeared demanding that it be turned off so a dying patient might go in peace. However, the Bentley engineers refused to interrupt their vital first test of what was an unconventional engine.

Bentley had been able to examine a pre-war Grand Prix Mercedes in detail during the war, and was also familiar with the 1912 Grand Prix Peugeots and the Rolls-Royce Eagle V12 aero engine, each of which provided inspiration for Bentley's new motor. With four cylinders, each with an 80mm bore and 149mm stroke, the new engine had a swept volume of 2,996cc – significantly bigger than the 12/40 DFP which had proved so successful before the war. But what really set it apart was the arrangement of its combustion chamber and valve gear.

Bentley adopted a hemispherical combustion chamber with opposed overhead valves, a layout which burned fuel more efficiently than the more conventional side-valve arrangement. To improve the engine's breathing, Bentley went for four valves in each cylinder rather than the normal two, after the fashion of both the Peugeot and Mercedes Grand Prix engines. Though the four valves had to be smaller to squeeze them into the combustion chamber,

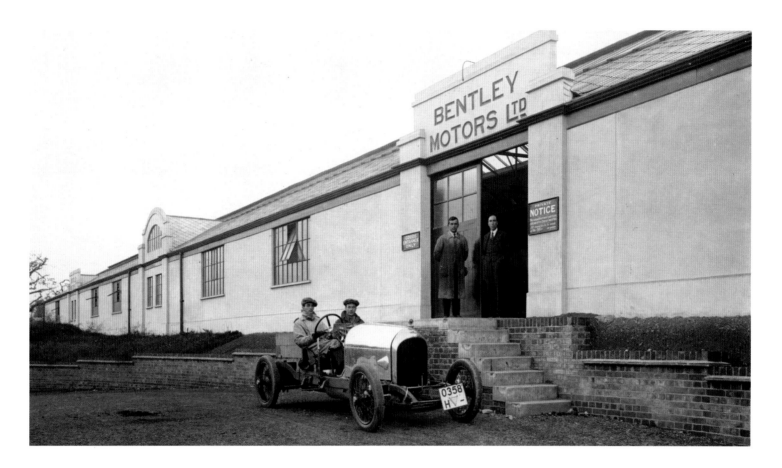

Above: The second Bentley 3 Litre outside the company's Oxgate Lane premises, close to the Edgware Road, around 1921.

they were capable of moving more intake and exhaust gases than two large ones.

Conventional engines had a camshaft low down at the side of the engine operating long pushrods which in turn operated the valves. The Peugeot engine had adopted twin overhead camshafts, but that was an expensive solution – and one which, for the Bentley application, would generate too much engine noise. Instead Bentley went for a single overhead camshaft driven by a shaft with spiral bevel gears at each end, mating with the front of the crankshaft at the bottom. The camshaft operated a line of rocker arms which in turn opened the valves. The cylinder block and heads were a single unit, another feature influenced by the Peugeot engine, ensuring there could be no problems with the sealing of the combustion chambers while the engine was in service.

The vertical shaft at the front of the engine which drove the camshaft also carried skew gears at its centre which turned a magneto for the ignition system, and the same gears also drove the water pump. On the prototype engines a further gear drive was arranged to drive two oil pumps in a dry-sump oil system.

The engine drove through a Ferodo cone clutch to a four-speed manual gearbox which was drawn up by Burgess, based on his design for the pre-war racing Humbers. The engine and transmission went into a chassis with a conventional ladder frame design that also featured some clever details such as the rearward position of the rear axle on its leaf spring, which extended the wheelbase and was said to reduce clutch judder. A mock-up of the chassis was built for the London Motor Show in the autumn of 1919 and generated a good deal of interest.

The first car was on its wheels by December 1919. It was driven out of the workshop by test driver Clive Gallop, sitting on a cushion placed on top of the bare chassis.

The impromptu test drive was cut short when Gallop's workshop coat became entangled in the exposed propshaft and started dragging him down into the chassis, but soon the bodywork was fitted and the complete car was subjected to a barrage of tests. EXP 1, as the first prototype was known, was put into the hands of motoring journalist S.C.H. Davis for road test in *The Autocar* in January 1920. Davis, who had first met W.O. during the war when they were both working on military aero engines, gave the car a very positive review.

The tiny workshop at New Street Mews was nowhere near big enough to house a production facility, so new premises were sought. For a while Tangmere Aerodrome in Sussex, a former Royal Flying Corps training field, was under consideration, but it was really much too large for the Bentley operation. Instead the company bought a plot of land in north London, between Cricklewood and the North Circular Road, where it established a new factory on Oxgate Lane. Behind the factory there were fields and a golf course, but Oxgate Lane joined the Edgware Road, one of the busiest roads into and out of London, and there was plenty of activity nearby. Just across the main road was Cricklewood Aerodrome, and the Handley Page aircraft factory. To the north lay the Staples mattress company, and to the south a motor-bus depot, the Smiths clock factory and the (unrelated) Smiths crisp works.

There was still plenty of detail work to be done to turn the original EXP 1 prototype into a production car. Two more prototypes, EXP 2 and EXP 3, were built at the Oxgate Lane works in 1920 and helped to develop improvements to the chassis and a new wet sump lubrication system –

after the scavenge pump of the original dry sump system proved to be unacceptably noisy. There were also changes to the camshaft drive system and the introduction of twin ignition using a pair of magnetos. The first customer chassis was delivered in September 1921.

Bentleys were racing that same year, with Frank Clement winning a Brooklands race in one of the prototypes in May. In 1922 Bentley sent a car to the Indianapolis 500, but it could do no better than finish thirteenth. Bentley entered the Isle of Man TT and performed well with almost standard production cars against purpose-built racing machines from Sunbeam and Vauxhall, finishing second, fourth and fifth and winning the team prize. An early customer, John Duff, stripped down his 3 Litre and broke a gaggle of speed

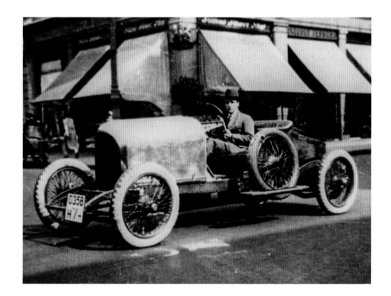

Above: W.O. in the second prototype, EXP 2. This car in this photo was completed in 1920, and is the oldest Bentley still in existence.

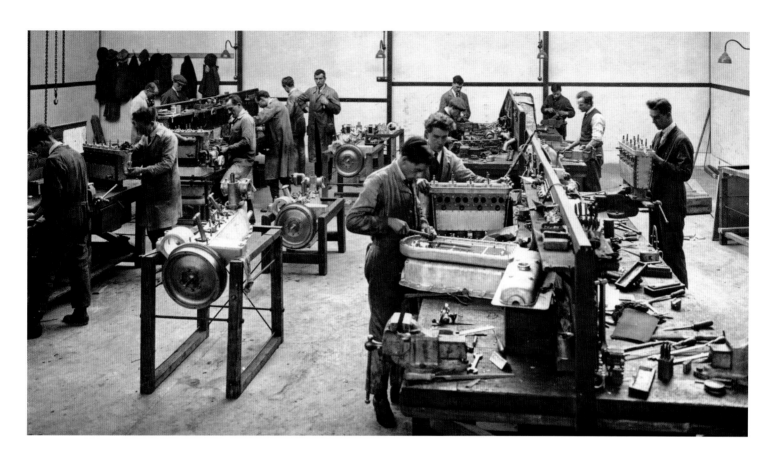

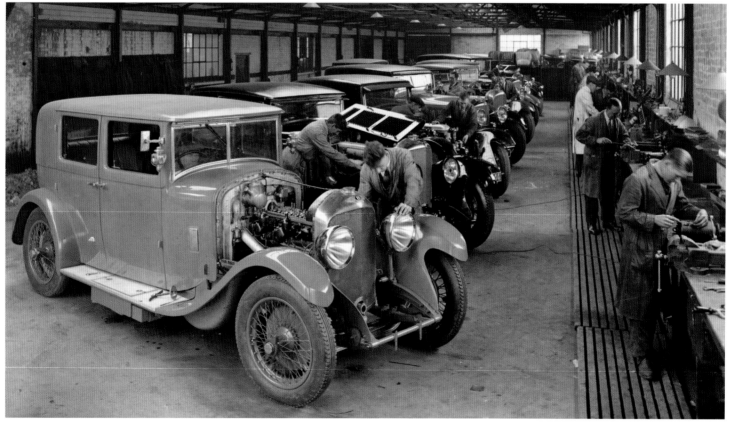

Top and above: Bentley production at Oxgate Lane, Cricklewood, in the 1920s. The factory was purpose-built for the firm; its engine shop and final inspection area are shown here.

records. Then in 1923 Duff heard of plans for the first 24-hour race at Le Mans, and approached the Bentley factory for help with his entry.

Bentley was a racer, but he was dead against the idea of a 24-hour race, suggesting that it was simply a bigger challenge than any car was designed to cope with. Duff persisted, however, and in the end Bentley agreed to provide some arm's-length assistance. Factory driver Frank Clement would act as Duff's co-driver, and two Bentley mechanics would be on hand to prepare the car for the race. The Bentley was the only foreign entry. It ran strongly in the early part of the race, with Duff holding second place. But the lack of four-wheel brakes proved a problem, leading both Duff and Clement to take to the escape road at the end of the Mulsanne Straight during the race, and the stony road surface led to smashed headlamps and a holed petrol tank. Clement had to borrow a bicycle and ride four miles from the pits to the stricken Bentley with cans of petrol and material for a makeshift repair. Back on track he broke the lap record in an effort to make up time, but the Bentley finished the race in fourth place.

The 3 Litre had proved successful as a racing car and a road-going sports car, but it lacked the refinement W.O. was always striving for and did not have the power of larger-engined rivals. The need for more power was imperative because customers were increasingly fitting heavy saloon bodies to Bentley chassis. The solution was to add two cylinders to the engine, making it an inline-six – a layout which is naturally better balanced and smoother running. Though it had much in common with the previous engine, it was more than just the four with two extra cylinders. Instead, the engine was redesigned with narrower bores and bigger main bearings, together with a new form of camshaft drive. Rather than the vertical shaft drive of the four-cylinder engine, the six had a pair of helical gears driving a short horizontal shaft at half engine speed, which carried three eccentrics. A pair of coupling rods linked each eccentric with a similar one mounted on the end of the camshaft at the top of the engine, so that as the crankshaft and half-speed shaft rotated, the cam drive was also turned. This curious arrangement, which owed a lot to steam engine practice, was introduced to quieten the camshaft drive, making the whole engine more refined.

The six-cylinder engine with 4.5-litre capacity went into a lengthened chassis with extra cross-bracing, and the first prototype was on the road by May 1924. Low-pressure 'balloon' tyres were just being introduced, and the new car was fitted with a set to test. In this form it was shipped to France for W.O. and his colleagues to drive to the Le Mans 24-hour race, where Duff and Clement were again driving the sole Bentley entry – this time with full works support.

There were plenty of modifications to the race car, based on the experience gained in the 1923 race. Headlamps were covered by wire-mesh stoneguards, and the fuel tank was also protected from flying stones. Four-wheel brakes, an innovation now being readied for Bentley's production cars, made braking stronger and more reliable.

Duff took the first stint, with the Bentley running behind a handful of larger-engined French cars early in the race. Regulations prevented topping up of any fluids before lap 20, and when Duff came in a lap early to refuel he was hurriedly sent out to attempt another lap – fortunately

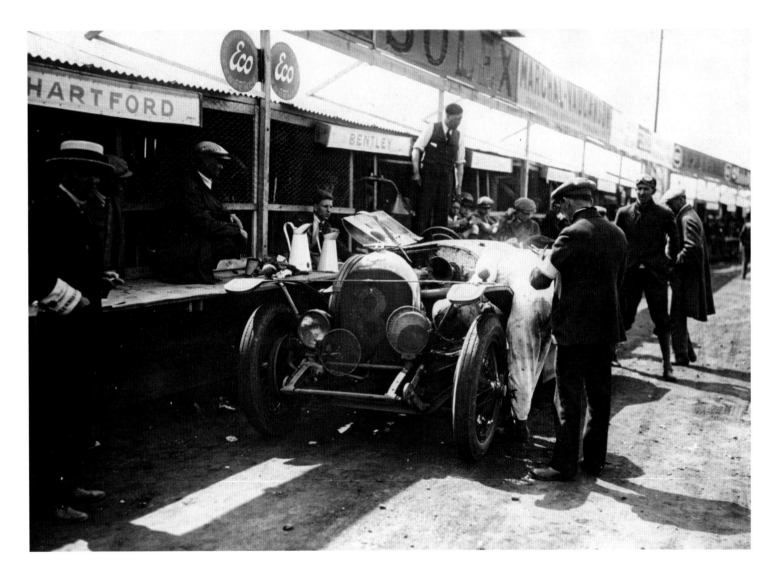

Above: After Bentley drivers John Duff and Frank Clement took
fourth place at Le Mans in 1923, they returned the following
year and won the race in a car that had undergone numerous
adaptions and improvements.

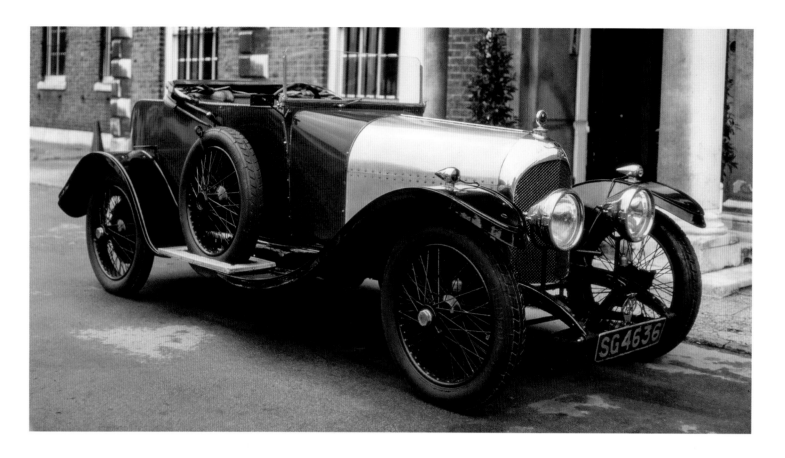

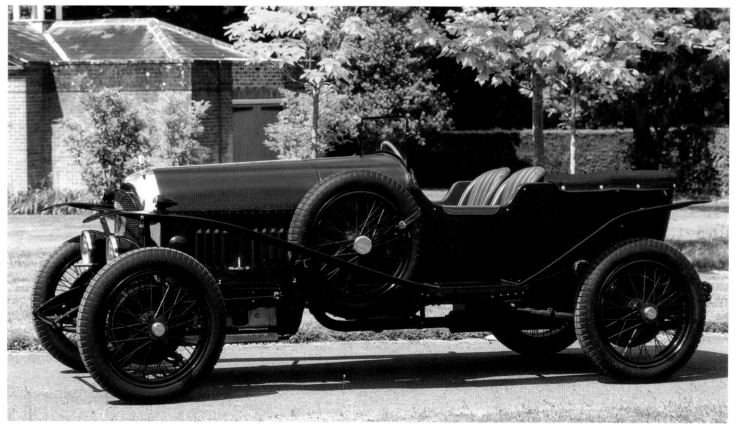

Top: The Bentley 3 Litre was a handsome car, and its sophisticated and powerful engine gave it an impressive turn of speed.

Above: John Duff's 3 Litre, which finished fourth in the first-ever Le Mans competition in 1923 – despite being damaged during the race.

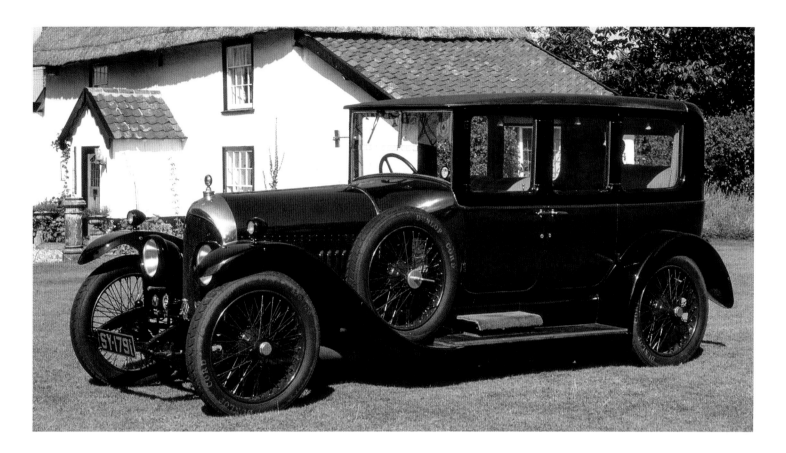

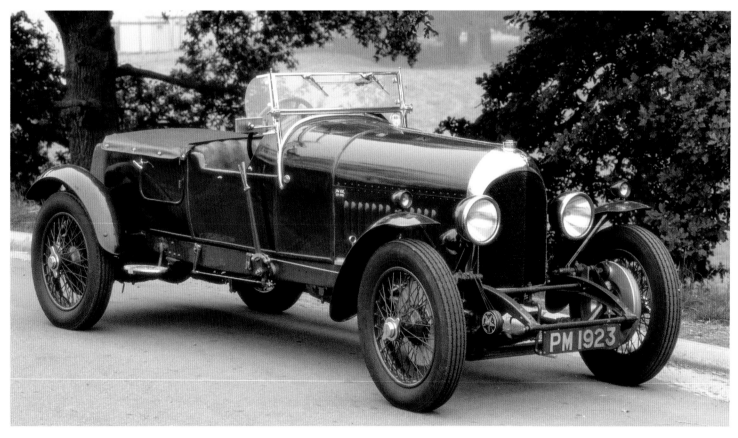

Top: Many 3 Litres were open tourers – but there were also saloons, like this 1923 car with Gurney Nutting coachwork.

Above: This 1923 3 Litre has a body made by the Connaught Coachworks, based near London's Covent Garden.

making it back to the pits without drama. As night fell the Bentley was back in the pits with difficulty selecting gears, but after half an hour the trouble was traced to a coachbuilder's staple that had somehow dropped into the gear selector mechanism. The Bentley ran third during the night, but when the two leading French Lorraine-Dietrich cars both hit trouble it moved into the lead. Clement extended the Bentley's advantage on Sunday morning with some fast laps, then at 2.30 p.m. the team called the car in for a precautionary tyre change. But the rear wheels proved very difficult to remove – some said due to sabotage by a rival team – and the Bentley lost a lot of time. Though it completed another five laps before the end of the race, the average speed had dropped so much due to the long pit stop that they did not count under the Le Mans rules. But the 120 laps the Bentley had already completed was enough to give the team victory from two Lorraine-Dietrichs by just one lap. At its second attempt Bentley had triumphed in one of the world's toughest races.

On the way back from Le Mans the new six-cylinder prototype had a chance encounter with another British prototype car, which W.O. and his Bentley colleagues recognised as a new Rolls-Royce. The two cars proved to have equal top speeds, and an impromptu race between them was only resolved in favour of the Bentley when one of the occupants of the Rolls-Royce lost his cap and the Rolls was forced to stop. Clearly the Bentley had no performance advantage over the new Rolls, which had been one of the objectives of the new engine, and if Bentley wanted an effective competitor for the new car from Derby a rethink was required.

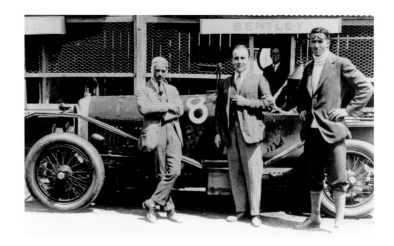

Above: W.O. Bentley (centre) poses with the company's factory driver Frank Clement (left), John Duff and the 1924 Le Mans-winning 3 Litre.

The decision was taken to substantially increase the capacity of the six-cylinder engine, widening the bore to 100mm so that it displaced 6,597cc. A single Smiths carburettor was fitted, chosen for its smooth running capabilities rather than its power potential, and the intake was on the opposite side of the block from the four-cylinder engine. An experimental 6½-litre car was built, with the new engine fitted on rubber mountings into the long-wheelbase chassis, and refinements such as a redesigned steering box: it went on display at the London Motor Show in October 1925.

By then Bentley had been back to Le Mans in an effort to repeat its 1924 success. This time there were two cars: Duff's 3 Litre, shared again with Clement; and a works entry driven by Bertie Kensington Moir and Dudley Benjafield.

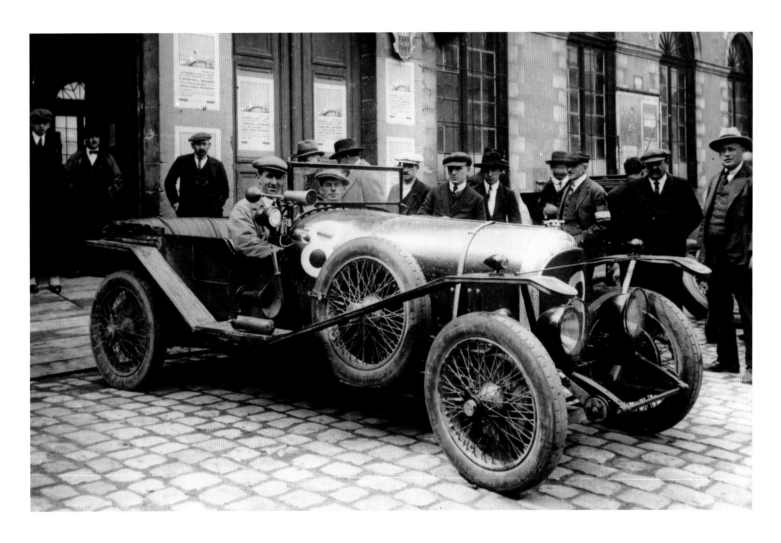

Above: The victorious 3 Litre, photographed at Le Mans in 1924 with
the drivers aboard. John Duff, at the wheel, looks suitably pleased.

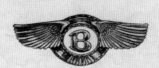

THE THREE LITRE
BENTLEY

3 MODELS FOR 1923—STANDARD MODEL, NEW
TOURIST TROPHY MODEL & LONG CHASSIS MODEL

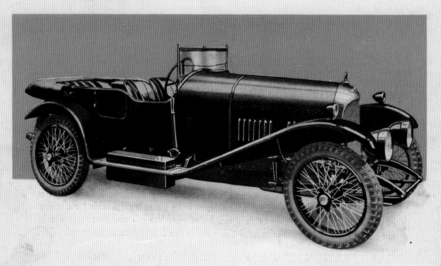

FOUR-SEATER ON TOURIST TROPHY CHASSIS ... Price **£1295** complete.

GUARANTEED FEATURES

SPEED   The Standard Short Chassis is guaranteed to attain a speed of 80 m.p.h. on Brooklands track.

The Tourist Trophy Chassis is guaranteed to attain a speed of 90 m.p.h. on Brooklands track.

The Long Wheelbase Chassis is guaranteed to attain a speed of 75 m.p.h. on Brooklands track.

PETROL CONSUMPTION   Every chassis is guaranteed to have a petrol consumption of 25 miles per gallon at an average speed of 30 m.p.h.

DEFECTS IN MATERIAL   We undertake to supply new, or repair free of charge any part that may fail owing to defective material or faulty workmanship during a period of **five years** from date of purchase.

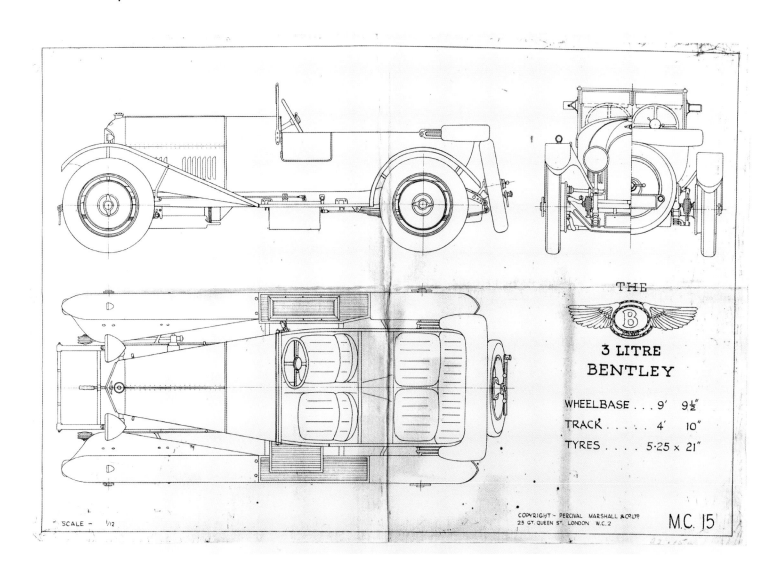

THE

3 LITRE
BENTLEY

WHEELBASE . . . 9' 9½"

TRACK . . . . . 4' 10"

TYRES . . . . 5·25 x 21"

SCALE - 1/12

COPYRIGHT ~ PERCIVAL MARSHALL & Co. LTD
23 GT. QUEEN ST. LONDON W.C.2

M.C. 15

Opposite: Front cover of a 1923 sales brochure for the 3 Litre. Bentley guaranteed the standard car was good for 80mph at Brooklands.

Above: General layout drawing of the 3 Litre with four-seat open tourer bodywork. Shorter and longer wheelbase chassis were also available.

The regulations had been revised again, this time requiring the cars to complete the first twenty laps with their hoods raised, and the Bentleys were filled with enough fuel for those twenty laps. But the calculation of the fuel quantity had been based on the cars' fuel consumption with the hoods lowered, the way they normally raced, and when the hood and windscreen were raised the cars burned fuel faster. Benjafield arrived back in the pits on foot after his car ran out of fuel after eighteen laps, and it wasn't long before Duff's car suffered the same fate. In theory refuelling was only allowed in the pits, but Duff smuggled some petrol out in a lemonade bottle and got his car going again, but it all came to nothing when the car was eliminated later in the race after a carburettor broke up and caused a fire.

Later that year there was an attempt on some long-distance speed records at the banked Montlhéry track near Paris, where one of the drivers was a wealthy amateur named Woolf Barnato. His money came from South African diamond mines, and he had spent some of it on a 3 Litre Bentley in 1925 which he raced successfully at Brooklands. But Barnato would soon become more than just one of Bentley's customers.

Though Bentley Motors had been enjoying considerable sales success with the 3 Litre, it had also been investing heavily in the development of the new engine and chassis for the 6½ Litre model, while at the same time building new facilities at Oxgate Lane. Preparing and racing cars was another major cost, though one which had major benefits in the publicity it generated for the brand. W.O. was convinced that the 6½ Litre would be a fine and profitable car, but he was concerned that it might easily consume all Bentley's resources before it was ever developed into a production reality. There was a real chance the company could fail before the 6½ Litre ever had the opportunity to prove its sales potential.

What W.O. needed was a wealthy investor who could keep the company afloat until the 6½ Litre started to pay its way. Following an abortive attempt to get a captain of the British motor industry, William Morris, interested in the Bentley operation, W.O. approached Woolf Barnato. Early in 1926 a new Bentley Motors company was founded with Barnato as chairman and chief shareholder, after his investment company poured over £100,000 into the car company. W.O. stayed on, now concentrating on the

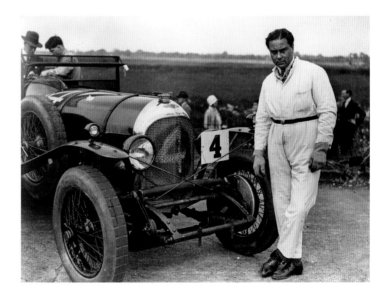

Above: Woolf Barnato's fortune came from diamond mining in South Africa. An enthusiastic amateur racing driver, he became the owner of Bentley Motors in 1926.

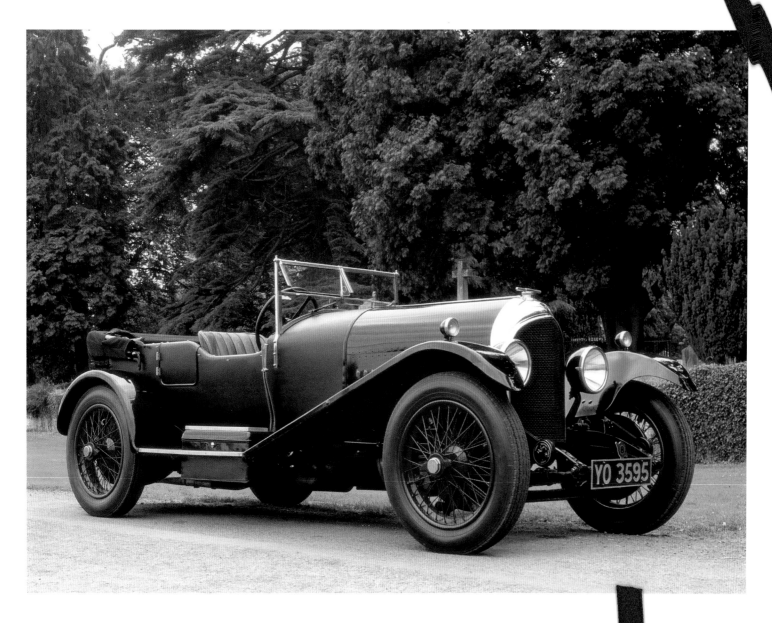

Above: This Bentley 3 Litre Red Label was built for Barnato in 1926
to factory competition specification and raced by him at Brooklands
in the Essex Motor Club Six Hours.

technical side of the business – a year or so later he gave up the title of managing director and became chief engineer. Barnato's cash injection meant that W.O. was once again in a position to develop his cars further.

In the spring of 1926 the Bentley team returned to Montlhéry several times, intent on setting 12-hour and 24-hour endurance records. W.O. was convinced that a Bentley could raise the record speed for a 3.0-litre car to more than 100mph (161km/h), generating masses of publicity for the company. The car they used was Benjafield's own 3 Litre, rebuilt at the factory and fitted with a new streamlined body which led to it being nicknamed 'The Slug'. It proved able to lap the oval Montlhéry track at over 100mph (161km/h) and set a record for 3,000km in 12 hours, 23 minutes and 57.04 seconds at an average 100.23mph (161.305km/h), then returned a couple of weeks later to break the 12-hour record at 100.96mph (162.479km/h) – but engine problems and a crash curtailed the longer distance record attempts.

Focus on the Montlhéry record breaking activities had compromised preparations for the Le Mans 24-hour race in June, an important event for Bentley after the disappointment of 1925 when neither of their cars made it to the finish. For 1926 a three-car team was planned, with two works cars and a private entry for Tommy Thistlethwaite, sharing with Clive Gallop. One of the works cars was in the hands of Sammy Davis and Dudley Benjafield, while the other was driven by Frank Clement and George Duller, a champion jockey and friend of Woolf Barnato.

As usual there were detail changes to the regulations, which now required the cars to carry 180kg (397lb) in ballast, equivalent to the weight of three passengers. The simplest approach was to tie sandbags to the seats, but Bentley mechanic Les Pennel realised that while the rules stated that the weight had to be carried, they didn't specify where. Instead of the sandbags he fitted steel tubes at the front and rear of the chassis, filled with lead, which met the ballast rules and at the same time helped to improve the cars' weight distribution and chassis stiffness. But despite that clever thinking the Bentley effort came to nothing once again: the Clement/Duller works car and the Thistlethwaite/Gallop private entry had both expired with engine trouble by Sunday morning, while Sammy Davis suffered a brake failure in the other works car – which finished its race stuck in the sand bank at the Mulsanne corner. After the race that car, known as 'Old Number 7', was bought by Benjafield and entered in the Georges Boillot Cup race in Boulogne, but again it crashed after trouble with the brakes.

By now it was clear that the 3 Litre Bentley was being pushed to its limits to remain competitive in racing, and it had already been shown to have inadequate power for heavy saloon bodies. With Barnato's funding now underwriting new model development, W.O. looked for a way to replace the 3 Litre with a more powerful new model. Visitors to the Olympia show in late 1926 would have noticed nothing particularly unusual as Bentley displayed a 3 Litre Speed Model and a long-wheelbase Mulliner coupé, alongside a 6½ Litre with a Barker sedanca body and a sectioned 6½-litre engine. But all the work behind the scenes centred around the new model.

At the same time, a proper racing programme was planned for 1927. After the 1926 Le Mans debacle W.O. had wanted to withdraw from racing altogether, but with

Right: A spinoff from the Belgian coachbuilder Vanden Plas was based at Kingsbury, northwest London, where it produced many fine bodies for Bentley chassis. This is a 1926 3 Litre.

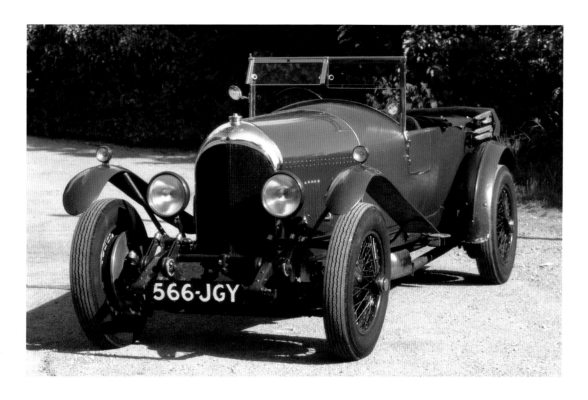

Below: This 1926 long-chassis Bentley 3 Litre features a 'faux-bois' (imitation wood-grain) finish on its wheels. It was created by Barker and Co. of London, which also made bodywork for Rolls-Royce and Daimler.

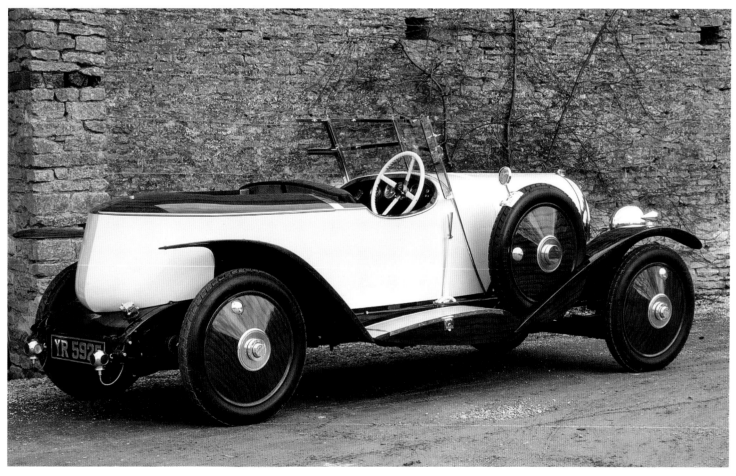

gentleman driver Barnato as chairman that was never likely. Instead the racing was put on a proper footing, with greater emphasis on a planned campaign and more analysis of the event regulations to identify the technical challenges.

Early evidence of this more professional approach came in May 1927 when Bentley entered the Essex Car Club Six-Hours race as a shakedown for that year's Le Mans 24 hours. But three of the four entries were fitted with new Duralumin rockers which broke up during the race. Henry 'Tim' Birkin refused to have the new parts fitted to his car so close to the start of the race and his 3 Litre, running the original steel rockers, survived to the end of the race. Despite gearbox problems Birkin finished third behind a Sunbeam and an Alvis.

Back at Oxgate Lane the replacement for the 3 Litre began to take shape. W.O. expanded the four-cylinder engine to just under 4.5 litres using the same bore and stroke as the six-cylinder 6½ Litre, and also introduced a new crankshaft with 55mm main bearings like those used in the six. Duralumin rockers and a one-piece cast sump were recent 3 Litre upgrades that were carried over to the new engine. Power went up from around 85bhp in the 3 Litre to about 110bhp for the 4½ Litre. The chassis was virtually the same as the 3 Litre, but with a few detail improvements.

The first prototype 4½ Litre, nicknamed 'Old Mother Gun', was prepared to race at Le Mans, where it would be driven by Frank Clement and Leslie Callingham. Benjafield and Davis again drove Benjafield's 'Old Number 7' 3 Litre, and there was a new 3 Litre for George Duller and French Baron André d'Erlanger. The race started well for the Bentley team, with Clement taking an early lead, and as

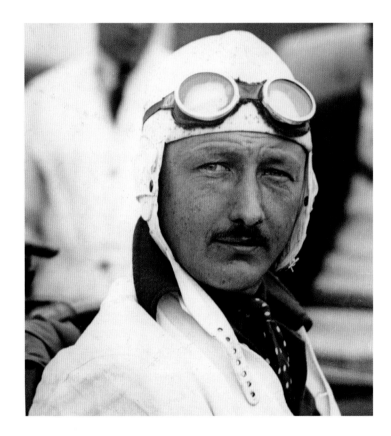

dusk fell the Bentleys were circulating in first, second and third place – when disaster struck.

The tricky Maison Blanche S-bend swerved around a white farmhouse which gave the bend its name, and which hid the second part of the corner as drivers approached. Pierre Tabourin spun his 2.0-litre Th. Schneider in the middle of the corner, bouncing off the crash barrier and ending up in the middle of the road at right angles to oncoming cars. The first rival on the scene was Callingham in the leading Bentley, who managed to avoid the crashed car but in the process put his own vehicle into a ditch. He was thrown out of the car, though fortunately without sustaining major injury. Next to arrive was Duller, who bailed out of his 3 Litre when he realised he could not avoid hitting the wreckage. Davis was next in the other 3 Litre: alerted, perhaps, by a fragment of wreckage or disturbed earth on the road he rounded the corner more slowly than the others, but even then could not avoid hitting the cars strewn across the road.

All three Bentleys had been severely damaged in a matter of minutes. The 4½ Litre and Duller's 3 Litre were beyond immediate repair, but Davis managed to get his car back to the pits. The chassis was bent and on one side a buckled wheel had to be replaced and the badly bent wing wired up. The headlamp was smashed, so Davis lashed a Smiths hand lantern to the chassis, and headed back into the race. The time lost had let a French Aries into the lead, but with only an hour to go the Aries succumbed to engine trouble and 'Old Number 7' was back in the lead. Benjafield even had time to stop at the pits to let Sammy Davis take over for the final lap to victory. The proprietor of *The Autocar* magazine, Sir Edward Iliffe, threw a party for the Bentley team at the Savoy in London where the car made a surprise appearance, unwashed and still bearing the scars from its crash.

Opposite: Sir Henry 'Tim' Birkin was one of the most talented drivers of his generation. Birkin was behind the development of the 4½ Litre 'Blower' Bentley.

Right: The 1927 Le Mans-winning 3 Litre, minus wheels and mudguards, is manhandled into the Savoy for the victory dinner. The car still shows damage from its mid-race crash.

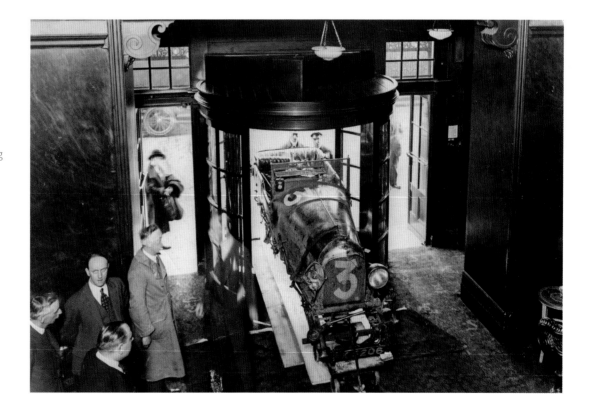

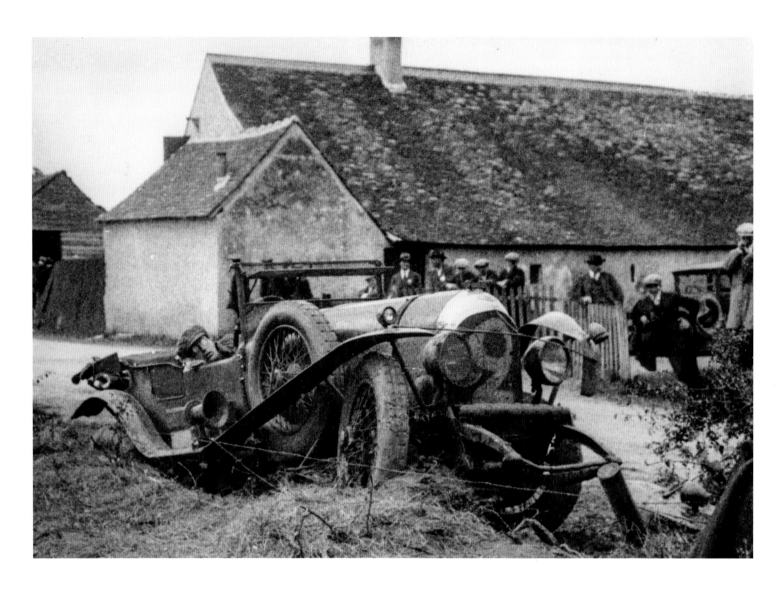

Above: An ugly mishap at Le Mans in 1927. Two of the three Bentleys competing that year crashed at the Maison Blanche bend on the evening of Saturday 18 June. The third car hit the wreckage but managed to keep going, and went on to win the race.

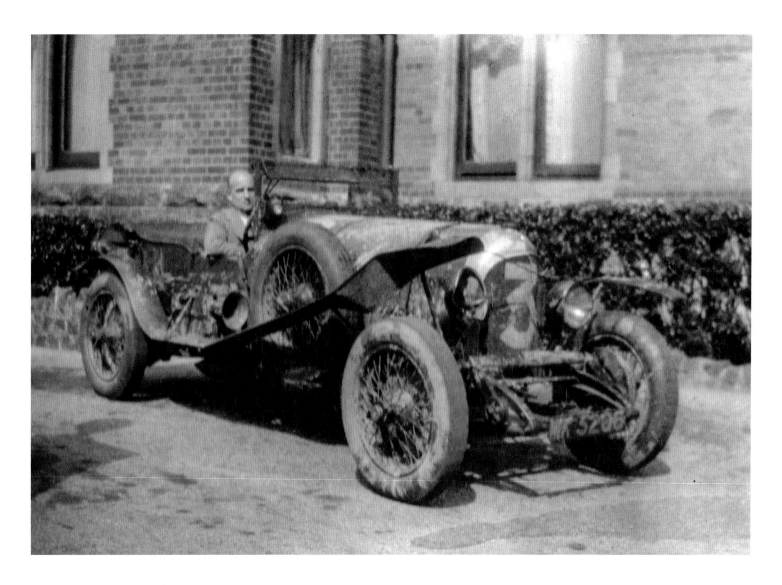

Above: The surviving, victorious Bentley 3 Litre at Le Mans in 1927,
driven by Dudley Benjafield. It won by an impressive twenty laps, but
the damage to its front wing and headlamp, sustained earlier in the
race, are clearly visible in this photo.

Clement and Duller won the Grand Prix de Paris race in the prototype 4½ Litre in August, and the production 4½ Litre was unveiled at the London Motor Show that October. The original 3 Litre model remained available but few were sold after the appearance of the larger-engined four-cylinder. The 6½ Litre was still the top model, costing around 50 per cent more.

For 1928 the Essex Six-Hours again acted as a pre-Le Mans trial, and this time Bentley came away from it with the team prize. At Le Mans the 'Old Mother Gun' 4½ Litre was shared by Woolf Barnato and Bernard Rubin, and there were new cars for Frank Clement/Dudley Benjafield and Tim Birkin/Jean Chassagne. Birkin put his car off the road after a puncture, and Clement's car broke its chassis. 'Old Mother Gun' suffered the same failure, but this occurred near the end of the 24 hours, and Barnato was able to crawl around the final lap to take Bentley's third Le Mans victory. Though Birkin entered his 4½ Litre in the German GP for sports cars and could only manage eighth place behind the mighty supercharged Mercedes, he finished first on the road in the Tourist Trophy – though he had to cede the victory on handicap.

After his German experience Birkin became convinced that a supercharged Bentley would win races, and approached supercharger expert Amherst Villiers to design a suitable installation. W.O., sceptical about the benefits, dictated that the supercharger had to sit right at the front of the car, outside the engine bay. Villiers made significant changes to the engine and supplied the Roots-type supercharger, and Birkin had the first 'Blower Bentley' built up from a 1928 4½ Litre at his own workshop. W.O.,

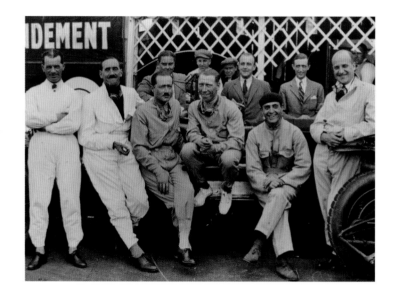

Above: Bentley Boys in 1927. Front row from left: Clement, Callingham, D'Erlanger, Duller (W.O behind), Davis and Benjafield.

meanwhile, was working on an alternative method of generating greater performance, by tuning the big six-cylinder engine to produce the Speed Six. The supercharged cars were not ready for Le Mans in 1929 but the Speed Six was, and Birkin was allotted to drive it alongside Barnato. The Speed Six proved to be the class of the field, winning comfortably ahead of three unsupercharged 4½ Litre cars: Bentleys filled the top four places. The team organised a formation finish to underline their superiority.

Birkin's Blower was ready in July and quickly proved fast but fragile. At the TT in August, now moved from the Isle of Man to the country roads near Newtownards in Ulster, there were five Bentley entries including a team of three supercharged 4½ Litres. W.O. raised some eyebrows by

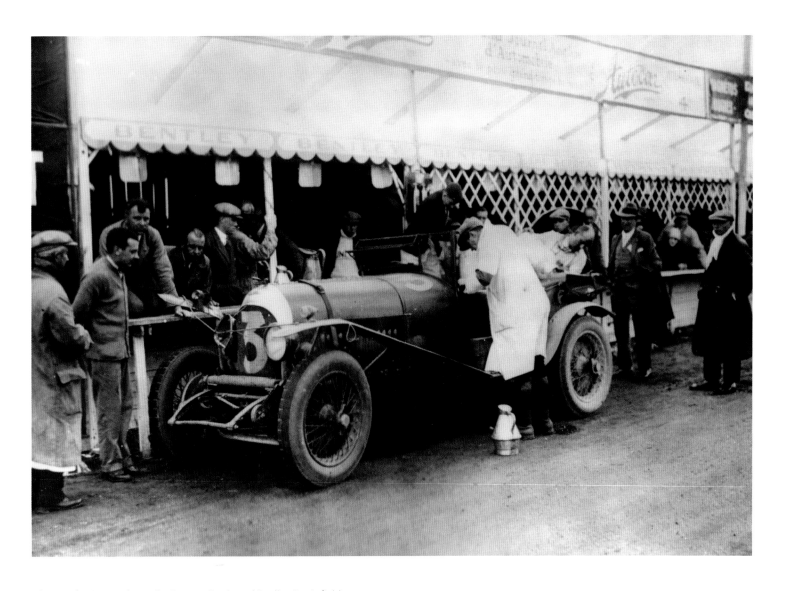

Above: The 3 Litre driven by Sammy Davis and Dudley Benjafield
undergoes refuelling and repairs in the pits at Le Mans in 1927,
on its way to a historic win.

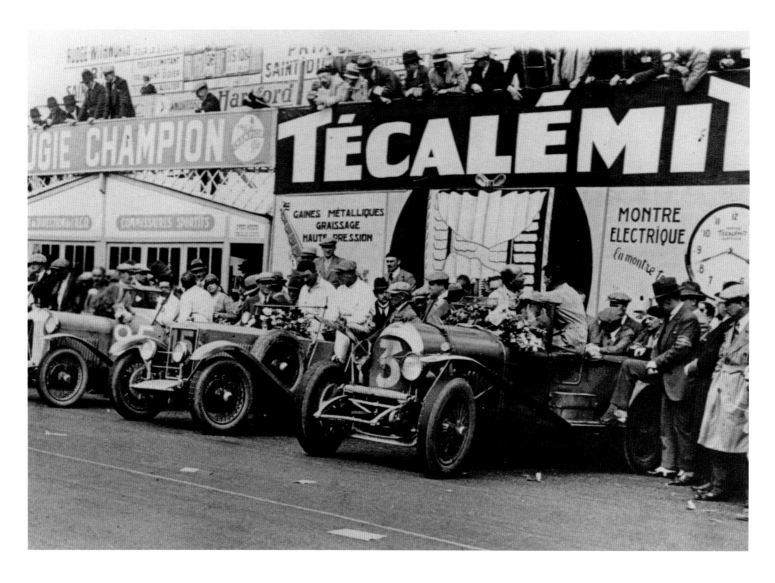

Above: The end of the 1927 Le Mans 24-hour race with the victorious Benjafield/Davis Bentley in pride of place. Cars from the French Salmson team came second and third.

Opposite: Established in 1923, the Le Mans competition, run over the Circuit de la Sarthe, soon gained a formidable reputation for the challenges it posed to cars and drivers.

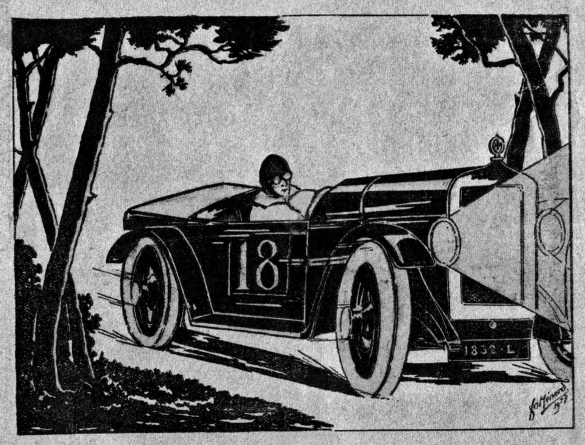

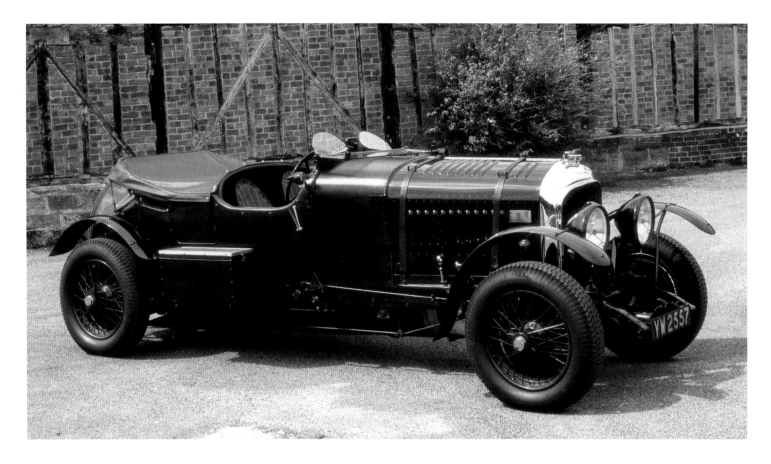

agreeing to act as riding mechanic to Birkin in his Blower. They finished second on the road but eleventh overall on handicap, while the fastest Bentley – a Speed Six driven by Glen Kidston – harried Rudolf Caracciola's Mercedes before crashing in the rain.

For the new British Racing Drivers' Club 500-mile race at Brooklands in October 1929 Birkin's Blower was given a new two-seat fabric body. In the race it was fast, lapping the banked track at 121mph (195km/h) and vying for the lead with Kaye Don's Sunbeam, but the engine spewed oil all over the bodywork and Birkin. Eventually it caught alight, and the body was all but destroyed.

Birkin enlisted financial support from the Hon. Dorothy Paget after his own resources ran dry, and over the winter the car was rebuilt at Birkin's Welwyn Garden City works. The new blue-painted single-seater body was designed by Reid Railton, with some early aerodynamic thinking. The familiar curved radiator grille was replaced by a smooth nose panel that extended forwards over the

top of the supercharger and carburettors, there was a cowl on top of the body that pushed air over the driver's head, and a fairing behind him to smooth out the airflow over the rear body. But Birkin didn't like the cowl, because it made it difficult for him to see the road and other competitors, so it was quickly replaced by a conventional aeroscreen.

The engine was based on the usual supercharged Bentley 4½-litre in-line four, but with a new counterbalanced crankshaft and robust H-section conrods designed by Amherst Villiers. In this form it generated about 240bhp. It was entered for the first Brooklands meeting of 1930 and, despite a damaged supercharger and clutch slip, Birkin finished second behind a Bugatti. In a longer race later that day, he achieved over 101mph (163km/h) average on his standing-start lap and over 126mph (203km/h) on a flying lap to win at 119.13mph (191.721km/h) overall. At a Brooklands Easter meeting handicap Birkin had to give J.G. Parry-Thomas's Leyland-Thomas special an 11-second head start, but still won by 150 yards (137m).

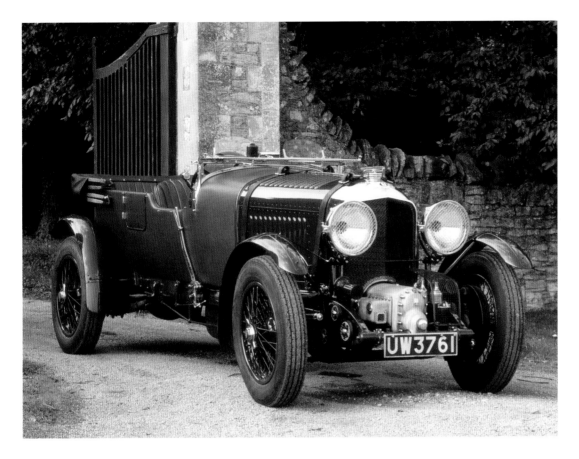

Opposite: One of the 1928 works racing cars, an unsupercharged 4½ Litre with Vanden Plas 'bobtail' bodywork. In 1929 this car finished third at Le Mans and second in the Brooklands Double Twelve.

Left: This 4½ Litre 'Blower' was tested by the motoring journal *The Motor* in 1930.

Below: A 1929 Speed Six with flamboyant Barker bodywork. Only four cars of this design were built, and three survive: this one fetched more than £300,000 at a UK auction in 2004.

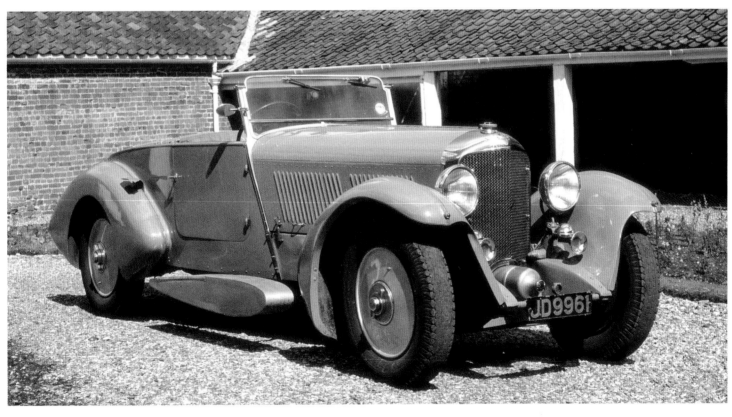

LE CIRCUIT PERMANENT DE LA SARTHE

Développement : 16 kil. 360

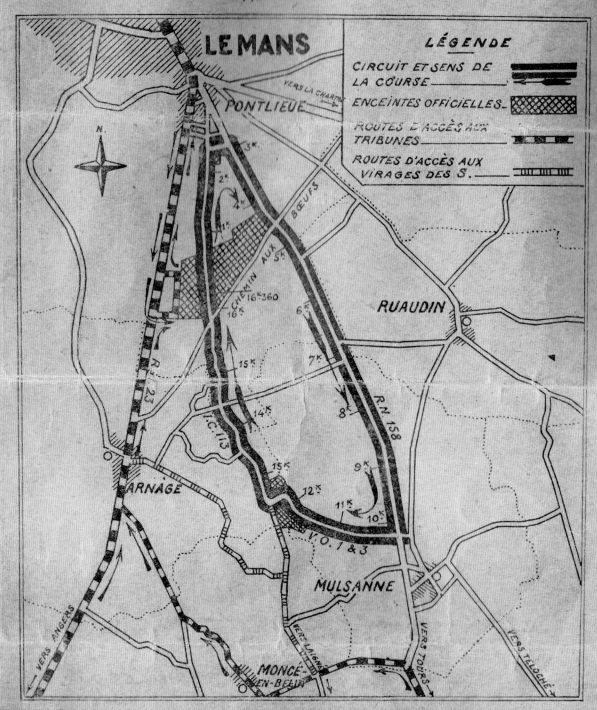

Légende:
- CIRCUIT ET SENS DE LA COURSE
- ENCEINTES OFFICIELLES
- ROUTES D'ACCÈS AUX TRIBUNES
- ROUTES D'ACCÈS AUX VIRAGES DES S.

Les nouveaux Insignes de l'Automobile-Club de l'Ouest

Les Sociétaires de l'Automobile-Club de l'Ouest peuvent retenir dans tous les bureaux du Club les nouveaux insignes dont le modèle est reproduit ci-contre.

Ces insignes ont été établis aux couleurs du Panonceau du Club : bleu et jaune.

Ils sont également mis en vente au Bureau de l'A. C. O., sous les Tribunes, aux prix suivants :

INSIGNE VOITURE :

Modèle émaillé	3 francs
Modèle émail	10 —

INSIGNE BOUTONNIÈRE :

Modèle émail	3 francs

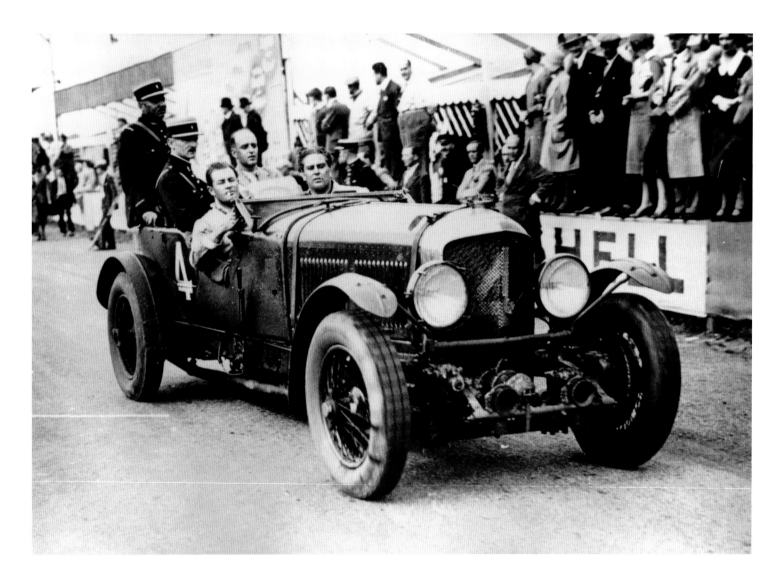

Opposite: This map from a 1930 Le Mans programme shows the layout of the circuit, in the public roads between the towns of Le Mans, Mulsanne and Arnage. Much of the same circuit is still in use today, augmented by sections of purpose-built track.

Above: The 1930 Le Mans race saw an epic duel between the Blower Bentleys entered privately by Dudley Benjafield and Tim Birkin, and Rudolf Caracciola's Mercedes SSK. All three retired, leaving the victory to the Bentley works team Speed Six of Woolf Barnato and Glen Kidston.

Later that day the single-seater raised the Brooklands Outer Circuit lap record to 135.33mph (217.793km/h). Birkin then hopped into a plane, flying to Le Touquet to keep a dinner engagement with Woolf Barnato.

Such was the life of the playboy drivers who became known as the 'Bentley Boys'. The company chairman had the most extravagant lifestyle of all, full of parties and foreign travel. In March 1930 he was having dinner in Cannes when the conversation turned to racing the famous Blue Train across France. A Rover and an Alvis had both recently beaten the overnight express from Saint-Raphaël to Calais, and Barnato bet he could do it easily. None of his guests would match his £200 wager, but he decided to prove his point anyway. Setting out from Cannes the

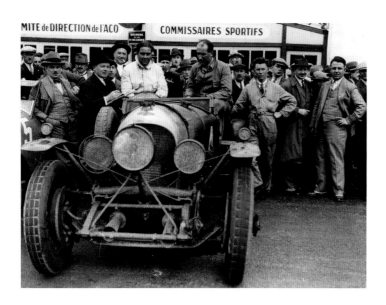

Above: Bentley made a habit of winning at Le Mans: Woolf Barnato (left) and Bernard Rubin triumphed in 1928.

following evening at 5.45 p.m., he reached Calais at 10.30 a.m., hours ahead of the train. So he pressed on, taking a boat across the channel and arriving at the Conservative Club in London at 3.20 p.m., four minutes before the Blue Train arrived in Calais. The French government, furious at their train being humiliated, banned Bentley Motors from the 1930 Paris Motor Show and fined the company £160 for racing on public roads. Rumour has it the fine remains unpaid to this day.

For many years it was believed the Barnato made the trip in a Speed Six with a striking one-off three-seater coupé body by coachbuilder Gurney Nutting. Terence Cuneo painted a famous picture of this car neck and neck with the train, a scene which certainly never happened because the train and car routes did not coincide. But it is now believed that Barnato used a Mulliner saloon-bodied Speed Six to beat the Blue Train, despite which the Gurney Nutting coupé is still widely known as the Blue Train Bentley.

Two Blowers started the Le Mans 24-hour race in June. Birkin shared his car with Jean Chassagne while Giulio Ramponi co-drove Dudley Benjafield's car. The works Bentley entries were three Speed Sixes – Woolf Barnato shared with Glen Kidston, Sammy Davis with Clive Dunfee, and Frank Clement with Dick Watney. The Blowers did not reach the finish, but Birkin and Benjafield set a blistering pace that Rudolf Caracciola's Mercedes-Benz was forced to match and the effort proved too much for it. The Mercedes retired, leaving the way clear for Barnato to win his third Le Mans 24-hour race.

Though Dorothy Paget soon withdrew her support for Birkin's racing team she did continue to fund development

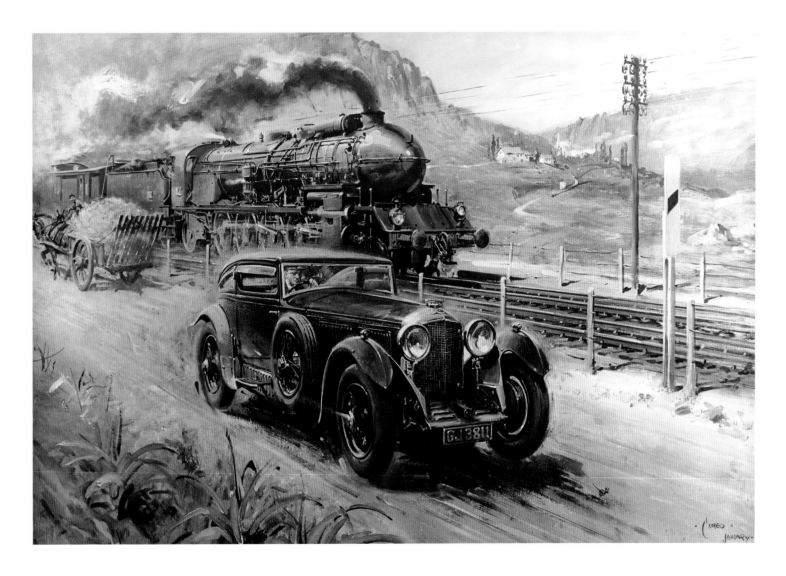

Above: Terence Cuneo's famous painting of Barnato's Gurney Nutting coupé racing the Blue Train. Cuneo has allowed himself a little artistic licence: it wasn't this car Barnato used to beat the train on its journey across France, and his route never ran alongside the railway track.

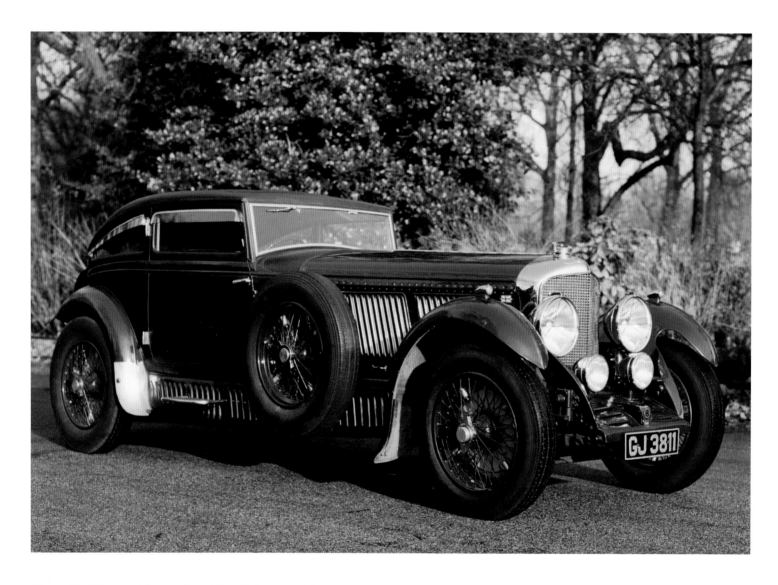

Above: Woolf Barnato's famous Speed Six with its unusual Gurney
Nutting fastback body. Though probably not the car Barnato used to
race the train in 1930, it is commonly known as the 'Blue Train' Bentley.

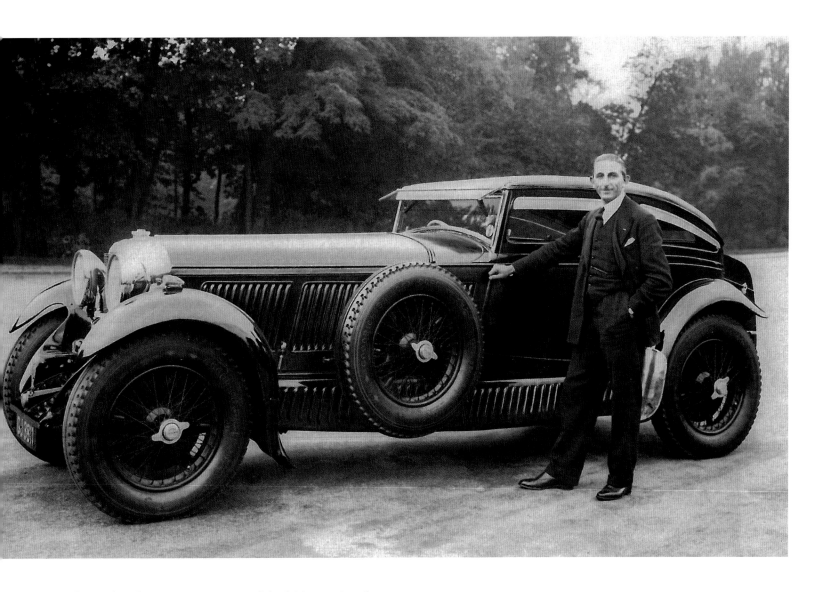

Above: Though Barnato was an accomplished driver – twice winner at
Le Mans driving Bentley cars – he also had a chauffeur, Cyril de Heaume.
He is seen here posing with the boss's Speed Six around 1930.

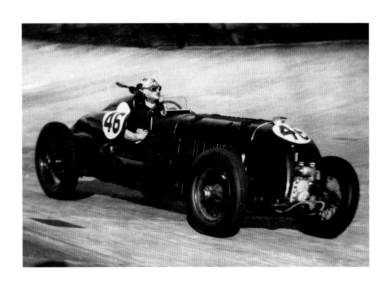

Above: Scarf flying in the wind, Tim Birkin pounds around the Brooklands banking in his 4½ Litre 'Blower Bentley'.

of the single seater, and work continued over the winter of 1930–1. Birkin consulted racer and engineer George Eyston, who had invented the Powerplus vane-type supercharger which would go on to break speed records in his MG EX120 in 1931. A Powerplus blower was fitted to Birkin's Bentley, with a warm-water feed from the radiator to prevent the intake from icing up. In this form the single-seater proved fast but fragile, and after it caught fire in testing Birkin refitted the original Villiers Roots blower.

The single-seater was repainted red for 1932. The cylinders were bored out 0.5mm, taking the engine capacity up to 4,442cc, and dry-sump lubrication was added with a scavenge pump on the nose of the supercharger, sending oil to a tank at the back of the car via a small oil cooler. The supercharger itself received a new aluminium casing and new rotors, increasing maximum boost to 12psi, and the two-inch sidedraught SU carburettors were replaced by huge downdraught SUs with 62mm throats. In this form the Bentley could consume a gallon (4.5l) of methanol/benzole/petrol fuel in 59 seconds, equating to fuel consumption of around 2mpg at racing speeds.

Birkin bettered the Brooklands lap record now held by Kaye Don with a 137.96mph (222.025km/h) in testing before the Easter meeting, but could not repeat the performance in competition – and his racing ended early with a cracked cylinder block. But he was back later in the year, recording 137.58mph (221.414km/h) on the way to winning a match race with John Cobb's Delage – during which the streamlined fairing parted company with the back of the car and flew high into the air.

That was the last time Birkin raced the Bentley. Three weeks later he drove a Maserati to third place at the Tripoli Grand Prix, and during a pit stop burned his arm on the exhaust pipe that ran along the side of the open cockpit while reaching for a cigarette. Just a few weeks later, possibly from blood poisoning resulting from the wound, or from a recurrence of the malaria he had contracted in Palestine during the First World War, or a combination of the two, Birkin was dead.

By then the world had been plunged into financial chaos, and it looked like the Bentley marque might be dead, too.

Opposite: 'Blower No.1' was Birkin's own car, most famous in this later form with characteristic narrow body and radiator cowling. Today it must be one of the most valuable Bentleys of all.

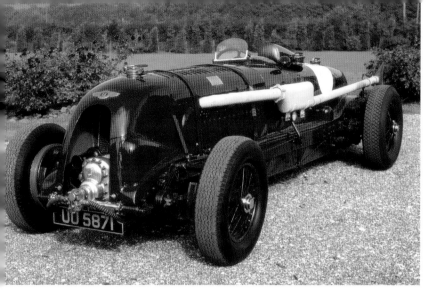

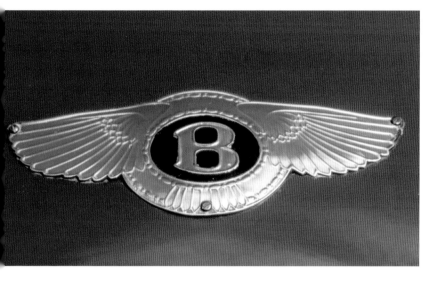

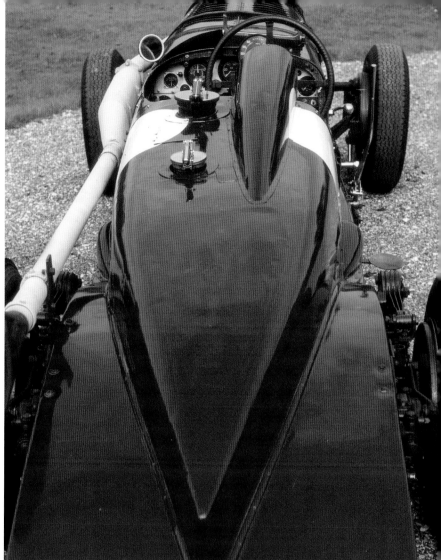

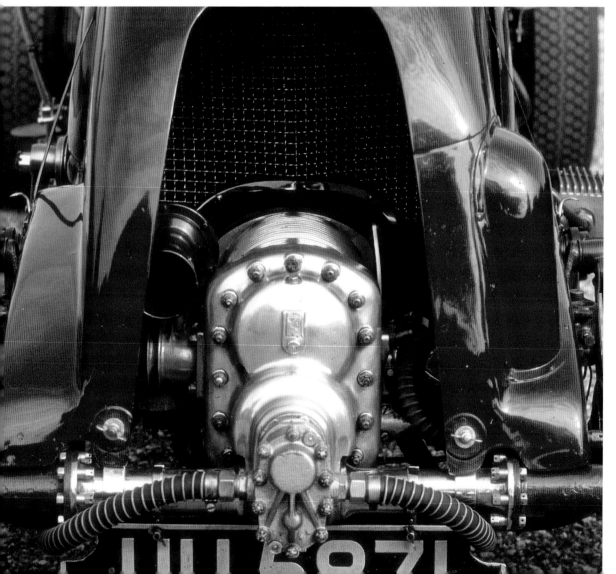

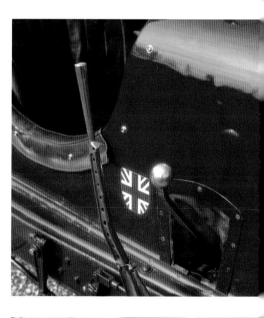

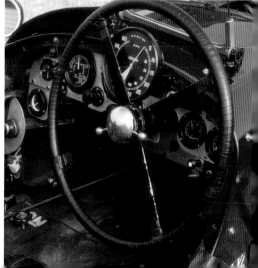

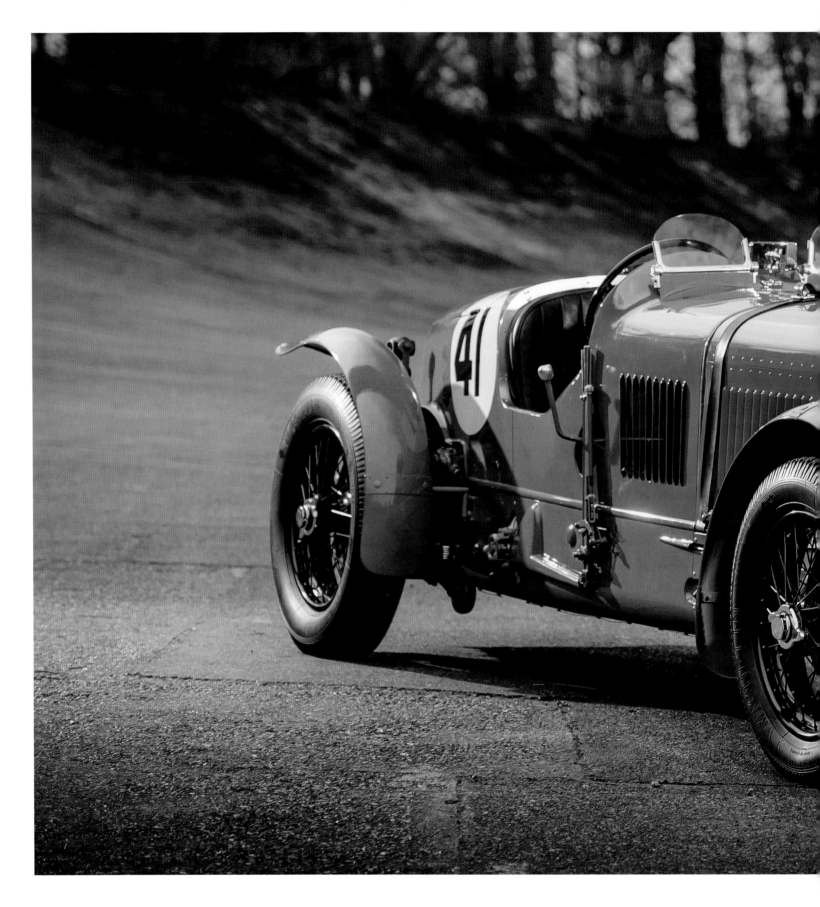

Above: Speed Six 'Old Number One' won the Le Mans
24-hours in 1929 and repeated the feat in 1930.

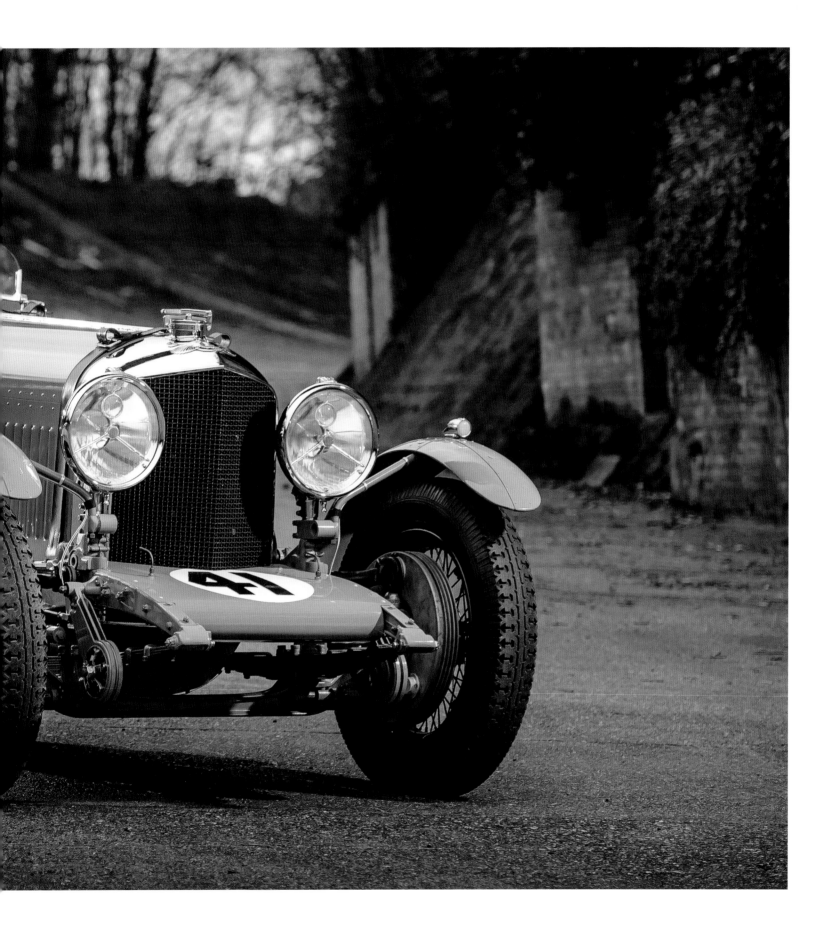

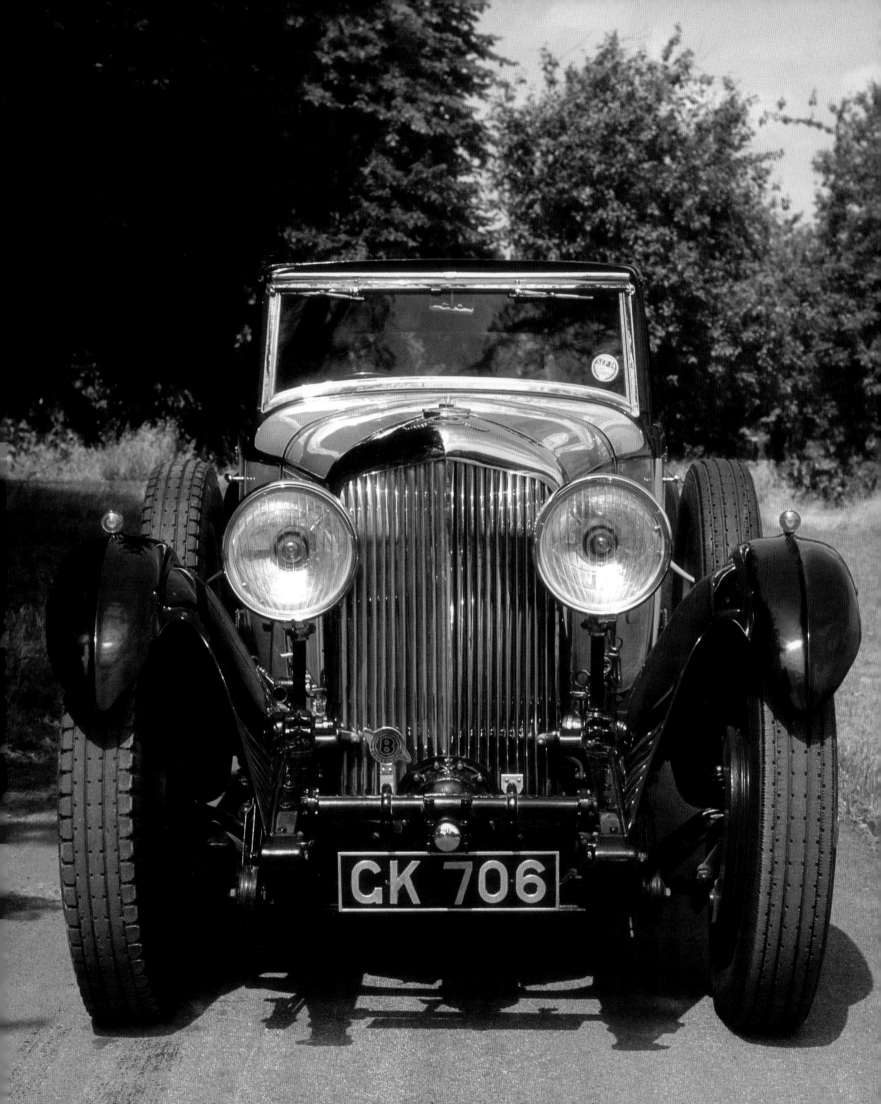

Chapter 3

CRISIS AND RESCUE

A few weeks after Bentley's triumph in the 1929 Le Mans 24-hour race, the company issued a statement announcing its withdrawal from motor racing. After three consecutive Le Mans victories the Bentley works team was now expected to win, and the only significant publicity to be garnered would be if the cars failed. At the same time Woolf Barnato let it be known that he himself was retiring from the sport, the two decisions being interlinked as the chairman of Bentley could hardly be seen racing a car from another manufacturer.

The announcements carried a wider implication for Bentley Motors. Barnato had bankrolled the company because it provided him with the means, and the excuse, for his racing activities. Now that racing was no longer in Bentley's interest, and Barnato's own fascination with the sport was not what it had been, the car manufacturing business had to begin to pay its own way.

That meant a shift in emphasis. Bentley Motors had focused primarily on sports cars from its inception, and had never managed to sell enough of them to make a profit which could pay back the company's loans. In the new, businesslike atmosphere sports cars were much less important, and instead the company concentrated on producing quality saloon cars and touring cars.

Despite the Wall Street Crash of late 1929, and the knock-on effect it had on economies around the world, Bentley embarked on the design of a new car aimed at an even wealthier customer. The first step was to take the existing 6.6-litre six-cylinder engine and widen the bore to 110mm, expanding the capacity to 8.0-litres. Many parts were cast in Elektron, a magnesium alloy, to save weight.

The carburettors were swapped back to the right-hand side: doing so matched their placement on the four-cylinder engines, made control cables easier to route, and reduced exhaust heat soak into the cabin. The first of these engines was tested in February 1930, and was then fitted to W.O. Bentley's own car, an experimental 6½ Litre nicknamed 'The Box' on account of its very upright saloon body.

For the production cars the new engine was partnered with a new chassis. In the four-cylinder cars the rigid mounting of the engine had helped to stiffen the front end of the chassis, but the adoption of rubber mountings for the 6½-litre engine to improve refinement had meant the front end of the chassis was more flexible than was ideal. This led to some unpleasant handling characteristics as the chassis distorted, allowing the front axle to shake and bounce. The redesign of the chassis aimed to improve its stiffness, using new tubular cross-members to provide a more positive link between the two main chassis rails. An extra cross-member was added to tie the two rails together at the front. The suspension springs were longer, to improve ride comfort, and the kick up over the back axle was pushed further back to so that the rear seat could be repositioned for more legroom – an important consideration when the owner of the car would be likely to travel in the back seat. A new gearbox with a split casing was introduced which was much heavier than before, but also a lot quieter in operation. To make maintenance easier the 8 Litre was fitted with a Tecalemit one-shot lubrication system: by pushing a plunger under the dashboard the driver could oil all the chassis lubrication points which had to be attended to manually on lesser cars.

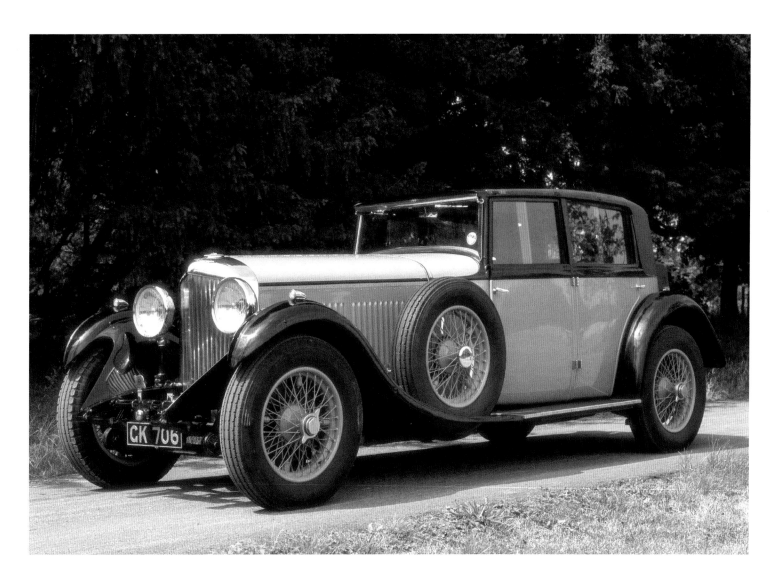

Above: The 8 Litre was Bentley's attempt to match the finest cars Rolls-Royce could offer. Huge, powerful and refined, it was an extraordinary car – but could only be afforded by the company's most wealthy customers. W.O. Bentley regarded the 8 Litre as an engineering triumph, and drove one himself for several years.

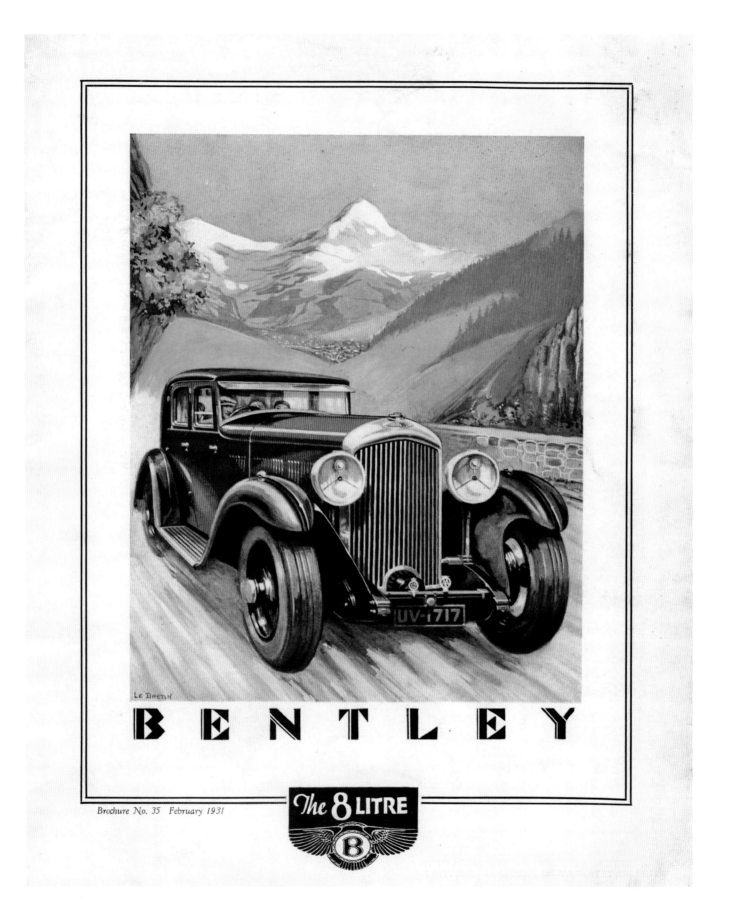

Above: Bentley's sales catalogue for the 8 Litre in 1931 showed the car
doing what it did best – rapid continental touring in comfort and style.

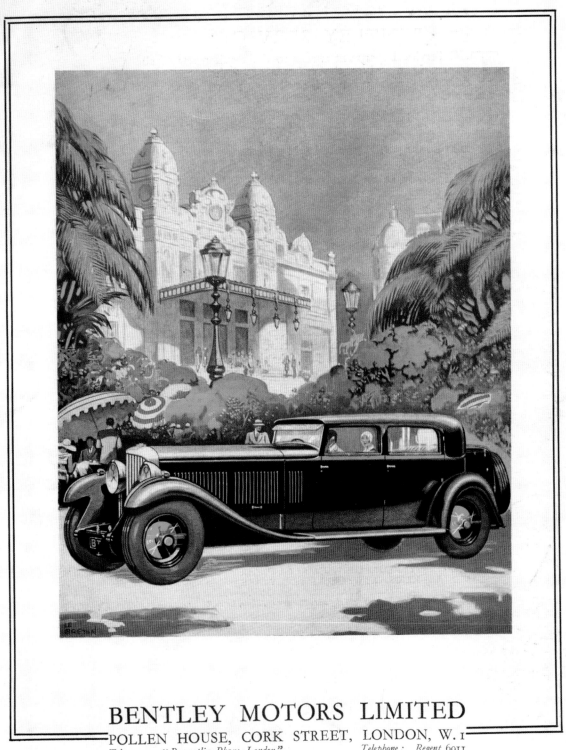

BENTLEY MOTORS LIMITED
POLLEN HOUSE, CORK STREET, LONDON, W. 1
Telegrams : " Benmotlin, Phone, London "   Telephone : Regent 6911
DIRECTORS
Woolf Barnato, W. O. Bentley, Sir Walrond Sinclair, J. K. Carruth H. Pike, R. S. Witchell

Above: The back of the same brochure shows the 8 Litre in its element –

as a comfortable saloon car of the utmost quality and elegance.

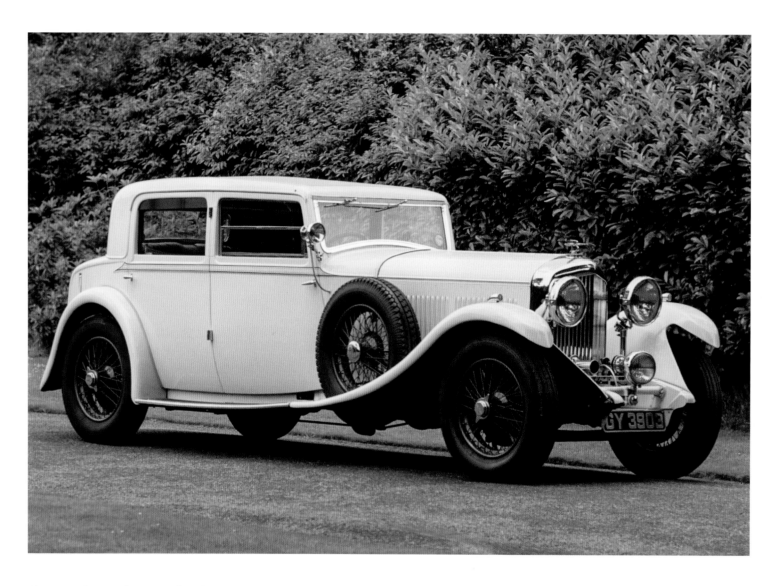

Above: By the time this H.J. Mulliner-bodied 8 Litre was delivered in 1932, Bentley Motors had been sold to a new owner, Rolls-Rolls, and sweeping changes in the company's direction were under way.

Six 8 Litre chassis were built for the car's unveiling at the Olympia Motor Show in October 1930, where Bentley announced a chassis-only price of £1,850 which was exactly the same as a short-wheelbase Rolls-Royce Phantom II, its most direct rival. *The Autocar* and *The Motor* both drove W.O.'s personal 8 Litre, fitted with an H.J. Mulliner saloon body, and wrote reports which were very positive. *The Autocar* managed to record a top speed of just over 101mph (163km/h), amazing for a saloon car of the era. Bentley guaranteed the 8 Litre would reach 100mph (161km/h) regardless of the coachwork fitted to it, and W.O. later said he thought the 8 Litre was the best car Bentley made during his time with the company.

Though the 8 Litre sold to wealthy individuals – the first one, with a formal H.J. Mulliner saloon body, was delivered to stage and film star Jack Buchanan in October 1930 – Bentley still needed to cater for buyers lower down the market. By now the 4½ Litre was very old-fashioned, and the company wanted a car which was more modern and also, crucially, cheaper to manufacture: the monoblock design of the original Bentley engines resulted in a lot of tricky machining. Work began on designs for a completely new Bentley engine in the summer of 1929, and single-cylinder prototypes were running by January 1930. Two specialist engine design companies, Weslake & Co and Ricardo (formerly Engine Patents), were consulted on the design. W.O. appears to have taken very little interest in the new engine as it abandoned the technically pure solution using four valves per cylinder and overhead camshafts, and instead retrogressed to an inlet-over-exhaust layout. Ricardo had achieved very good results with this sort of

engine, and had soon built a single-cylinder prototype which, when scaled up to a 4.0-litre inline-six, would generate more power than the existing 4.4-litre engine in all but its most highly tuned form.

Rather than build a new chassis to go with the new engine, a modified version of the 8 Litre chassis was used. This was strong and stiff, but very heavy. Inevitably the smaller engine produced a lot less power than the vast engine in the 8 Litre, and it meant that the 4 Litre model lacked the performance many people expected of a Bentley, though it was still more than a match for its biggest rival, the 20/25hp Rolls-Royce. Motoring journalists did, though, comment favourably on its smoothness and silence.

The new car was unveiled in May 1931, but by then the financial position at Bentley Motors had become critical. The following month Bentley managing director Jack Carruth telephoned and then wrote to Arthur Sidgreaves, his opposite number at Rolls-Royce, outlining Bentley's position and suggesting 'a working arrangement between our two companies'. After careful scrutiny of Bentley Motors' finances, Rolls-Royce declined to become involved.

A week later Bentley Motors was due to pay interest on two of its loans, but had nothing to pay it with – and after putting his hand in his pocket to cover Bentley's bills for almost five years, Barnato had finally had enough. As Bentley was not in a position to pay the interest the loans were called in, amounting to a £65,000 liability. In early July a receiver, Patrick Frere, was appointed to wind up the company and sell off its assets. Now that Barnato's interest in racing had waned, it was probably his least painful way of divesting himself of the company.

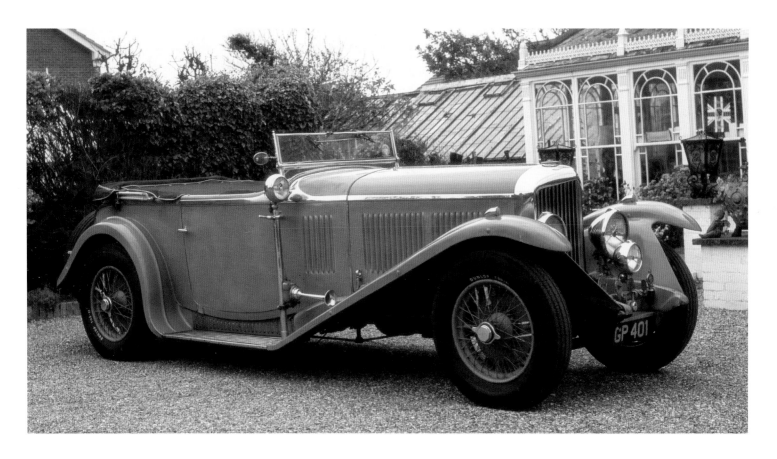

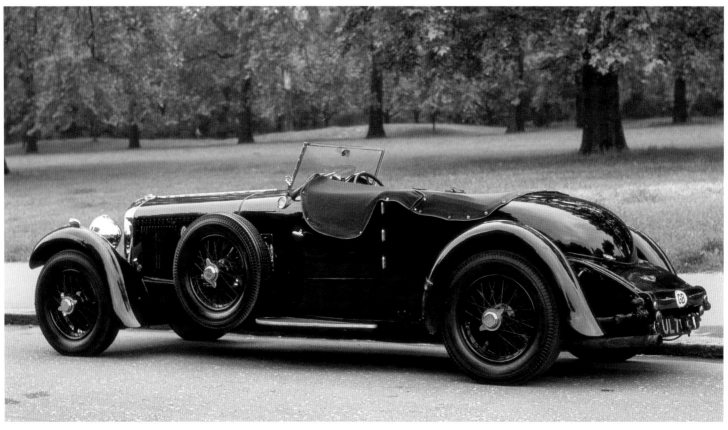

Top: This short-chassis 8 Litre with Vanden Plas bodywork was built in 1931 for Woolf Barnato to use on his Californian honeymoon.

Above: A very different 8 Litre, with sports tourer bodywork by London coachbuilder Corsica, which was added in 1937.

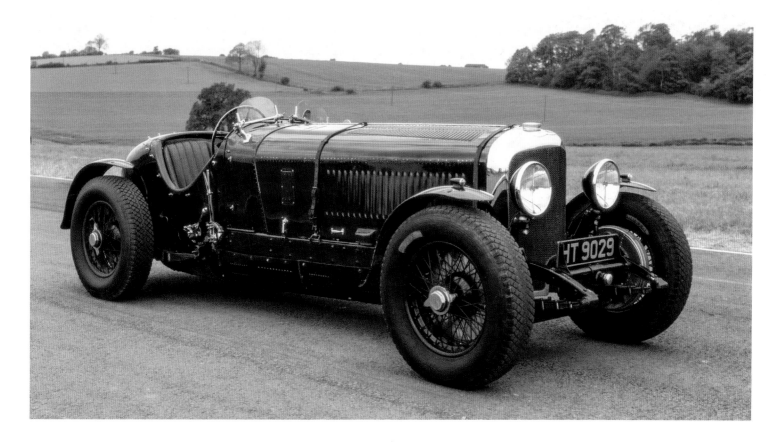

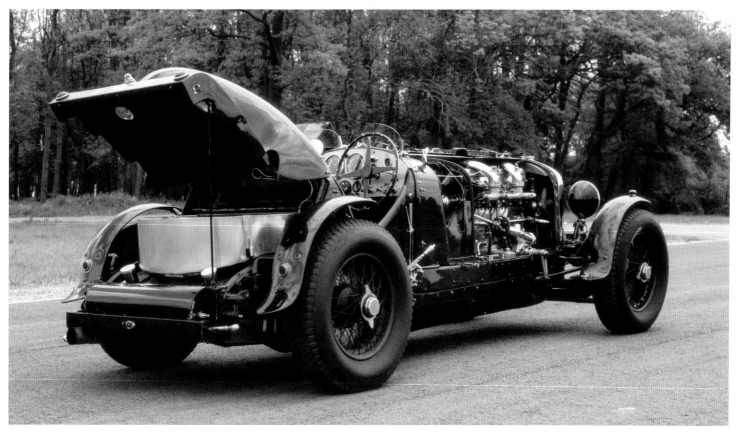

Top and above: A special, turbocharged 8 Litre built by John 'Jumbo' Goddard. At its tail is a massive fuel tank.

Following pages: W.O. Bentley's own company car – a 1930 8 Litre with a saloon body made by H.J. Mulliner.

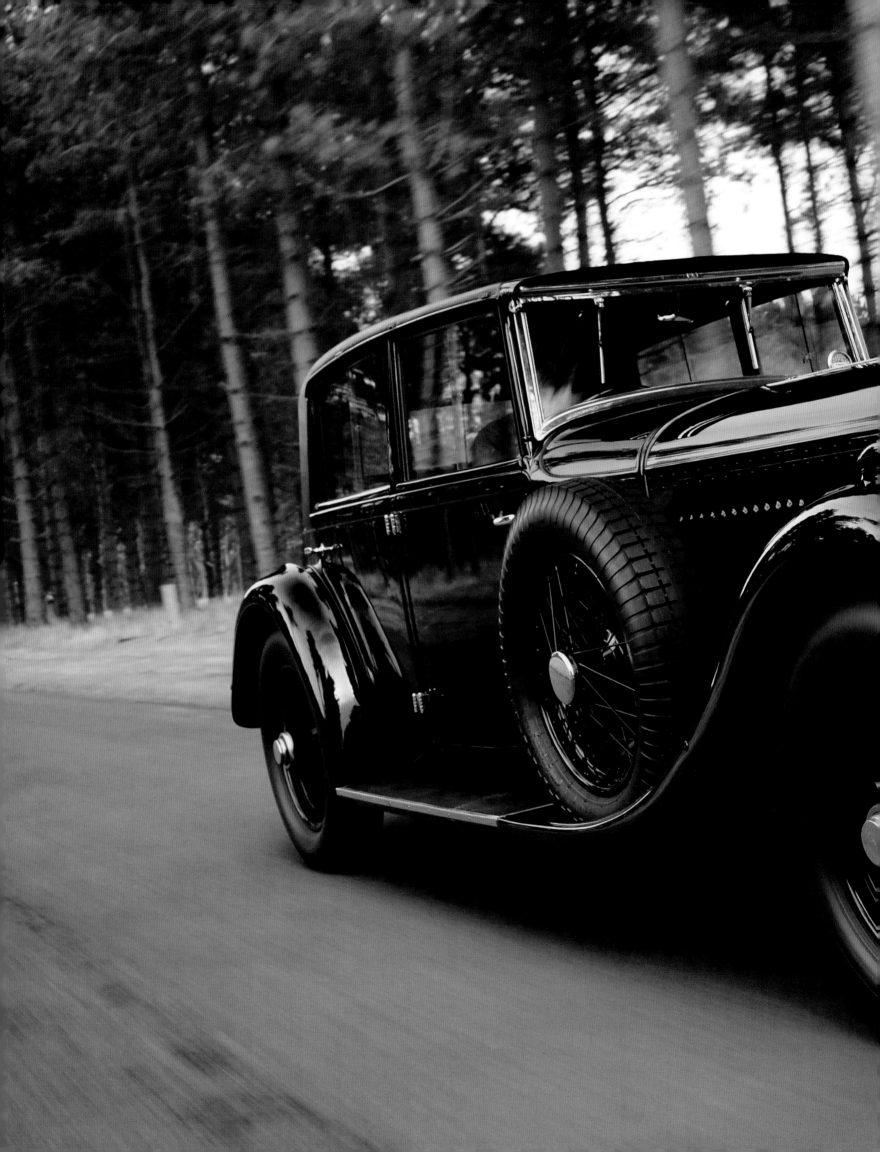

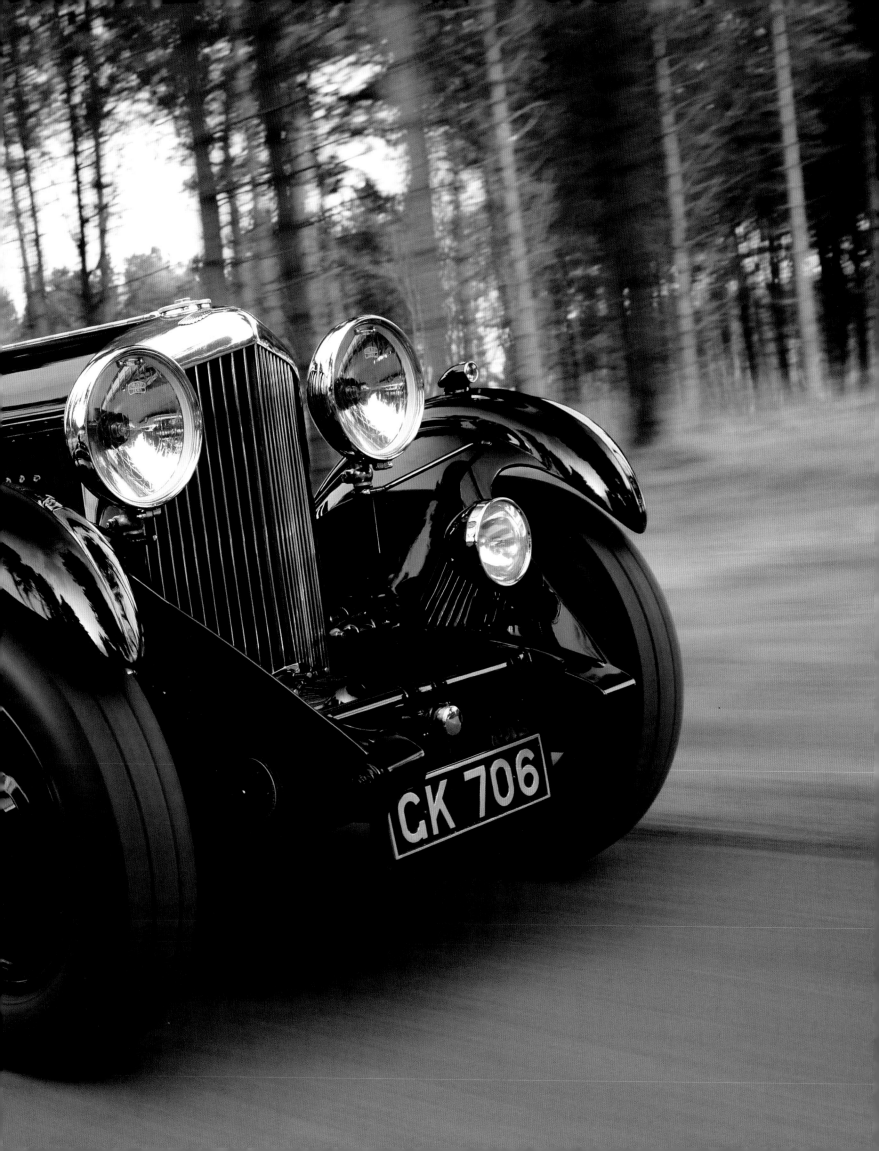

Frere looked for a new owner to take over the company in its entirety – and while one obvious suitor, Rolls-Royce, was clearly not an option, Frere found another, in the London-based Napier engineering company. Napier had been founded in the early 19th century by Scotsman David Napier and built its reputation on precision engineering work, such as the construction of printing presses, ammunition manufacturing equipment and industrial cranes. The company moved into car production in 1900 after the third generation of the family, Montague Napier, entered into a partnership with Australian businessman S.F. Edge. Encouraged by Edge, Napiers were early competitors in motor sport and the first cars to be painted in 'British Racing Green'; the company also built aero engines which were used in racing and record-breaking specials like Malcolm Campbell's Bluebirds, John Cobb's Napier-Railton and Henry Segrave's Golden Arrow. During the First World War Napier built trucks, ambulances, aircraft and aero engines at its factory in Acton. After the war a return to car making with the T75 proved unsuccessful. Napier was keen to get back into the motor business, and the acquisition of Bentley, based just a few miles away from its own London base, would have provided an ideal opportunity.

Napier initially offered £84,000 for the whole Bentley Motors company. The deal included the services of W.O., who had signed a contract tying him to Bentley Motors. The Napier deal seemed virtually certain to go through, and was reported in the newspapers and in the motoring press. With permission from the receiver, W.O. and some of his engineering staff started work on a design for a new six-cylinder 'Napier-Bentley'.

At a hearing in the High Court before Mr Justice Markham in November 1931 the Bentley Motors assets were due to be formally transferred to Napier. After final negotiations, Napier's offer had come to £103,675. But, to the surprise of both Bentley's and Napier's counsel, a barrister representing an organisation called the British Central Equitable Trust came forward to announce that he was empowered to make an offer for Bentley Motors which was greater than that put forward by Napier. After consulting with his client Napier's counsel improved the offer, and before the counsel for the British Central Equitable Trust could respond the judge declared that he would not sit as auctioneer, and instead invited the submission of sealed bids from both sides that afternoon. When the bids were opened it was revealed that Napier had improved its offer to £104,775, but the rival bid was £125,256. Bentley was bought by the British Central Equitable Trust, and all that remained was to find out who this unknown organisation was acting for. Even W.O. had no idea.

A few days later the identity of the mystery buyer was revealed. Though it had turned down Jack Carruth's partnership offer earlier in the year, Rolls-Royce still had some interest in Bentley. When it became clear that a sale to Napier was likely, Rolls-Royce must have been keen to avoid giving a rival to its aero engine business an opportunity to compete in the motor business as well. By buying Bentley, Rolls-Royce headed off a Napier-backed challenge which would have been a much more serious competitor than the underfunded independent Bentley operation had ever been – despite the quality of, in particular, the 8 Litre. Napier never did return to car making.

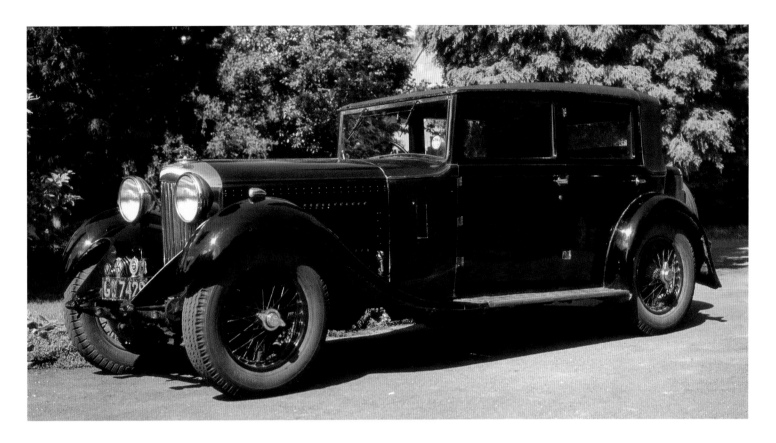

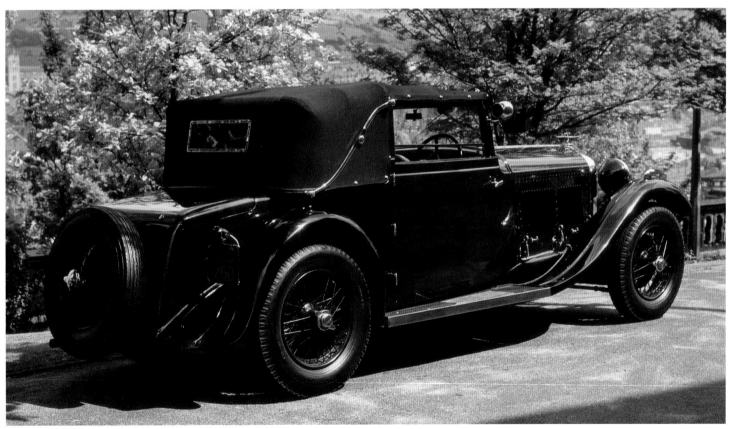

Top: The 4 Litre was Bentley Motors' last new model as an independent. This version has Thrupp & Maberly coachwork.

Above: A 4 Litre with a drophead coupé body by Freestone & Webb – probably the last Bentley to be made at the Cricklewood factory.

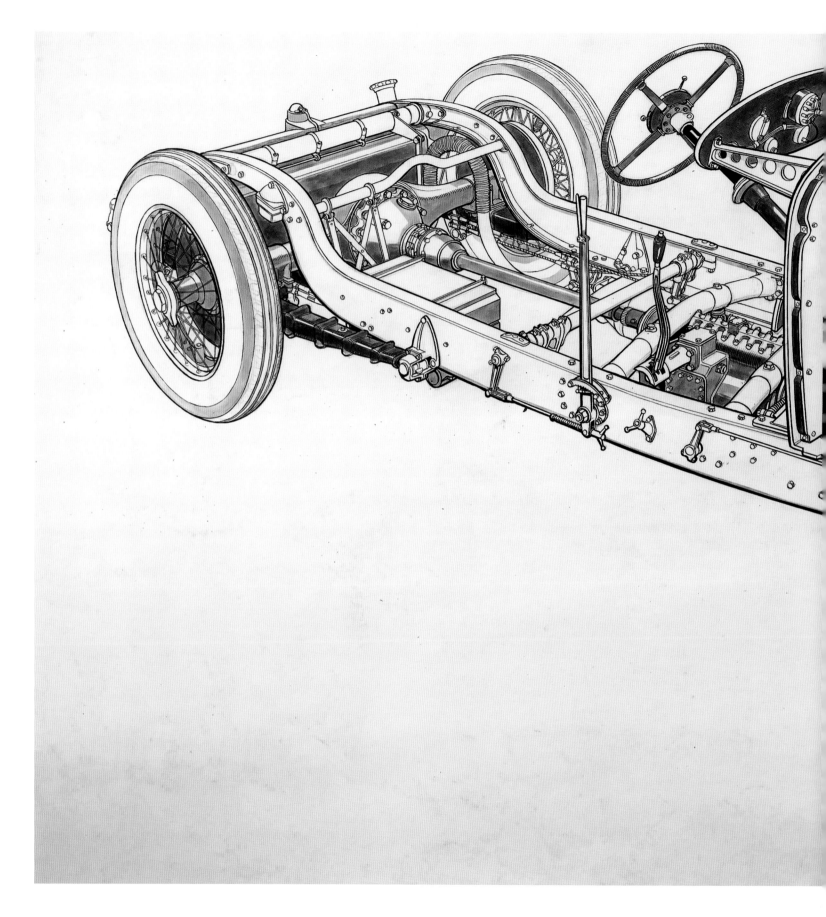

Above: A cutaway drawing of the 4 Litre chassis revealing its engine based on work by Ricardo, which differed fundamentally from previous Bentleys' overhead cam designs.

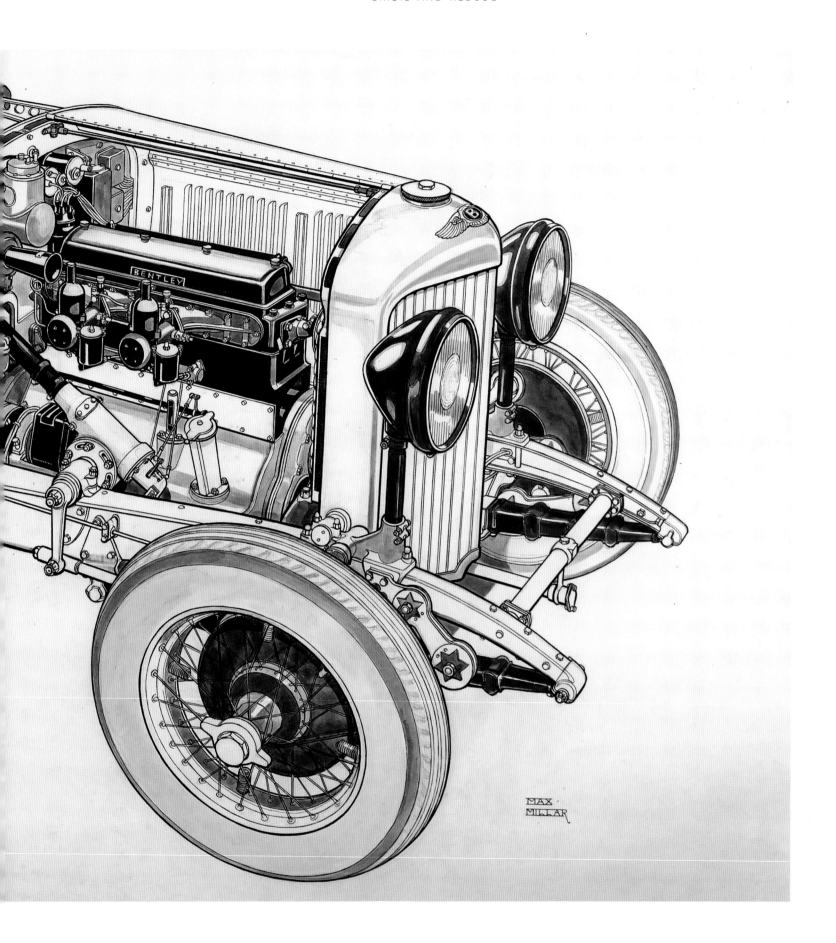

With Rolls-Royce in charge there were sweeping changes at Bentley. There was no interest from the new owners in restarting production of the existing Bentley cars – the 8 Litre was a direct competitor for Rolls-Royce's flagship 7.7-litre Phantom II, and the unloved 4 Litre was not selling anyway. The Cricklewood factory, established in 1920 and expanded as the company grew in size and stature during its first decade, was summarily closed, and the men who made the first generation of Bentleys all lost their jobs. For a while it seemed as though Rolls-Royce was content to let the Bentley name fade away into obscurity.

W.O., tied to Bentley by his contract, met with Sir Henry Royce to discuss the future. But despite their similar backgrounds – both had started out as railway apprentices and built businesses based on their own philosophies of engineering, and both had interests in motor cars and aircraft engines – there seemed little common ground. Royce is said to have dismissed Bentley as a 'commercial man'; and this, coming from someone who prized quality of engineering above all else, ranked as something of an insult. W.O. was obliged to work for Rolls-Royce until at least 1935, and he acted as a liaison between Rolls-Royce's sales office in London and the Derby factory. He also spent a lot of time test-driving prototypes of new Bentley and Rolls-Royce cars all over Europe. But he was kept away from the design team that was engaged in creating a new generation of cars that would bear his name.

It was not until 1933 that this next generation of Bentleys appeared. The 3½ Litre owed virtually nothing to previous Bentley practice, and took the brand into a different market sector with a different kind of customer.

The imposing radiator grille shape was the same as that on the Cricklewood Bentleys, but behind it everything was new. New to Bentley, anyway: in fact the 3½ Litre owed a lot to the Rolls-Royce 20/25, Derby's most popular model in the inter-war years. It also had links to another Rolls-Royce project which had never made it into the limelight.

This was Project Peregrine, which had been envisaged as a smaller, cheaper car to sit below the 20/25 in the Rolls-Royce range. But by 1930 Derby's engineers had calculated that the Peregrine would actually cost much the same to produce as the 20/25. Selling it at a lower price would not have been profitable, so the project was abandoned. Now that a new Bentley was needed in double-quick time the Peregrine was resurrected to provide the basis for it, though it was given more than just a Bentley radiator grille.

Originally Peregrine had been planned to receive a new supercharged 2.75-litre engine, but with development time short chief engineer Ernest Hives instead proposed a reworked version of the existing 3.7-litre Rolls-Royce straight six. To give it the sporting edge expected of a Bentley the compression ratio was raised, a more aggressive cam profile was employed, and there was a new crossflow cylinder head. Twin SU carburettors replaced the single Rolls-Royce carb fitted to the same engine in the 20/25, giving a power output of about 110bhp – about 10bhp more than the Rolls. The new engine was coupled to a four-speed manual transmission with synchromesh on the top two gears. There were leaf springs and servo-assisted mechanical drum brakes on all four wheels, and at both ends of the car the chassis was curved over the axles to drop the body down.

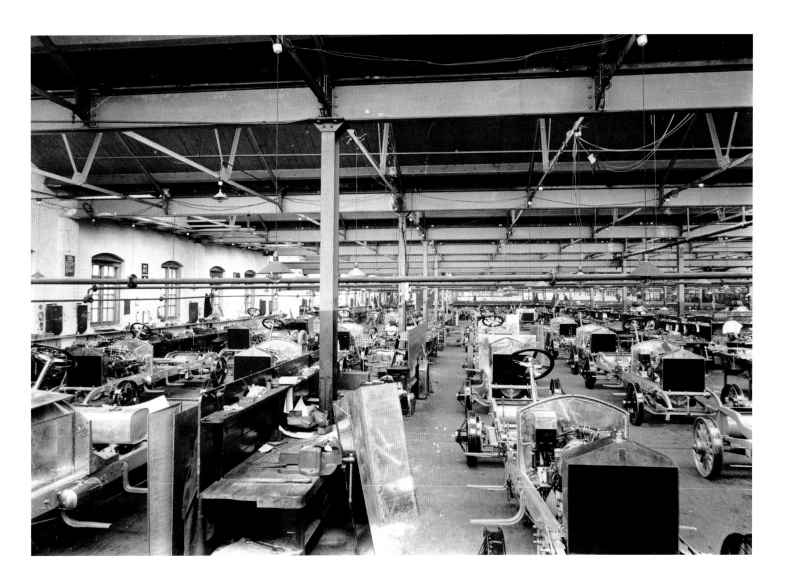

Above: Rolls-Royce Silver Ghosts in production at the company's
motor works at Nightingale Road, Derby, around 1912. A new
generation of Bentleys would be produced there from 1933.

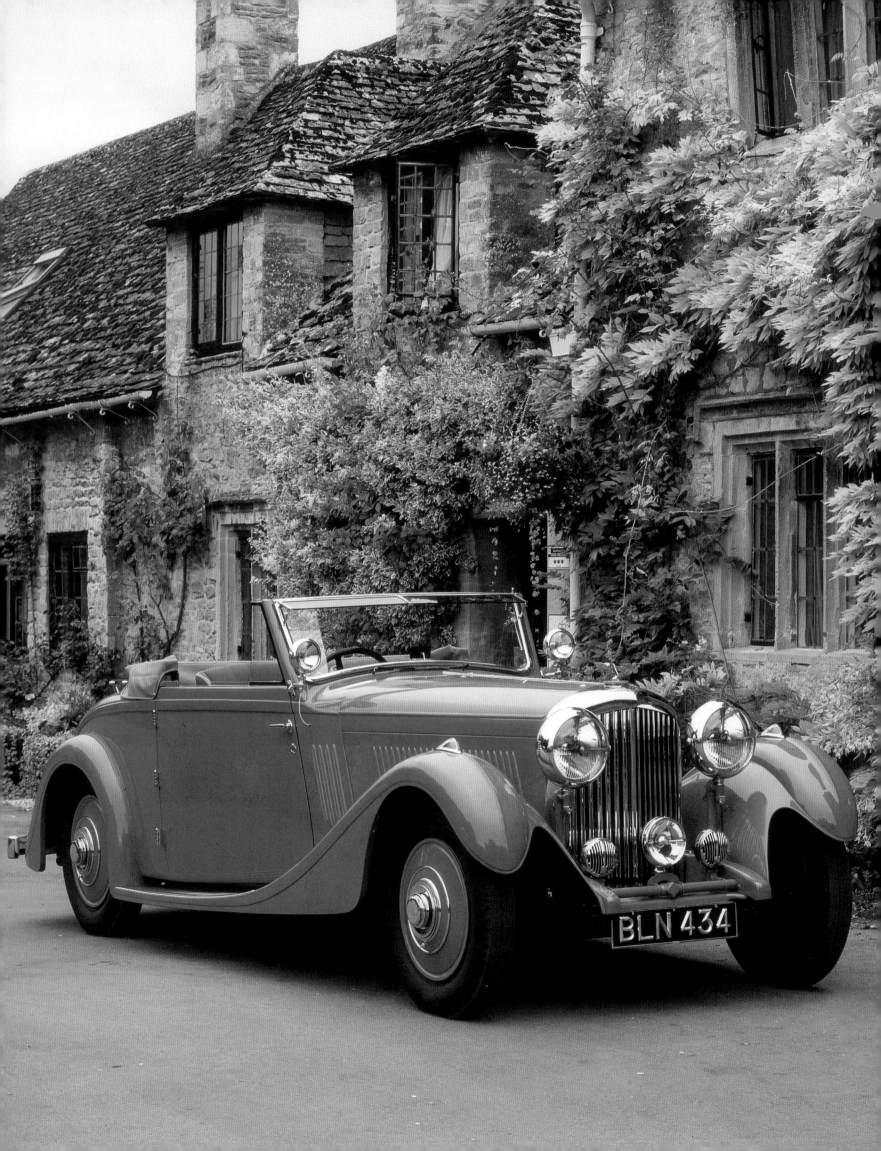

All the design and engineering of the new car was carried out by Rolls-Royce, under the direction of Hives and Henry Royce. Though W.O.'s contribution was limited to testing of prototypes, he was impressed by the final product, writing that he would "rather own this Bentley car than any car produced under that name."

The new Bentley 3½ Litre was launched at the London Motor Show at Olympia in 1933. It was sold as 'The Silent Sports Car', though in truth there was little that was sporting about it apart from the reputation of the Bentley name. But it was a quality car with performance well beyond the average that could cruise smoothly and quietly, and it had a genuine appeal to upper-crust customers.

With the Cricklewood factory gone, Rolls-Royce built the chassis at its Derby factory, so the 3½ Litre models quickly became known informally as 'Derby Bentleys'. As with most cars of the era they were bodied by independent coachbuilders – including many of the finest names of the time, such as Barker, Freestone & Webb, Gurney Nutting, Hooper, Mulliner, James Young and Vanden Plas. But nearly half of the 1,100 cars built were bodied by Park Ward at their factory in Willesden, not far from the old Bentley factory in Cricklewood.

W.O.'s contract was up for renewal in April 1935, and he must have been in two minds about whether or not to stay with Rolls-Royce. He still had an influence, albeit a small one, on the products that bore his name, and he was being paid handsomely, by an established and renowned employer, for an agreeable job that was well within his capabilities. W.O. was now in his late forties, had just married for the third time – his first wife died during the Spanish flu of 1919, his second divorced him in 1931 – and the stability of the employment offered by Rolls-Royce must have been attractive. The draft new contract included a significant salary increase. But Bentley was still, with some justification, aggrieved that Rolls-Royce were ignoring his technical ability, and had never offered him a position on the board of the reconstituted Bentley Motors.

The new challenge Bentley was looking for came from an unexpected source. London lawyer Alan Good was in the process of rescuing the ailing Lagonda company, and asked W.O. to join as technical director. The deal was done shortly after the 1935 Le Mans race, which Lagonda won with an M45R Rapide – the first victory for a British car since Barnato and Kidston won in a Bentley Speed Six in 1930. W.O.'s departure from Rolls-Royce left him, he later said, with a sense of freedom. He designed a new V12 engine for Lagonda in 1937, and after the war masterminded a new Lagonda saloon with a 2.6-litre six-cylinder engine. When David Brown bought Lagonda in 1947 and merged it with Aston Martin, the Lagonda-Bentley engine ended up powering a generation of Astons, from the DB2 to the DB Mark III. W.O., meanwhile, left Lagonda and set up as an independent engineering consultant. He moved to the Surrey countryside and into semi-retirement, returning to Oxgate Lane in 1969 for an event celebrating the fiftieth anniversary of Bentley Motors. He died in a nursing home at Woking, Surrey on 13 August 1971, at the age of 82.

Bentley Motors continued without its founder. Rolls-Royce had designed the 3½ Litre to be a road car, with no

Opposite: 1934 3½-litre drophead coupé with bodywork by James Young.

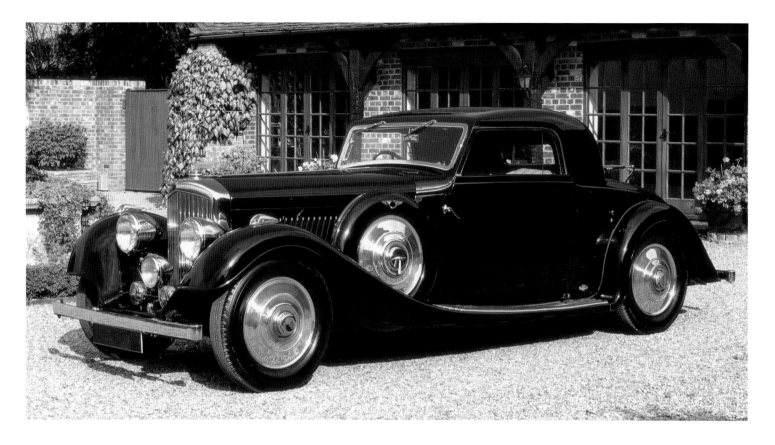

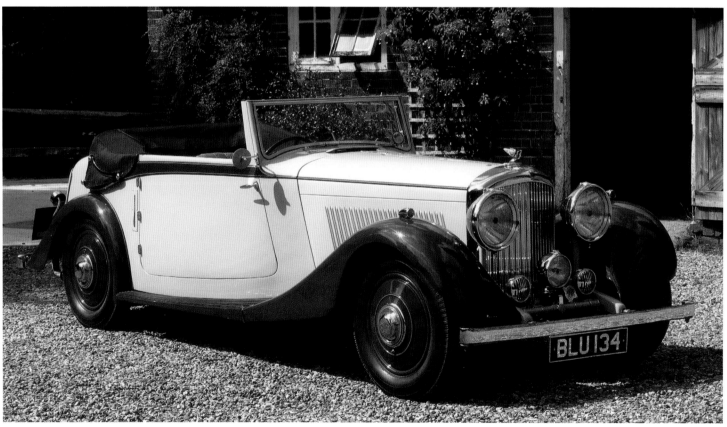

Top: 1934 3½ Litre with rakish two-door coupé bodywork by Carrosserie Kellner, whose workshop was on Paris's Champs-Elysées.

Above: British firm Park Ward's coachwork for the Derby Bentleys was more traditional: this is also a 1934 3½ Litre.

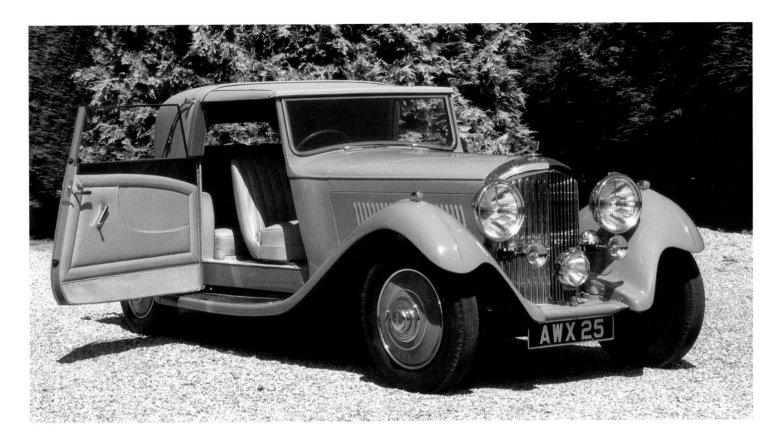

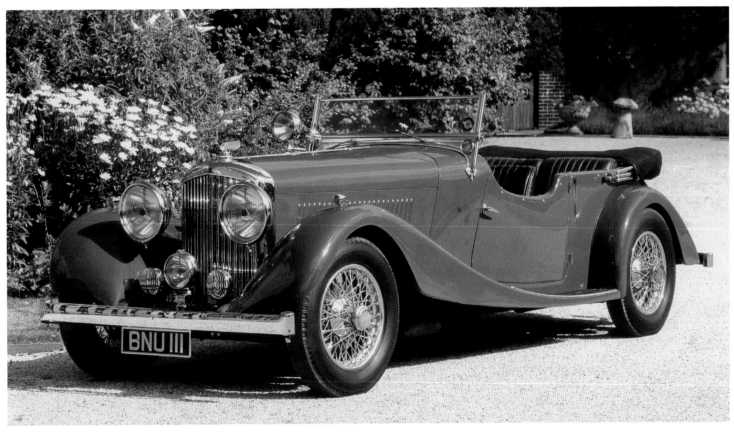

Top: Sedanca coupé coachwork by Gurney Nutting made the most of the 3½ Litre's bold domed grille.

Above: Another variant on the 3½ Litre theme, this time with four-seat open tourer coachwork by Vanden Plas.

thought of competition, but a single racing version was built in 1934 for the experienced racing driver Eddie Hall. With the physique for tough, long-distance races, Hall had made a specialism of the RAC Tourist Trophy. The TT had moved to Ulster in 1928, using a road course more than thirteen miles long between the towns of Newtownards, Comber and Dundonald. It was renowned as one of the best and most challenging circuits of its day, and motor racing author Doug Nye called it "the British Nürburgring". Hall had finished second in his class in 1930 in a 4½ Litre Bentley before switching to smaller MGs, one of which he then entered in the Mille Miglia in 1934 with new wife Joan as co-driver. They went to Italy to recce the route in a sports-bodied 3½ Litre Bentley which had been delivered to Hall that March. The Bentley lapped the open public roads of the Mille Miglia course twice, exceeding 100mph (161km/h) on the sections which were free of other traffic. Throughout it all the Bentley proved to be faultless, needing only an adjustment to the brakes along the way. Then in June the Bentley was pressed into service in Hall's successful effort to climb the highest peaks of Scotland, England and Wales between sunrise and sunset, covering 470 miles (756km) in a little over 11 hours. Hall was so impressed he wanted to try racing the Bentley in the TT race that was coming up in September, and asked Rolls-Royce to offer support.

As we've seen, in W.O.'s era the Bentley marque built its reputation on success in motor racing, and the factory was very much part of it. At Rolls-Royce it was a different story: the last racing car that had had factory involvement was built in 1906, when C.S. Rolls himself won the Ulster TT

in a Light 20. Despite some misgivings Rolls-Royce agreed to offer some assistance, and fitted Hall's 3½ Litre with a new, lightweight two-seater body. It was in with a good chance, because the TT organisers had decided to outlaw supercharged engines and return to cars which more effectively represented the machines people could really use on the road.

The race was run on a handicap basis, which meant some of the smaller cars were given a head start on the big Lagondas, V8 Fords and Hall's Bentley. Early in the race Charles Dodson's six-cylinder MG Magnette led the way, but Hall caught him and pulled out a half-minute lead. After fuel and tyre stops Hall was half a lap down on Dodson with an hour of the race to run. The Bentley reeled in the MG lap after lap, still gaining even when it began to rain. At the start of the last lap the gap was 42 seconds, but all Hall could do was reduce the deficit to 17 seconds by the end. Another lap and the Bentley would have taken the win. Hall and the Bentley were back in Ulster the following year, fighting a long duel with Johnny Hindmarsh in a 4½-litre Lagonda. The Lagonda challenge faded, but again Hall's Bentley lost out to a smaller car on handicap, this time Freddie Dixon's Riley.

For 1936 Hall's Bentley was given a new 163bhp 4.25-litre engine and the bodywork was revised in the hope that it would be more aerodynamically efficient. The Bentley also now carried a 40-gallon (182-litre) fuel tank in the tail, which meant Hall could run the whole of the TT without refuelling. That year the race was wet, which would have helped reduce tyre wear, and Hall had no need to stop at all – but he still couldn't catch the fastest of the Rileys on

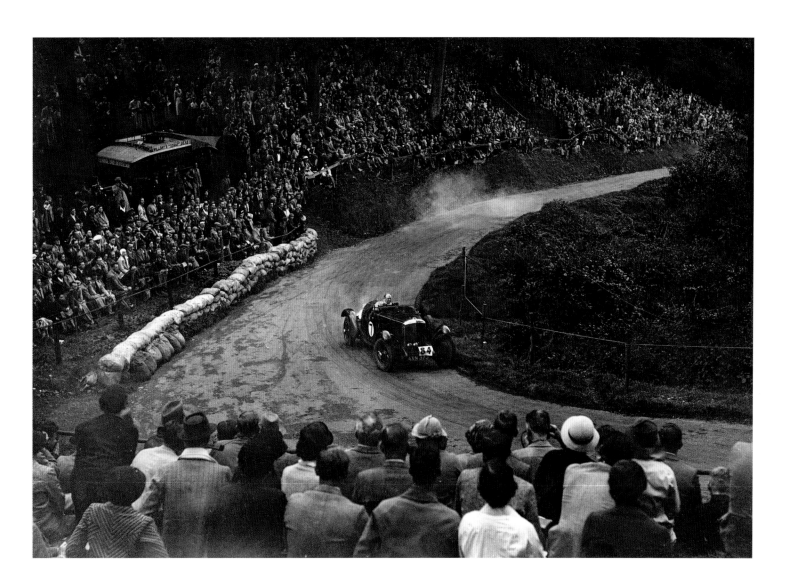

Above: The Derby Bentley was never conceived as a racing car, but
that didn't stop some owners. Wealthy, highly successful amateur
competitor Eddie Hall's 3½ Litre takes a tight line at the Shelsley
Walsh Hill Climb in 1935.

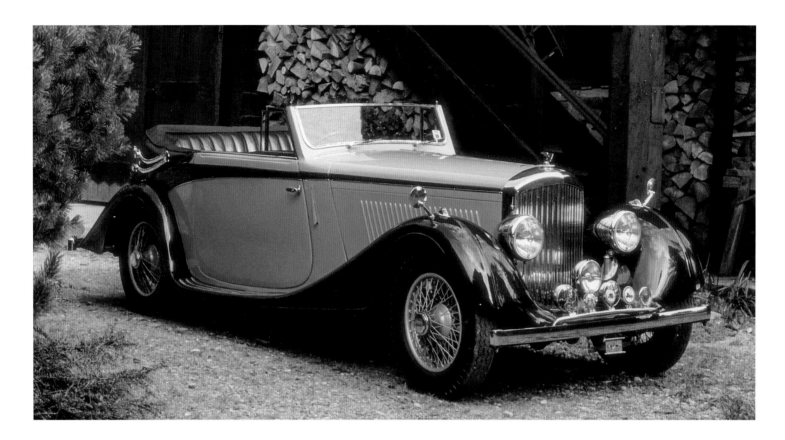

handicap and finished second once again. Even then Hall wasn't done, and he wheeled the Bentley out again after the war, driving non-stop for the whole of the Le Mans 24-hour race to finish a creditable eighth overall.

The 4.25-litre engine that had gone into Hall's Bentley for the 1936 TT was available as an option on the production cars from March that year. The bore was widened from 3.25in to 3.5in, taking the capacity to 4,257cc. Further improvements came in 1938 when improved steering by Marles was fitted, and there was the option of overdrive. As with the 3½ Litre, most of the cars were bodied by Park Ward, and many adopted steel bodywork instead of the older aluminium panels over an ash wood frame. The last few of the 1,234 4¼ Litre Derby Bentleys were delivered as late as 1941, though a new Bentley model had been announced in 1939. This was the MkV, based on the latest Rolls-Royce, the Wraith. Nobody is really sure where the 'MkV' designation came from – clearly the MkIV would have been the 3½ Litre/4¼ Litre cars, and some people suggest MkI/II/III were prototypes that never made it to

Above: The 3½ Litre was replaced by the 4¼ Litre for 1936. This car has coachwork by Carrosserie Vanvooren.

production. A more likely explanation suggests that the early numbers were the Cricklewood Bentleys – MkI was the four-cylinder 3 Litre and 4½ Litre, the MkII was the six-cylinder 6½ Litre and 8 Litre, and the MkIII was the side-valve 4 Litre.

Whatever the truth of the designation, the MkV featured a revised engine, much improved suspension and a brand-new chassis design. The most significant of these innovations was the new front suspension, which dropped the leaf-sprung beam axle which had been Bentley practice right from the start in favour of a new independent layout. Each wheel was mounted on a pair of wishbones, the lower one wide-based to resist braking forces and the upper one formed from the actuating arm of a lever-type damper. A coil spring was mounted inside the chassis on each side, and the two front suspension assemblies were linked by an anti-roll torsion bar which picked up on the front of

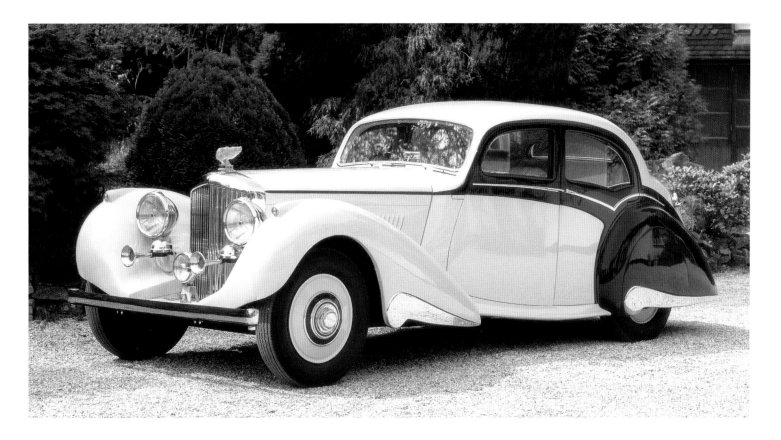

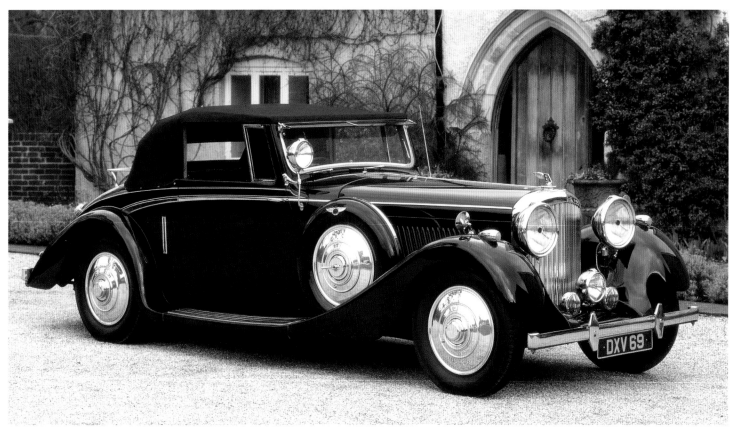

Top: The lines of this 4¼ Litre with 1938 pillarless sports saloon body by Carlton are emphasised by striking two-tone paintwork.

Above: Another 4¼ Litre Derby Bentley, this time with drophead coupé coachwork by Hooper.

each lower wishbone and ran across the front of the chassis ahead of the radiator.

The new independent suspension had two great advantages. First, shocks felt at one front wheel were not transferred so strongly to the other, as they were when the wheels shared a substantial beam axle. Second, unsprung weight was much reduced. Both these factors improved the ride quality and front-end grip, and made the steering more precise and less prone to kick-back on rough roads

The rear suspension was of the conventional type, with a live axle suspended by leaf springs. The chassis was a new design with deep channel section side-members stiffened by a massive cruciform brace. Refinements included brakes assisted by a vacuum servo to reduce pedal pressures, and a four-speed gearbox which now had synchromesh on the top three gears. The gear lever was between the driver's seat and the door. The engine was broadly the same in layout as the previous inline-six, but with improved bearings for greater reliability. Because of the independent suspension there was now room at the front of the car to mount the engine much further forwards, improving interior space and reducing heat soak into the car.

About twenty MkV chassis were built for an extensive test programme, but it's thought only a dozen were fitted with bodies before the Second World War halted production. One of the completed cars had a streamlined body designed by Georges Paulin and made by the French coachbuilder Vanvooren using thinner-gauge steel to reduce weight, and was given the name Corniche. The car was extensively tested, but was destroyed by a bomb in Dieppe while waiting on the dockside to return to England.

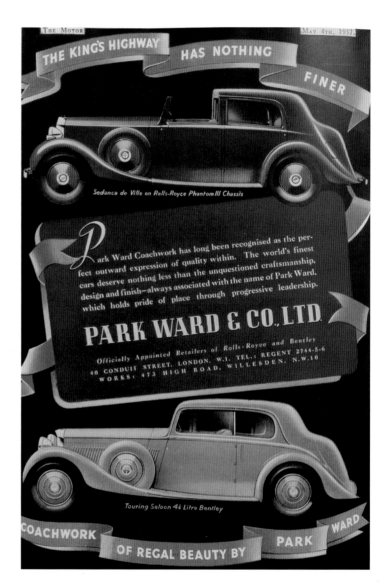

Above: This 1937 Park Ward coachwork advert featured a 4¼ Litre.

Opposite: Vanden Plas bodywork on the 4¼ Litre had a traditional feel. The quality of the finish, inside and out, was always impeccable.

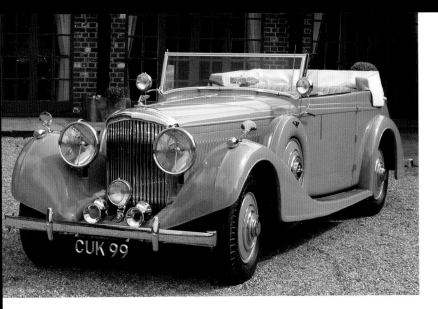
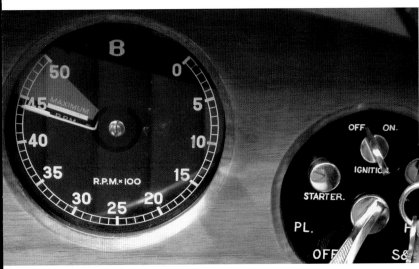
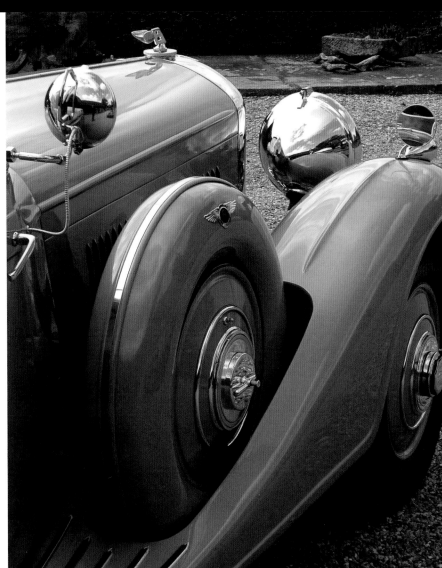
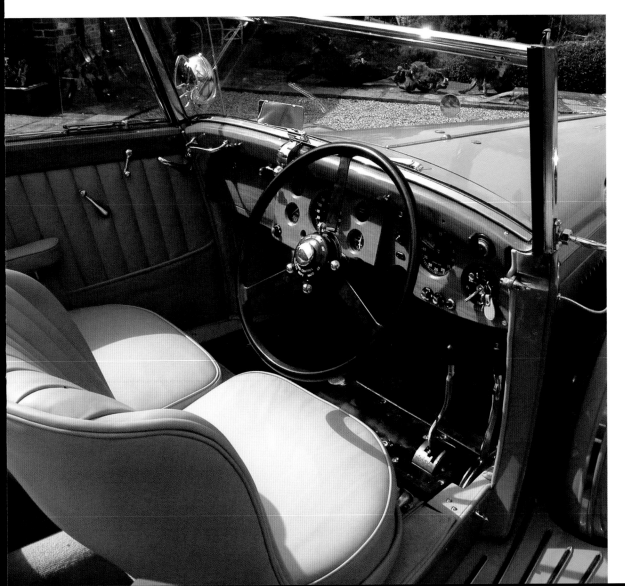
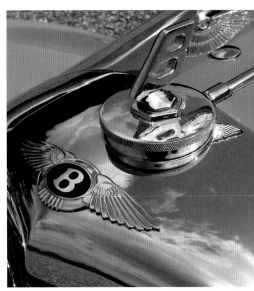
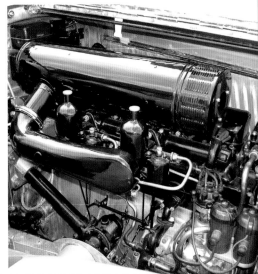

During the war Rolls-Royce concentrated on production of the Merlin aero engine used by the Spitfire, Hurricane and Lancaster aircraft. Production began at Derby in 1936 but by 1938, with war looming, the government was setting up 'shadow factories' to duplicate essential war work so that an attack on a single factory would not cause catastrophic disruption. The Derby site was, in fact, bombed in a surprise raid by a Dornier 217 in 1942. Engine and aircraft production lines were set up in shadow factories across the country, and Rolls-Royce established a parallel production facility for the Merlin at Crewe in Cheshire.

Crewe, 50 miles northwest of Derby, was chosen because it was remote from the concentration of motor industry production facilities in and around Birmingham and Coventry, virtually all of which had turned to aircraft production, aero engine production and other essential war work, and were a target for enemy bombers. Crewe had good road and rail links to the rest of the country, and plenty of usable land. Construction of the shadow factory at Pyms Lane, Crewe began in July 1938 and the first Merlin engine was completed by the end of the year. At its peak in 1943 the plant employed 10,000 people, and it made more than 26,000 engines by 1946.

After the end of hostilities Rolls-Royce concentrated its aero engine operations at Derby and moved Bentley and Rolls-Royce car production to Crewe. The first cars to emerge were the Bentley MkVI, a revised version of the stillborn MkV, and its long-wheelbase Rolls counterpart, the Silver Wraith. The MkVI was available with a 'Standard Steel' body, built by Britain's largest independent mass-manufacturer of car bodies, Pressed Steel in Cowley. The

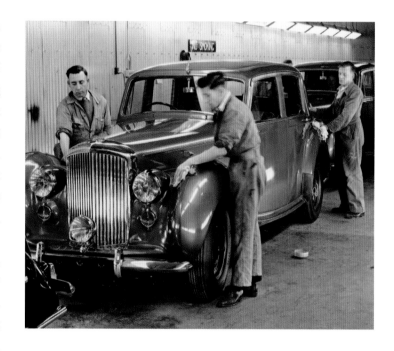

Above: The postwar MkVI was the first Bentley available with bodywork produced by the factory rather than by a separate coachbuilder.

bodies were sent to Crewe where they were fitted to the chassis, painted and trimmed. It was the first time a Bentley had been available from the works as a complete car – though the MkVI could still be ordered in chassis-only form and supplied to a coachbuilder for bespoke bodywork, as had always been the way with previous Bentleys.

The engine was expanded from 4,257cc to 4,566cc by enlarging the bore in 1951, and in this form the MkVI continued in production until 1952. By then Bentley had survived the Great Depression, financial chaos, takeover and the Second World War – and was about to produce one of its greatest-ever cars.

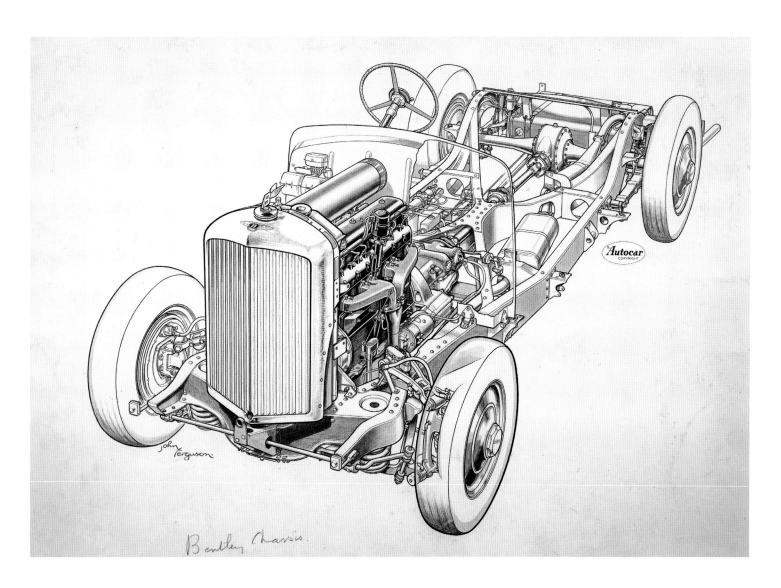

Above: The chassis fitted to the MkVI was much more modern than those on previous Bentleys. Front suspension was independent with coil springs, and there was a substantial cruciform brace to improve structural stiffness.

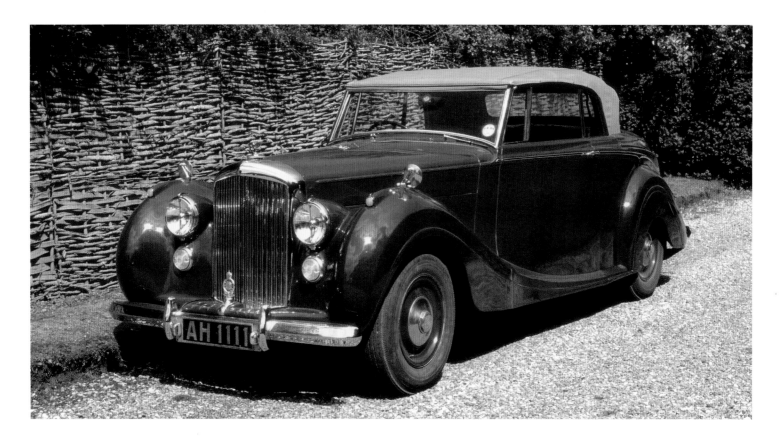

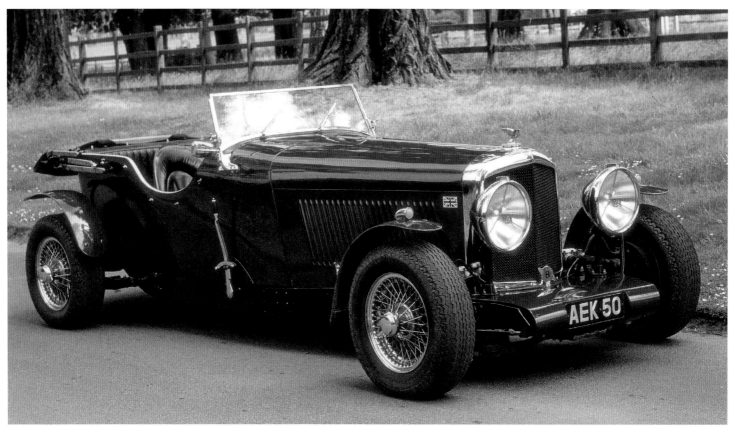

Top: This drophead foursome coupé by Mulliner, on a 1947 MkVI chassis, displays a graceful, traditional style.

Above: In later years many MkVI chassis were rebuilt as specials with sports bodies like this one.

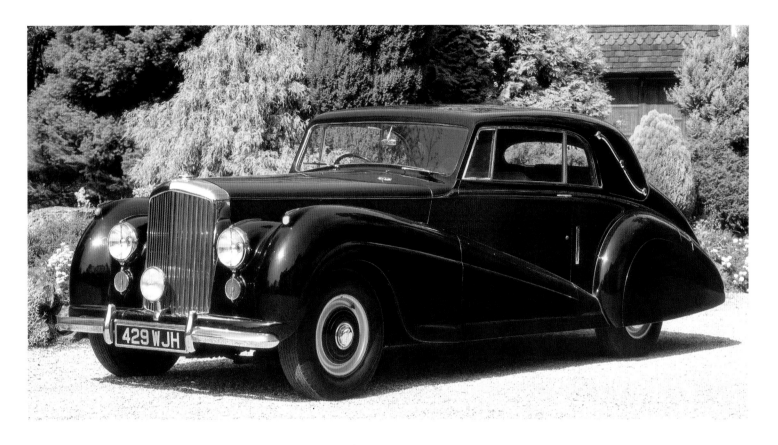

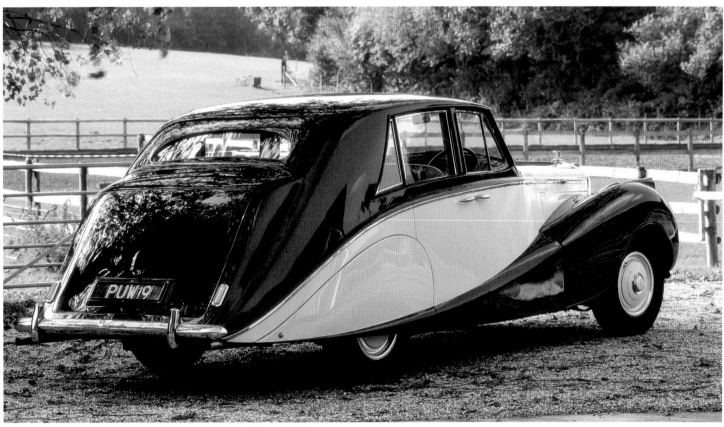

Top: This 1951 MkVI has two-door coupé bodywork by Park Ward of Willesden, London.

Above: Hooper's Empress-style coachwork, seen here on a 1952 MkVI, has gloriously flowing lines.

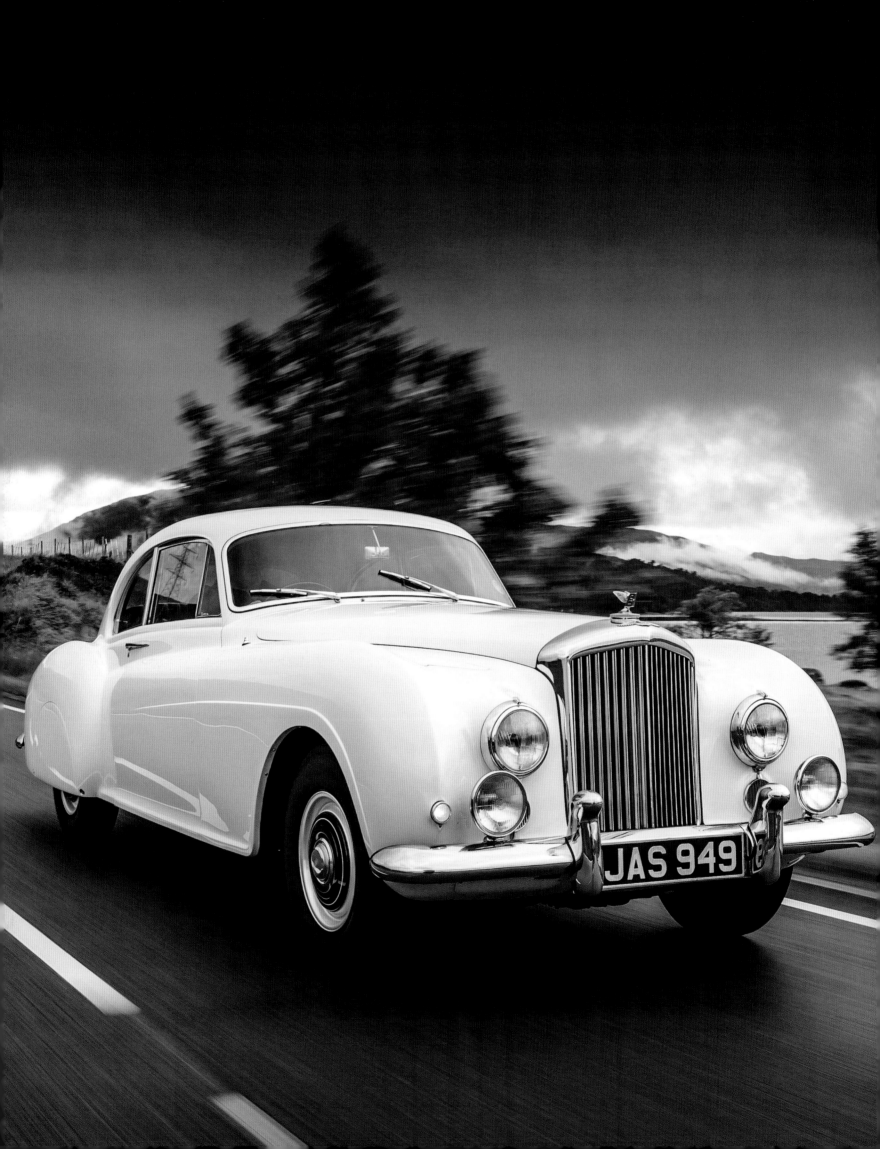

Chapter 4

GOING CONTINENTAL

The Derby Bentleys had plenty of Rolls-Royce engineering but they were still noticeably different to the cars bearing the Spirit of Ecstasy, and at first the intention by the new owners of the Bentley marque was to maintain a clear distinction in appearance and character between the two brands. The MkVI had been built on a shorter wheelbase than its close cousin, the Rolls-Royce Silver Wraith, and it had been the only Crewe product that could be bought as a complete car thanks to the availability of the Standard Steel body. Rolls-Royces remained exclusively coach-built. The MkVI also spawned a new derivative which had no Rolls-Royce equivalent, and would begin a line of Bentleys that would become renowned as some the brand's most iconic cars – the Continentals.

Development of the first Bentley to officially wear the Continental badge began in 1950, but the idea behind it was a pre-war one. The concept originated with what is probably the most famous Derby Bentley of them all, built for Greek shipping magnate André Embiricos in 1938. Embiricos already owned a 4¼ Litre Bentley with cabriolet coachwork by Jean Antern, and now wanted something rather faster and more focused. Walter Sleator of Bentley's French distributor Franco-Britannic Automobiles put Embiricos in touch with another French coachbuilder, Pourtout, whose designer Georges Paulin was making a name for himself with elegant shapes designed with aerodynamic efficiency in mind, including the Talbot Lago SS 'Goutte d'Eau' (water drop) and the 1937–38 Peugeot Darl'mat racing cars.

Paulin's design for Embiricos was radical. The proud Bentley radiator grille, which had been created for the 3 Litre back in 1919, carried forward on every model and recreated for the Derby Bentley, was now dropped. In its place there was a swept-back cowl, with simple vertical wires covering the aperture. Low-set, faired-in headlamps either side merged with the curvaceous front wings which swept back behind the wheels to the front edges of the two rear-hinged doors. There was a divided windscreen that was heavily raked, and a low, curving roof. The rear wheels were enclosed with spats, and the drooping roof combined with a narrowing rear cabin into a tight, tapered tail. Paulin tested the shape in a wind tunnel, following in the footsteps of Hungarian engineer Paul Jaray who had pioneered this type of testing in the 1920s, to ensure that it delivered significant gains in aerodynamic efficiency from its smooth form and small frontal area.

With a higher-than-standard final drive ratio the Embiricos Bentley proved to be capable of a rousing 120mph (193km/h), and in 1939 it covered 114 miles (183km) in an hour on the banking at Brooklands. It also proved to be able to manage 20 miles (32km) per gallon (4.5l) of fuel at a constant 80mph (129km/h), underlining the efficiency of the Paulin body shape. After the war Embiricos sold the car and the new owner entered it for the Le Mans 24-hour race in 1949, where at eleven years old it still finished a creditable sixth overall, and it went on to finish the race twice more in 1950 and 1951.

Though the Embiricos car was one Bentley driver's vision of a fast touring model, it seems to have been the inspiration behind a factory project, the Corniche, a prototype of a fast, streamlined saloon developed alongside the regular MkV saloon just before the Second World War. The Corniche was fitted with a tuned engine, and the lightweight, low-

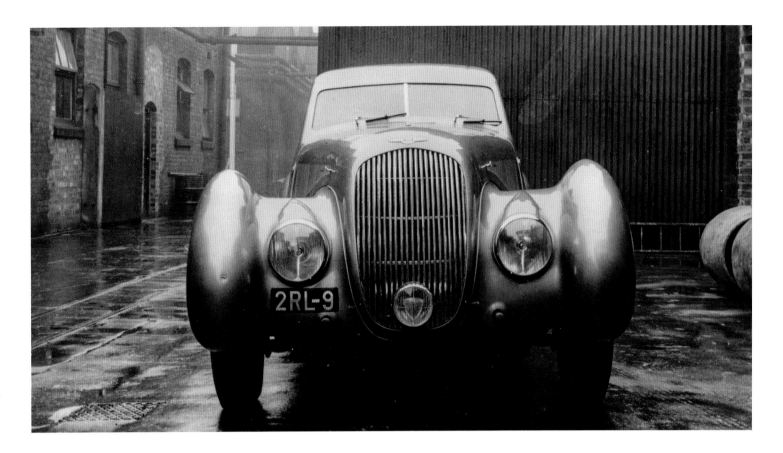

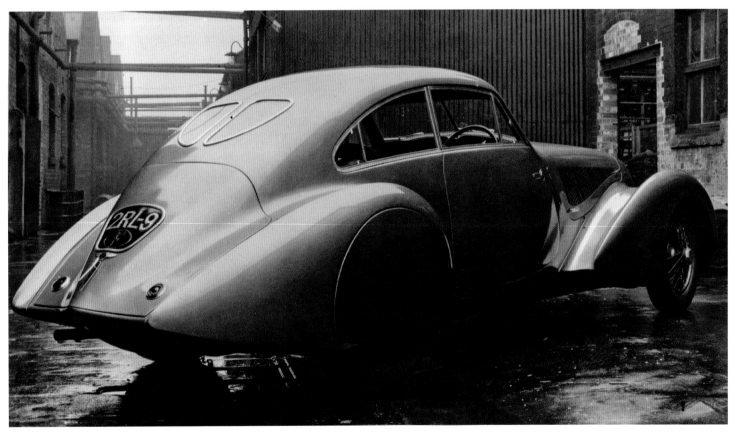

Top and above: The Embiricos Bentley was built in 1938 with striking coachwork designed by Georges Paulin for the French firm Pourtout.

Following pages: The style and ethos of the pre-Second World War Embiricos car influenced the Bentley Continentals that would follow later.

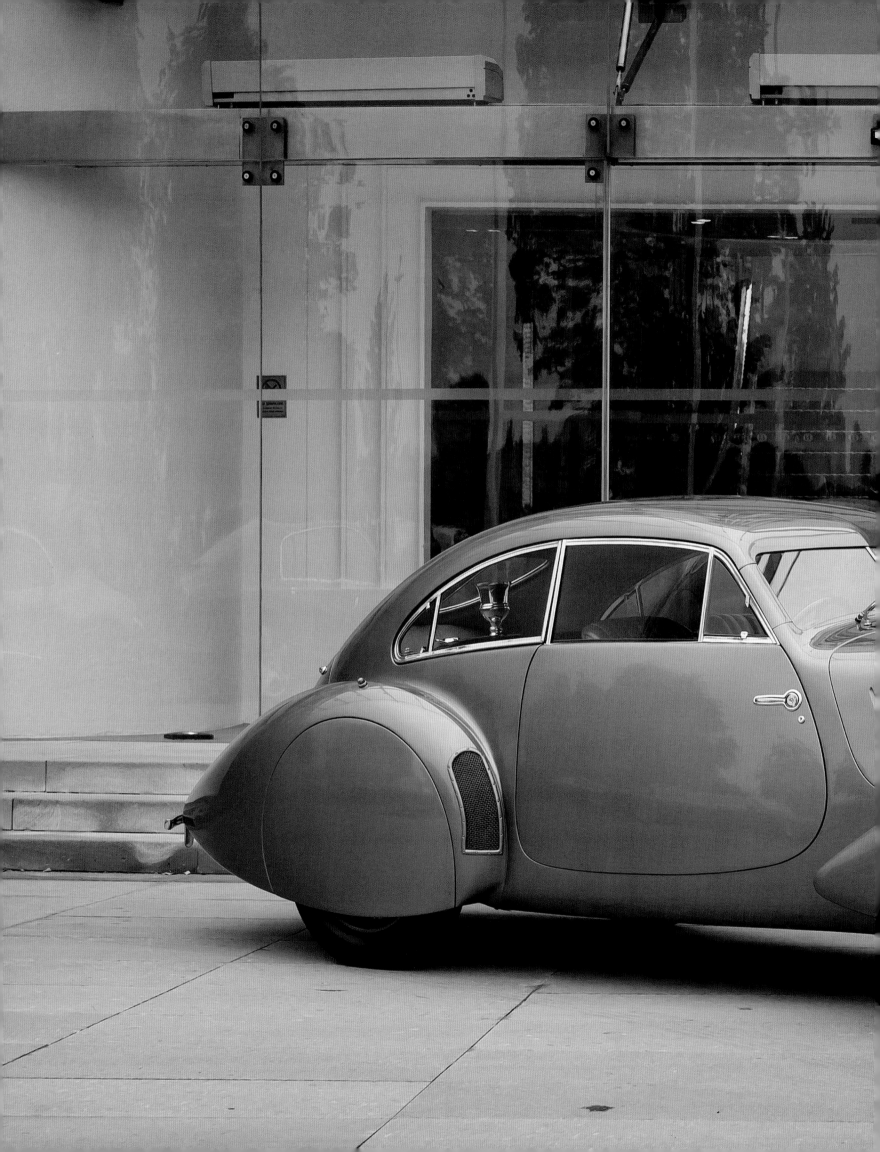

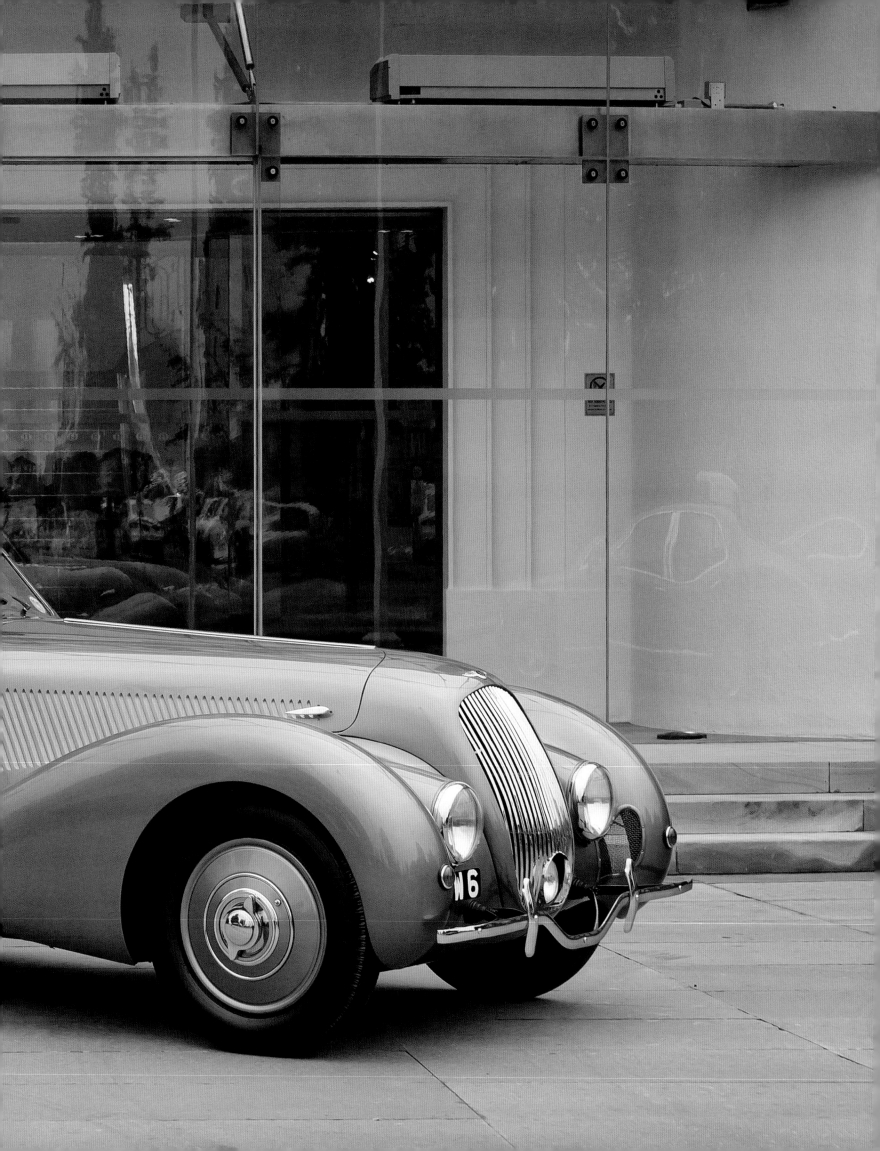

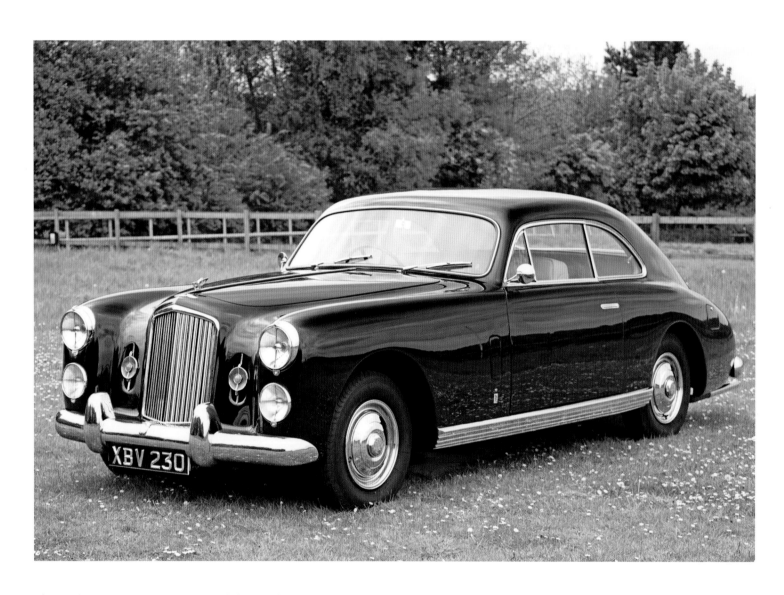

Above: The Bentley Cresta was another link in the chain between the Embiricos car and the Continental. Styling was by Pinin Farina.

drag body was again designed by Georges Paulin but this time made by Vanvooren of Paris. At the same time there was some thought about producing a straight-eight Bentley, and two prototypes, called Scalded Cat and Cresta, were built just as war brought car manufacturing to an end.

After the war the concept of a faster, more exclusive Bentley was revived, first by Walter Sleator and a French colleague, Jean Daninos of Forges et Ateliers des Constructions d'Eure-et-Loir (FACEL). Sleator and Daninos successfully petitioned Bentley for a revised version of the MkVI chassis which was more suited to the kind of low, lithe bodywork they were keen to fit. To lower the whole car the steering column was mounted at a shallower angle and engine ancillaries were repositioned so the bonnet line could be lowered. The Turin styling house Pininfarina created a full-width, two-door fastback body, and the car became known as the Cresta – reviving the name of a pre-war prototype. Chassis records suggest 11 were built, some by Pininfarina and some by FACEL. The last was Daninos' own car, which carried revised bodywork, again shaped by Pininfarina, which would inspire the creation of his own Facel-Vega car in the 1950s.

In 1950 Crewe began work on Corniche II, as it was at first known, at the Clan Foundry experimental section in Belper, a few miles north of Derby. It was based on the low-line chassis created for the Cresta and fitted with a big-bore 4,566cc engine with a higher compression ratio and a more efficient exhaust, which produced a distinctive rasp. The changes to the engine increased power by 25bhp, and this was delivered through a close-ratio gearbox to a rear axle with a higher final drive ratio of 2.79:1.

The styling of the new car was refined by aerodynamic testing of quarter-scale models in a wind tunnel at Rolls-Royce's Flight Test Establishment at Hucknall in Nottinghamshire. Though the shape of Corniche II had been inspired by the Embiricos car it was quite different, in some ways more modern and in others more traditional. The front end was brought up to date by blending the wings into the body of the car in the 'full width' style that had been pioneered in America, but unlike the Embiricos car the Corniche had a traditional Bentley grille. To ensure that the grille interfered as little as possible with the airflow it was 1.5 inches shorter than that on the Standard Steel body, and was canted backwards at a noticeable angle. The windscreen was a two-piece affair to allow a significant curvature, and at the back the wings formed small fins which had been shown in testing to improve directional stability.

Target top speed for the Corniche II was 20 per cent more than the Standard Steel saloon, in other words around 120mph (193km/h). Few tyres then available would stand up to cruising at that kind of speed while carrying the weight of a full-size car like the Bentley, so it was essential to keep the finished weight of the vehicle to a minimum. The two-door body was built by H.J. Mulliner using aluminium panels and its new 'lightweight' process which replaced conventional wooden body frames with light alloy extrusions, resulting in a car that was around 10 per cent lighter than a Standard Steel saloon. Weight was also saved by using aluminium alloys elsewhere in the Corniche II – for the tubular seat frames, the bumpers and the window frames. There were no attempts to lighten the chassis so all the weight savings came from the bodywork.

In August 1951 the first prototype car was completed, receiving the registration number OLG 490, from which it quickly acquired the nickname 'Olga'. Early tests in England and France showed that the gearing was too high as the car could not reach maximum engine revs in top gear, so a revised gearbox and 3.07:1 axle were fitted. In this form Olga proved capable of nearly 120mph (193km/h) on the banked Montlhéry track – it would have achieved more in a straight line – and while it was only a couple of tenths of a second quicker than the Standard Steel saloon on the 0-50mph (80.5km/h) sprint, its acceleration at higher speeds was considerably better.

The new model was put into production in June 1952, by which time the Corniche name had been dropped in favour of Continental, a name which had been loosely applied to some coachbuilders' body styles but had never before been used as Bentley model name. There were detail alterations to the production cars, including a roofline an inch lower than Olga with a Triplex one-piece windscreen, chrome-plated brass window frames, and Lucas rather than Marchal auxiliary lamps – except for cars sold in France, where the local Marchals were preferred. Most of the 207 cars made had steel bumpers instead of alloy, and some were fitted with extra brightwork and plusher, but heavier front seats which no doubt improved comfort for the occupants, but chipped away at the Continental's lightweight philosophy. H.J. Mulliner bodied most of the cars, but six had bodies by Park Ward, five by Franay in France, three by Graber in Switzerland, and one by Pininfarina.

Just 27 Continentals were built before a series of revisions to all the Bentleys was accompanied by a new range of chassis numbers starting with an R, and they became known as R-types. The Standard Steel R-type was much the same as the MkVI as far back as the rear doors, but the back end of the body was new. The R-type had a 6-inch extension to the chassis behind the rear axle to accommodate a larger luggage boot, which also had a much bigger opening to make loading and unloading easier. Automatic transmission was now an option, using a four-speed General Motors Hydramatic unit, and there were refinements such as an automatic choke to make cold-start and warm-up simpler. In this form the R-type continued in production until 1955. By then the Continental had adopted a 4.9-litre engine with an even bigger bore, which would soon be standardised across the Bentley range.

The new engine was featured in a new model known as the S-type. For the S it received a revised cylinder head with six ports, which improved breathing, and there was a new intake manifold carrying the latest specification SU carburettors. The four-speed automatic transmission, still a GM design but now made under licence at Crewe, was standard fit, but there was a rare manual gearbox option until 1957.

The S was given a new chassis, longer and based on welded box sections which improved torsional stiffness by as much as 50 per cent in exchange for a tiny increase in weight. The front suspension was revised with reshaped wishbones which allowed the wheels to steer through a greater angle, reducing the turning circle. At the rear the springs were repositioned and there was better location for the rear axle. There was hydraulic activation for the brakes, front and rear, for the first time on a Bentley, though the

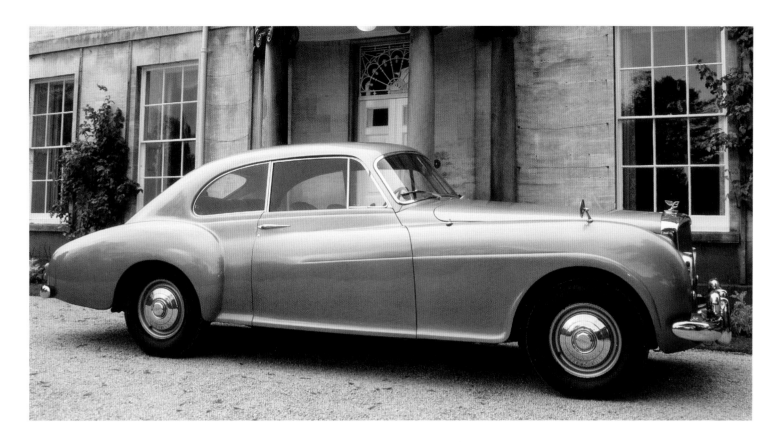

Above: 'Olga' was the name given to the prototype of what became the Continental. It boasts a number of unique features not present on the production cars.

Right: The R-type Continental was the fastest four-seater money could buy in the mid-1950s. This car is from 1953.

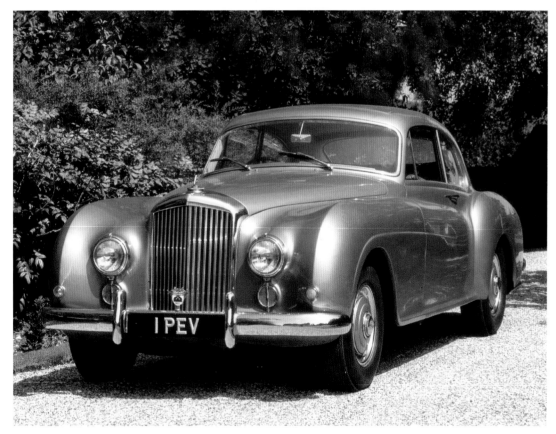

rear brakes also had a parallel mechanical connection to help provide better feel through the brake pedal. The drums were smaller so that they could fit inside 15-inch instead of 16-inch wheels.

As before, a Standard Steel body was available, manufactured by Pressed Steel in Oxford. The main part of the structure was steel but the closing panels – doors, bonnet and boot lid – were all aluminium alloy. The shape of the Bentley S was mirrored almost exactly in the Rolls-Royce Silver Cloud, apart from the difference in radiator grille shape, a deliberate policy of rationalisation which was an about-face change from the early years of Rolls-Royce's ownership of Bentley. It kept costs down, but would ultimately come to endanger the whole future existence of the Bentley marque.

Production of the last R-type Continentals overlapped with the introduction of the S saloon because of the lead time involved in coachbuilding the bodies, but late in 1955 Bentley announced a Continental version of the S which – like its predecessor – featured a lower steering column, higher compression ratio, longer final drive ratio and high-speed tyres. The H.J. Mulliner fastback body style from the previous Continental was adapted for the new car's increased wheelbase, and the shape was mildly updated with a higher waistline and a less pronounced rear wing. Detail changes suggested the Continental's original focus on aerodynamic efficiency and (comparatively) light weight had all but disappeared: the rear wheel spats fitted to the first Continental to reduce aerodynamic drag were dropped, and inside, the lightweight front seats made way for plush armchairs.

Only a few of the R-type Continentals had been built with anything other than the H.J. Mulliner fastback body style, but the S saw a wider range of suppliers and styles than before. London-based Park Ward, which had become a subsidiary of Rolls-Royce in 1939, adapted its existing two-door saloon and drophead bodies to the longer chassis, and there were two-door saloons from James Young and Freestone & Webb.

By the mid-1950s hydraulic power-assisted steering was common on luxury American cars, and Bentley followed suit by offering it on the S from 1956. Without it the steering needed a cumbersome four and a half turns from lock to lock. When power assistance was specified the gearing of the steering system was raised slightly, but even then there were more than four turns between locks, though effort was significantly reduced. The Rolls-Royce chassis engineers were concerned about the so-called 'sneeze factor', chief engineer Harry Grylls' view that an accident could be caused by inadvertent movement of the steering wheel on a car with very light, direct steering. Consequently they avoided making the steering too direct, an affectation that stuck with Bentley and Rolls-Royce for many years.

In 1957 H.J. Mulliner persuaded the factory to allow a four-door Continental for the first time, which it called the Flying Spur. The Spur had a family resemblance to the two-door Continental, but in addition to easier access to the rear of the passenger compartment it also offered

Opposite: The S1 Continental had a modified version of the R-type Continental body with a longer wheelbase and improved steering, suspension and brakes. It went into production in 1955.

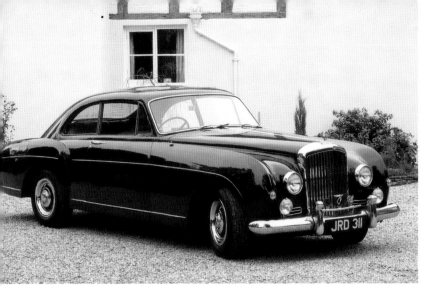

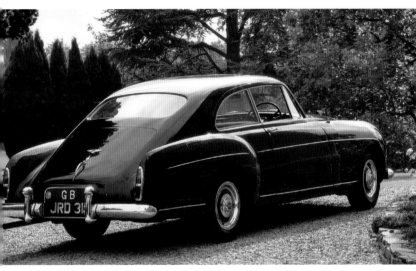

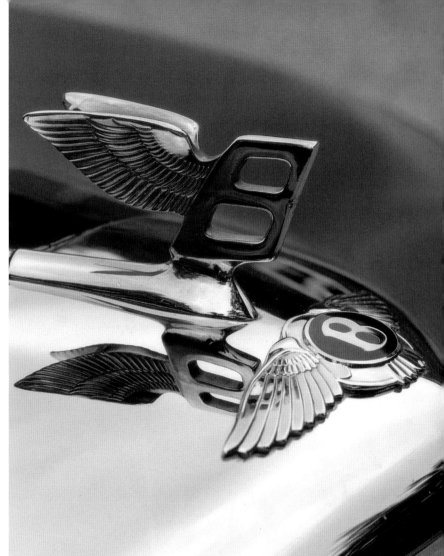

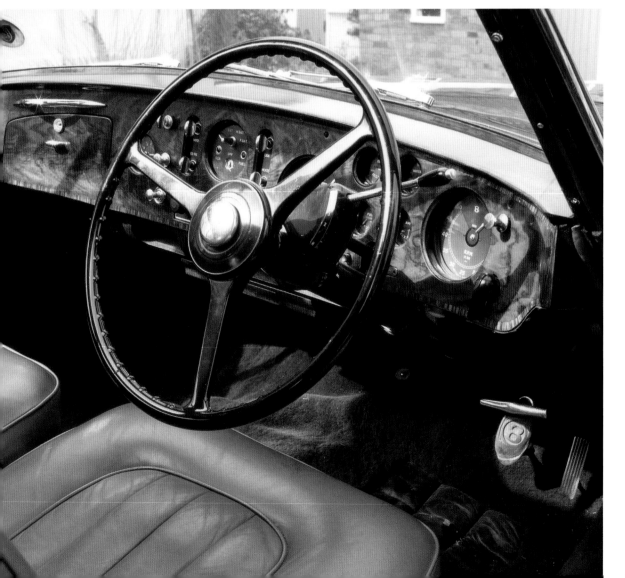

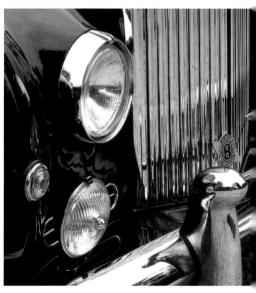

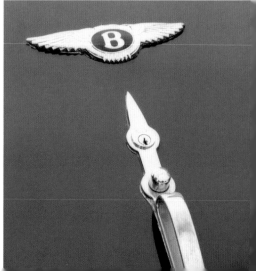

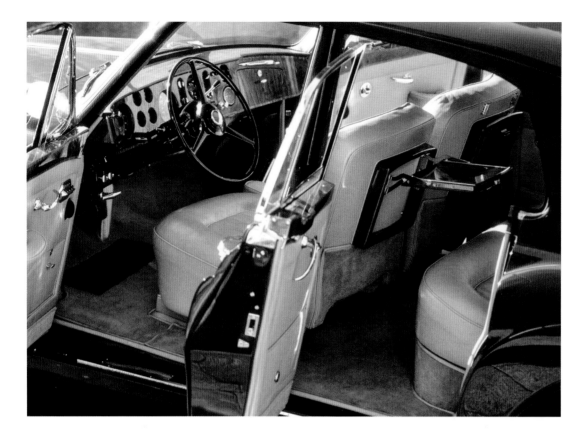

Left and below: The Flying Spur was named by Arthur Talbot Johnstone, H.J. Mulliner's Managing Director, after the heraldic symbol of his family. Seen here in its 1962 S2 form, it was a four-door sporting saloon with the Continental's style.

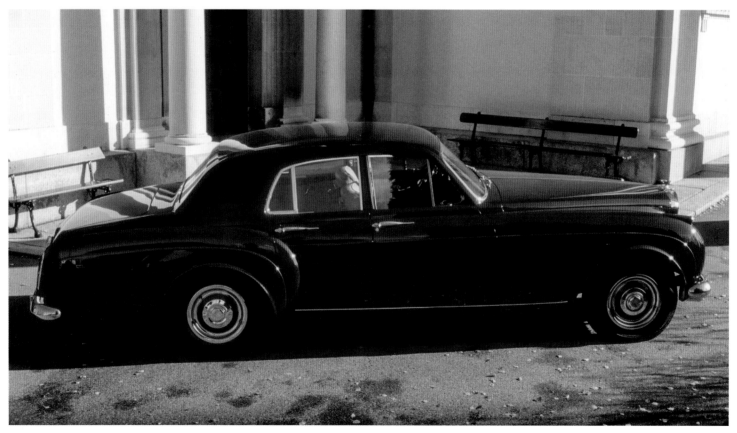

better rear legroom and more luggage space. Originally the design had a large quarter window behind each rear door, but later a 'blind rear quarter' version was offered with a much smaller window which provided greater privacy for rear-seat passengers. A companion mirror was mounted on the inside of the thick rear pillar which resulted. James Young built its own four-door Continental, and a third version was offered by Hooper – a much more modern, but arguably less elegant design.

Bentley introduced a long-wheelbase option for the saloon the same year, the extra four inches of wheelbase providing greater legroom in the rear compartment for those customers who preferred to lounge in the back and let a chauffeur do the driving. Only 47 long-wheelbase cars were built, compared to 3,217 of the standard-length S. There were more than 80 long-wheelbase Silver Clouds, but overall the Bentley was the bigger seller by quite a margin.

The 4.9-litre engine had been gradually improved throughout the life of the S, adopting a higher compression ratio of 8:1 as better-quality fuel became available, and moving to 2-inch SU HD8 carburettors and bigger inlet valves to improve breathing. The result was a further increase in power, though by now Rolls-Royce and Bentley had stopped issuing an official power figure to avoid a disadvantageous comparison with some rivals who exaggerated their figures – something Crewe was not prepared to do. Informed estimates put the output of the last 4.9-litre engines around 160–170bhp, and an experimental engine had been built with fuel injection which had recorded 210bhp on a test bed, though at the cost of some refinement. But even with these improvements the engine was nearing the end of its

potential for development. It had served Rolls-Royce well: the basic design had been around since the Twenty of 1922. For the future, and to meet the challenge of American rivals, the company needed a new engine with greater capacity and more development potential.

Increasingly those American rivals had turned to V8 engines. BMW had done the same with its 'Baroque Angel' 502, and Mercedes-Benz would follow suit with the 600 in 1963. Rolls-Royce and Bentley came to the same conclusion, and had already begun developing a new V8 engine. Early prototypes were known as L380, the number indicating that this engine had a 3.8-inch bore, giving it a capacity of 5.2 litres. For production the bore was enlarged to 4.1 inches, giving a capacity of 6,230cc for the L410. There were rumours that, as with the GM automatic transmissions, these were American designs built under licence, but in fact the new engine had been designed entirely by Rolls-Royce. The new motor was a 90-degree V8 with a gear-driven camshaft down the centre of the vee, and pushrods on the inside of each cylinder bank operating the valves by rockers on top of the cylinder heads. With a deep-skirted alloy block and alloy heads it weighed about the same as the outgoing iron-block six-cylinder – but even breathing through two 1.75-inch SU carburettors it produced considerably more power.

There was plenty of modern thinking in the new engine. As well as the all-alloy construction, with 'wet' cast-iron cylinder liners, there were hydraulic tappets which used engine oil pressure to maintain the valve clearances, leading to quieter running and reducing servicing requirements. The engine was oversquare, with a bigger bore than stroke, keeping the height of the engine down and reducing piston speeds to maintain reliability even at higher engine rpm.

The new V8 went into a revised Bentley called the S2 – so the earlier cars quickly became known retrospectively as S1s. There was also a virtually identical Rolls-Royce Silver Cloud II. The chassis was much the same as before apart from new engine mountings to suit the V8 engine, but because the engine was wider there was no room for the steering box, so it was repositioned outside the main chassis rail and driven by a gear system at the base of the steering column. The one-shot chassis lubrication system was dropped in favour of long-life grease. Once again, there was a Continental version with a slightly higher rear axle ratio for refined fast cruising, and new four-shoe front drum brakes. The radiator shell was lower and now had a slight forward lean.

H.J. Mulliner was swallowed up by Rolls-Royce in 1959, the same year that the Bentley S2 appeared. The four-door Continental Flying Spur body was retained with only minor changes, but the fastback two-door body was dropped in favour of a more practical two-door saloon shape with a larger luggage boot, a tidied-up version of what had been created for a small number of S1 Continentals. Park Ward now concentrated on drophead coupés, with a new and far more modern design by Norwegian stylist Vilhelm Koren. The echoes of the separate front and rear wings that still remained in most of the coachwork designs were swept away and instead there was a 'straight through' wing line, a single curve that ran right down the side of the car from the headlamps – which were pushed outwards away from the grille – to the tail lights. The new body was largely steel

and welded together, making it a strong and stiff structure despite the lack of a fixed roof. Inside there was a new dashboard which grouped the main instruments in front of the driver, and leather-covered padding at the top and bottom of the dashboard. It was a brave, modern design, and one which proved very popular – which must have given the Crewe styling department pause for thought.

2,308 S2s were built between the model's introduction in 1959 and its replacement by the S3 in 1962, 388 of them Continentals. Virtually the same number of the S2's sister model, the Rolls-Royce Silver Cloud II, were built over the same period. It was an early indication that the appeal of the Bentley marque was waning as it had less and less individual appeal, but there were no signs that Rolls-Royce was about to deviate from the rationalisation policy that made the Bentley S and Silver Cloud virtual twins.

The S3 was launched in October 1962, bringing with it a new four-headlamp front end with flashing indicators set into the wings on the standard bodies, and smaller bumper over-riders. The two pairs of headlamps raised the total power available from 120 watts to 150, increasing the main beam penetration and at the same time improving the spread of light on dipped beam. Under the bonnet there were some useful detail improvements, including a switch to 2-inch carburettors, the adoption of a new Lucas distributor with an automatic vacuum advance system, and a higher 9:1 compression ratio in countries where 100-octane 'Five Star' fuel was available. Performance and fuel economy both improved slightly as a result. There were also improvements to the steering to make the cars easier to manoeuvre at low speed.

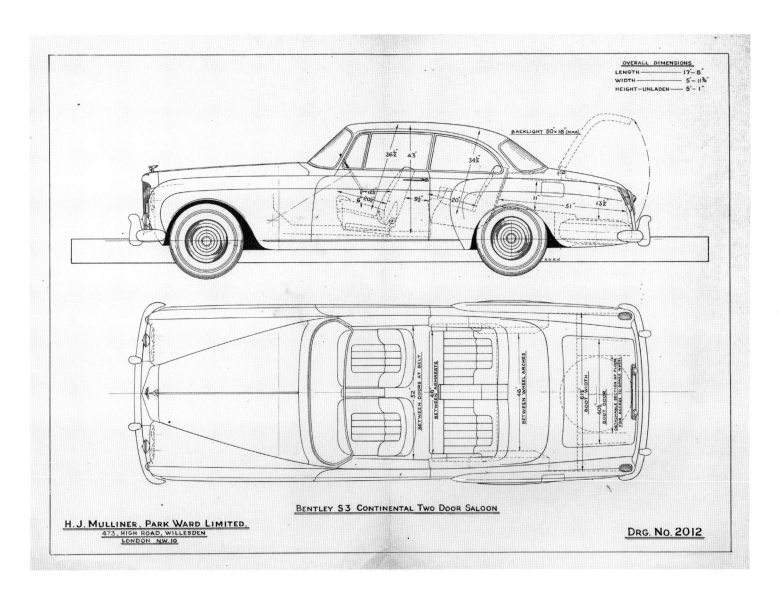

Above: Park Ward and H.J. Mulliner had been Rolls-Royce subsidiaries since (respectively) 1939 and 1959. By the time the S3 Continental appeared in 1962 they had been merged, and were operating out of the former Park Ward factory in Willesden.

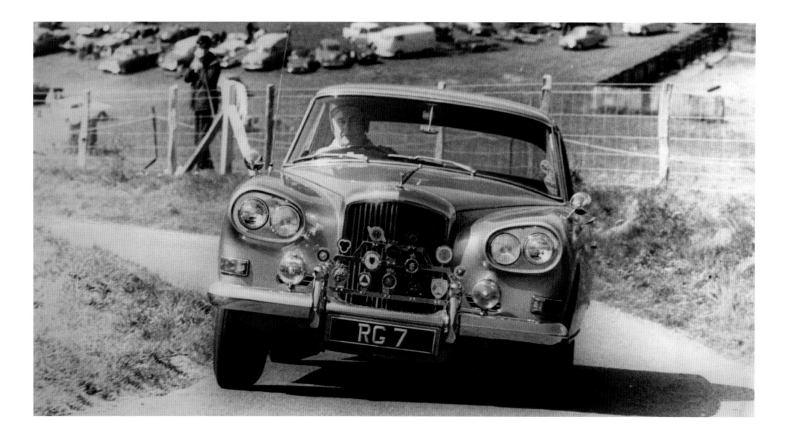

The Continental still had four-shoe front brakes and a special instrument pack including a tachometer, but otherwise it was virtually identical mechanically to the S3 saloon. H.J. Mulliner and Park Ward had now been merged to form Mulliner Park Ward, which operated from Park Ward's Willesden base. The former H.J. Mulliner Continental body, now with the four-headlamp front end, was initially offered again on the S3, but only 11 were built before a fixed-roof version of the Koren-styled Park Ward two-door replaced it in 1963. On this car the four headlamps were accommodated in slanted pairs, which gave the front end a very distinctive appearance. The Flying Spur continued, and there were also some two- and four-door Continentals bodied by James Young. A Continental-

Above: Norwegian stylist Vilhelm Koren joined Park Ward in 1957, and went on to create a very modern look for the company's S2 Continentals.

specification chassis was also available in Rolls-Royce Silver Cloud III guise, with the bodies adapted to match the Rolls grille. As it turned out, there would not be another model exclusive to Bentley until the Continental name returned nearly thirty years later.

The car that replaced the S3 was very different, with a new and far more modern method of construction, new suspension, and a modern new style. While this new car would open up a whole new era for Bentley, it would also edge the marque closer and closer to extinction.

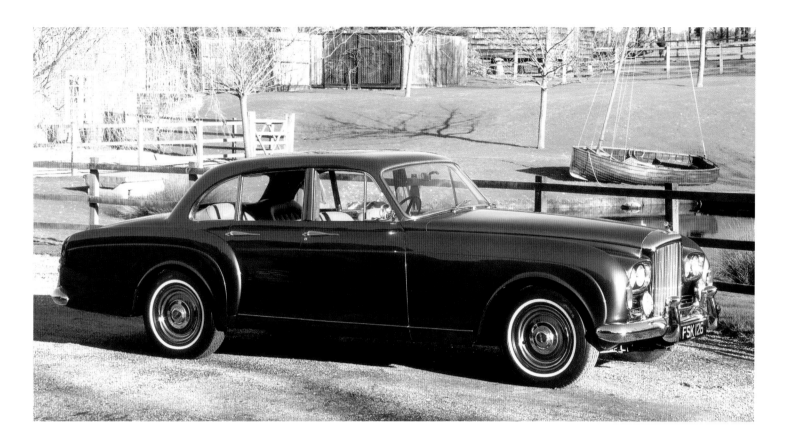

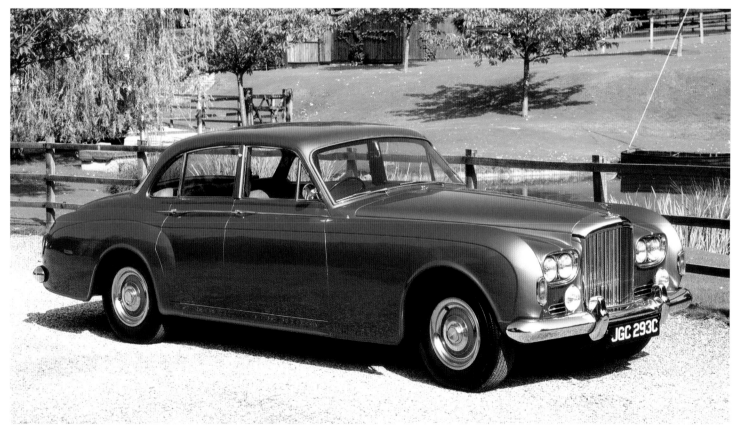

Top: Mulliner's S3 Flying Spur was available in six-light form (three windows each side) as here, or with bigger C-pillars for more privacy.

Above: Coachbuilder James Young's four-door Continental looked heavier and more staid – which some buyers preferred.

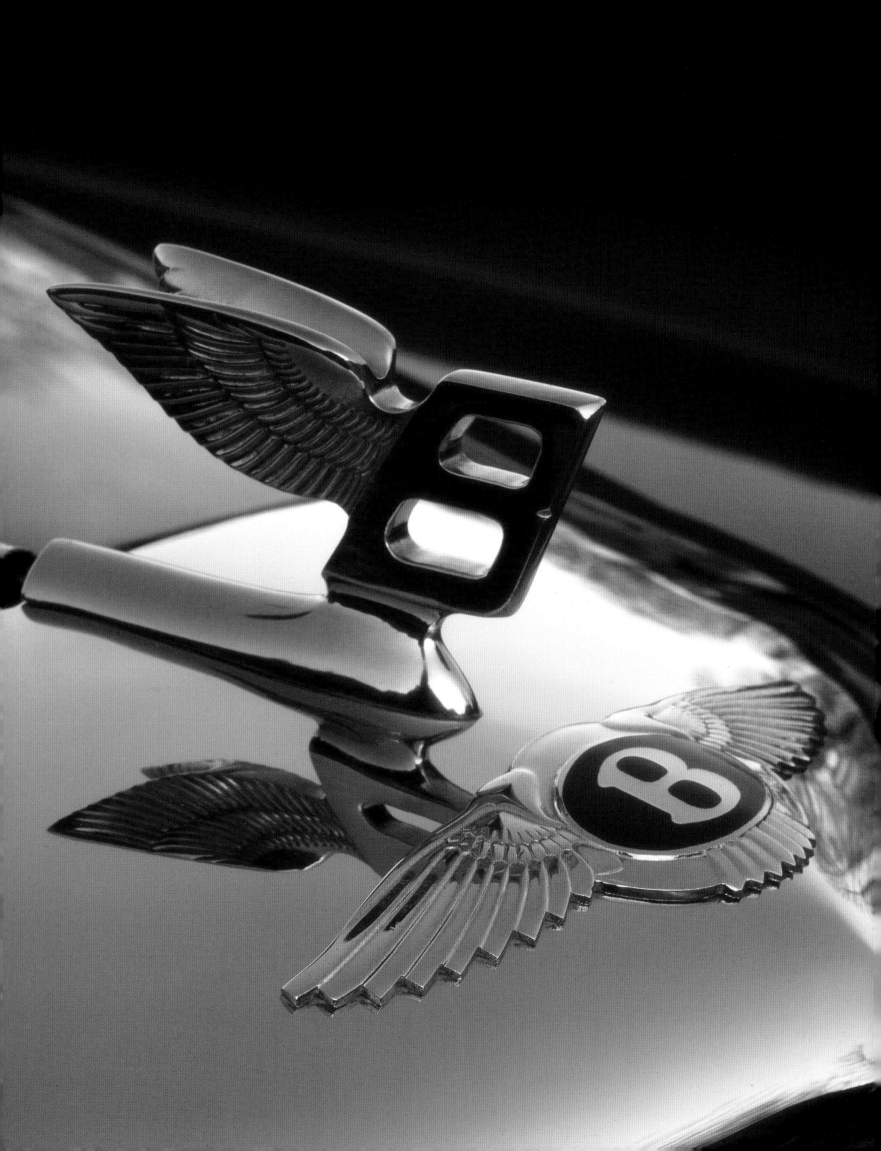

Chapter 5

BADGE ENGINEERING

Elegantly styled and manufactured with the highest quality they may have been, but by the mid-1960s the cars that were emerging from Crewe – the Bentley S3 saloon and Continental, and the Rolls-Royce Silver Cloud III – were beginning to look old-fashioned. Their styling harked back to an earlier age, and some of the engineering under their skins was positively antique – like the retention of the leaf-sprung live axle in an age when a quality car might be expected to have independent rear suspension, or at least coil springs and more positive location for the axle. The relatively new, all-alloy V8 was the standout feature, but more was needed: the next generation of Rolls-Royce and Bentley cars had to represent a sizeable leap forward.

At the time there was a fundamental change taking place in the way cars were constructed. The conventional chassis frame, derived from the construction of the horse-drawn carriage, was being replaced by a modern 'chassisless' structure variously known as monocoque, unitary or unibody construction. This had been pioneered in the 1930s, and reached the mainstream during the 1950s in cars like the Mini and the Ford Consul/Zephyr/Zodiac. Bentleys had always used the conventional construction method, with a separate chassis forming the structural basis of the car and providing mountings for the engine, transmission and suspension. The body then sat on top of the chassis, forming the passenger compartment of the car but contributing little or no additional strength or stiffness to the structure as a whole. The big advantages of this method were its low cost and easy adaptability.

In unitary designs, structural members such as box-section sills were built into the body itself, making the separate chassis redundant. The floor, transmission tunnel, pillars and bulkheads shared the loads. This more efficient use of the body material meant that the whole car could be lighter, and there could be a lower floor and more interior space. The big drawbacks were the amount of investment required in tooling to make large panels like the body sides and floor, and the difficulties the new system presented for coachbuilding bespoke bodies. The investment question was easy to answer if the body was produced in large numbers, but as Rolls/Bentley volumes were relatively low this meant the body, and therefore the tooling, would have to remain in use for at least ten or fifteen years. The problem of bespoke bodies was not as big as it may have appeared, as the market for coachbuilt cars had been shrinking for many years. Before too long the only coachbuilder working on Bentley and Rolls-Royce vehicles would be the in-house firm of Mulliner Park Ward, which had already made some moves towards a more modern style of construction with the all-welded S3 Continental bodies. The benefits of unitary construction for the next generation of Rolls/Bentley saloons far outweighed the disadvantages.

With all this in mind, Rolls-Royce's experiments with unitary bodies had begun in the 1950s. When the V8 engine was still secret, in 1958, it went into a prototype Rolls-Royce saloon called Tibet, which had modern full-width styling to go with its up-to-date unitary construction. Another project was the Bentley Burma – also a unitary car, but this time smaller and powered by a 4.0-litre six-cylinder petrol engine. The motor was an aluminium block version of the B60, developed by Rolls-Royce for military and commercial use, and related to the four-cylinder Austin Champ engine

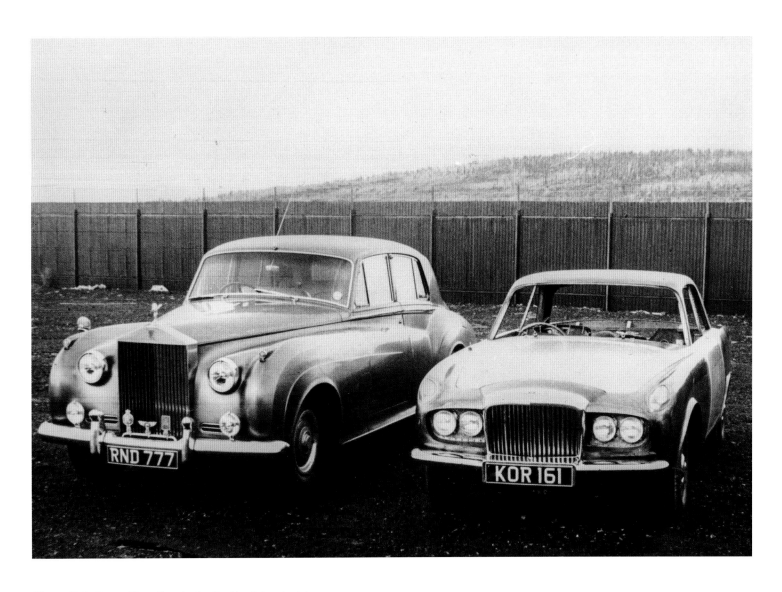

Above: Rolls-Royce Silver Cloud – the Bentley S-type's sister –
alongside the Korea prototype, one of several attempts to
develop a smaller Bentley.

and the straight eight that had powered the rare Phantom IV. Neither Tibet nor Burma, nor a two-door car derived from Burma and codenamed Korea, were carried forward to production in their original forms, but the thought process that started with those projects contributed enormously to the first Rolls/Bentley unitary production car that would arrive in the mid-1960s.

Rolls-Royce also collaborated with British Motor Corporation (BMC) to fit the Burma engine into a Vanden Plas Princess in place of its usual 3.0-litre Austin engine. The body was restyled with the addition of a Bentley grille, vertically stacked quad headlamps and new tail lights to produce the Bentley Java. Later versions adopted side-by-side headlamps in a more effectively resolved front end, and the styling of this vehicle was another stepping stone towards the new production car. Though the Java never appeared as a Bentley, BMC did adopt the Rolls-Royce engine for the Vanden Plas Princess 4 Litre R – though that proved not to be a sales success. A subsequent Bentley Bengal project based on the ADO61 Austin 3 Litre also never got beyond the design stage.

All these projects helped to refine the new unitary saloon car. Project SY – presumably Crewe had run out of southeast-Asian codenames – combined the best of Tibet, Burma and other projects in one. The result was a handsome four-door saloon, styled by Bill Allen and Martin Bourne under the direction of chief designer John Blatchley. As the style of the times dictated, it was squarer and simpler in appearance than Crewe's previous cars, with more restrained exterior dimensions but plenty of interior space thanks to the new type of structure.

The new car was announced at the Paris Motor Show in 1965. The Bentley version was known as the T-Series, following on from the previous S-Series, while the Rolls-Royce was called the Silver Shadow – though originally the intention was to call it Silver Mist, until a German speaker pointed out the unwelcome connotations of that name. The only points of differentiation for the Bentley versions were the badges, the rounded Bentley grille and the bonnet. There was also a £50 price difference, supposedly because the Bentley grille was cheaper to make, but that was hardly significant to anyone who had the resources to afford either the Rolls or the Bentley. Those who chose the Bentley probably did so not because it was cheaper, but because they preferred a car with a little less obvious ostentation than a Rolls-Royce.

The T-Series not only had a fresh, new shape: it was just as modern under the skin. The 6.2-litre V8 engine that had made its debut in the S2 and Silver Cloud II in 1959 was carried over to the new car with some modifications. New cylinder heads made maintenance simpler by allowing the spark plugs to be taken out from above, instead of forcing the mechanic to remove front wheels and engine bay side panels to get at the plugs from underneath. Home-market cars had the Crewe-built GM Hydramatic four-speed automatic transmission linked to the engine with a simple fluid coupling, as had been used on the previous cars, while export cars got the latest GM400 three-speed unit with a torque converter, which would eventually be adopted for all models. The gear selector was a lever on the steering column, with an indicator on top of the column to show which driving mode was selected.

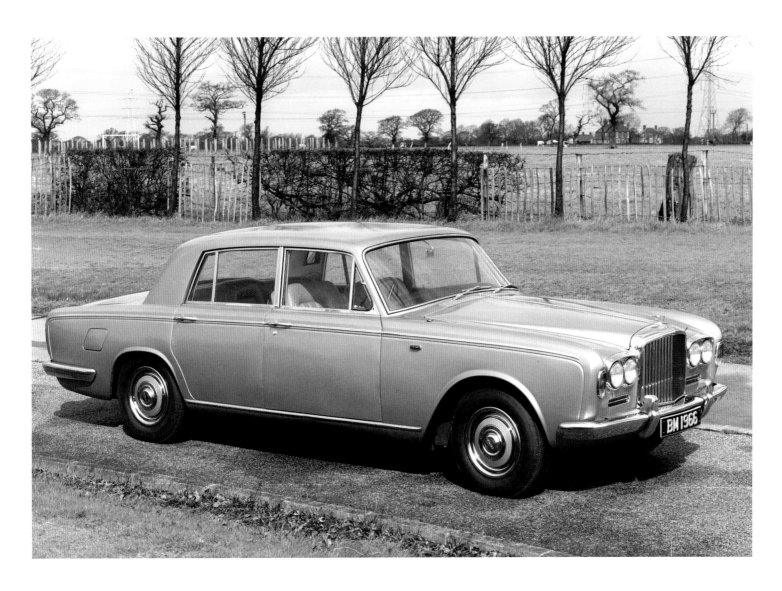

Above: Investigations into creating smaller, more modern cars culminated in the announcement in 1965 of the Bentley T-type, and its Rolls-Royce sister, the Silver Shadow.

The front suspension was by coil springs and wishbones as before, but the rear suspension was all new and far more advanced than on the previous generation of cars. The old-fashioned live axle and leaf springs had finally been consigned to history, and in their place came an independent suspension system using coil springs and semi-trailing arms mounted on a stout subframe. Self-levelling was provided using Citroën-type hydraulic struts, at first fitted to all four corners, but later on the rear only as it was established that the front struts made little difference to the operation of the system. The great benefit of the self-levelling system was that the suspension springs could be soft to give a good ride, but if a heavy load was carried – a full complement of passengers and their luggage – the system would prevent the rear of the car from drooping under the weight. The high-pressure hydraulics which operated the self-levelling also powered the brakes, which were fade-resistant discs all round in place of the drums fitted to previous cars. The interior was as luxuriously appointed as any previous Bentley, with a walnut-faced dashboard, thick Wilton carpet and fine leather in abundance.

Though traditional coachbuilding was now a thing of the past, two-door cars based on the T-Series/Shadow platform were built by Mulliner Park Ward and James Young. The Bromley-based James Young company produced a two-door saloon which closely followed the lines of the four-door, leaving it looking rather staid. It made fifteen Bentley versions (plus another thirty-five with Rolls grilles) before shutting up shop for good in 1967. Mulliner Park Ward persevered, however, launching its own two-door saloon in 1966. Unlike the James Young version this had redesigned doors and rear wings, with a dip in the waistline just aft of the door shut line which gave a hint of the flowing wing shapes of previous generations. The reworked styling made the Mulliner Park Ward cars much more attractive, and they sold better as a result.

Eighteen months after the Mulliner Park Ward two-door saloon was announced, it was joined by a two-door drophead coupé. The delay was caused by the extra work needed to ensure that the body was still stiff enough, even without the bracing provided by a fixed roof. The huge convertible roof was electrically operated and its multi-layer construction meant the cabin was quiet and snug when it was erected. Unfortunately the bulky roof could not be arranged to lie flat around the back of the cabin when it was folded, as on previous dropheads, because the new rear suspension springs took up the space the hood needed, so instead it stacked up behind the cabin like a huge Silver Cross pram. Building and fitting the roof, ensuring perfect operation and a lack of draughts or leaks, could take the Willesden factory up to a month. At this stage both drophead and two-door saloon were still known as T-Series or Shadows, depending on their grilles, but that would soon change.

All the Mulliner Park Ward cars were expensive to build because they were subject to a prolonged manufacturing process. The body panels were pressed and the shells built up in London, and they were then sent to Crewe for the mechanical parts to be added. The part-complete cars were then returned to Mulliner Park Ward for final finishing and trimming to take place. In 1967 the T-Series saloon cost £6,910 (including purchase tax) but the Mulliner Park

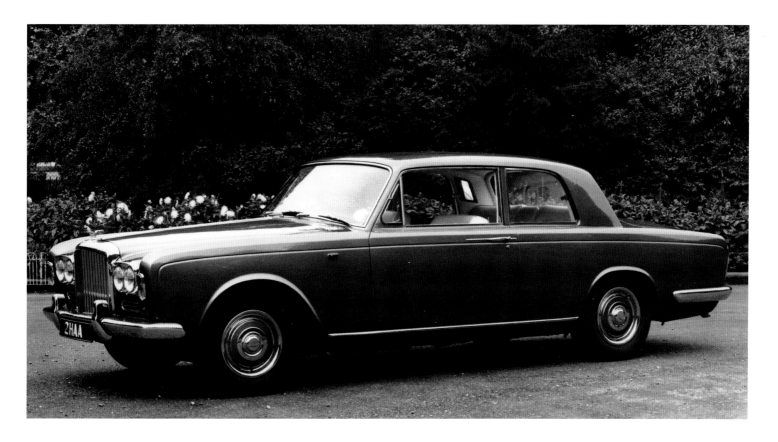

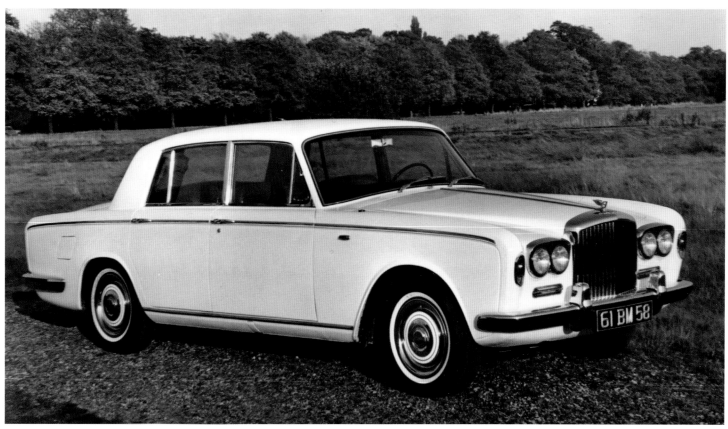

Top: The T-Series and Shadow were also available with two-door bodies: this is the rare version with James Young coachwork.

Above: There was little to differentiate the Shadow from the T-Series, and the Rolls-Royce version was a much bigger seller.

Ward cars were considerably more expensive: the two-door was listed at £9,958 and the drophead was £10,500, more than even the most expensive contemporary Ferraris and Mercedes, and twice the price of an Aston Martin.

In 1968 the rear suspension of all the cars was stiffened, a rear anti-roll bar was added, and the steering was quickened, to answer criticisms of vague handling and a ride that made some rear-seat passengers car-sick. The following year air conditioning, already available as an option, was added to the standard specification. While the Silver Shadow was made available in a long-wheelbase version there was, as yet, no T-Series equivalent. Interior changes to meet new North American safety legislation followed, with more padding around the dashboard, and different switches. Then in 1970 the engine was stroked to take the capacity out to 6,750cc, compensating for power lost by detuning the engine to meet increasingly stringent North American emissions regulations – which were having a similarly deleterious effect across the motor industry. A 7,269cc V8 with an even longer stroke had, in fact, been tested at Crewe in the 1960s, though it was never fitted to a production car.

Since the late 1960s Rolls-Royce's aero engine business, still located at Derby, had been working on the RB211, a key mid-range jet engine family with an advanced design using new carbon fibre materials to improve its power-to-weight ratio. The RB211-22 was chosen for the Lockheed Tristar in 1968 and planned for delivery in 1971, but as the new decade dawned it became clear that the engine was underperforming, late and over budget. By January 1971 Rolls-Royce had run out of money to complete work on the engine, and in February that year it went into receivership. The British government nationalised the company because of its importance to British industry – it was one of the largest firms in Britain, employing over 80,000 people – and set about rescuing the RB211 programme and returning the company to profitability. The motor car division, including Bentley, was separated as a new business, Rolls-Royce Motors Limited.

The first announcement from the new company, later that year, was a name for the two-door cars – Corniche, a revival of the name used on the pre-war and post-war prototypes that led to the first Continental production cars. In May 1973 the car company was floated on the stock market – to a rather muted reception – and as a result it became entirely independent of the reconstituted aero engine business, which was now known as Rolls-Royce (1971) Limited. The trademarks associated purely with the cars – in particular the Spirit of Ecstasy and the Rolls grille, together with the Bentley logo and grille shape – were taken over by the car company, while the rights to the Rolls-Royce name and logo were retained by the aero engine firm. A detailed agreement was drawn up enabling the car company to use them on its vehicles.

Despite the upheaval behind the scenes, there was plenty for the styling and engineering teams at Crewe to be getting on with. Numerous minor revisions to the T-Series/Silver Shadow were being made, often due to tightening emissions and safety legislation, and there were early thoughts about the next generation of saloon cars. On top of that there was a new flagship model, which would see the light of day in 1975.

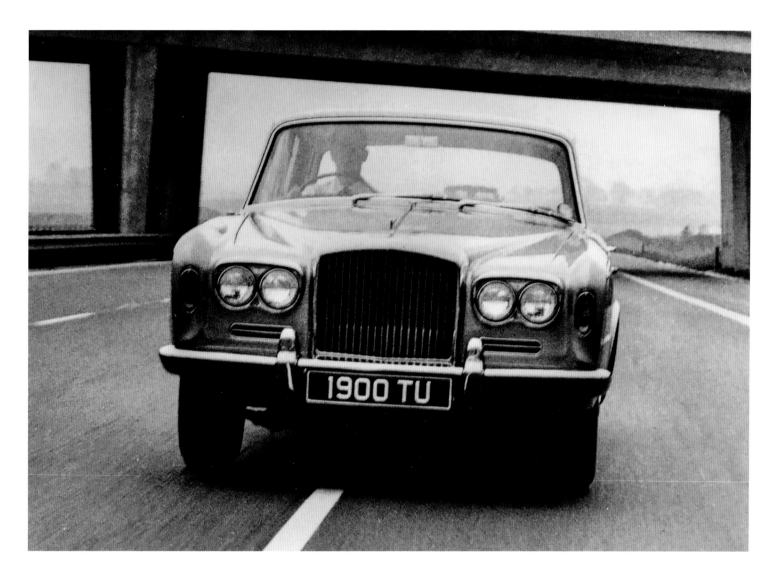

Above: The Bentley T1 was luxurious, quiet-running, and slightly less ostentatious than its more commonly seen Rolls-Royce equivalent, the Silver Shadow.

Following pages: Mulliner Park Ward's two-door T-Series became the Corniche. The model would go on selling into the 1990s.

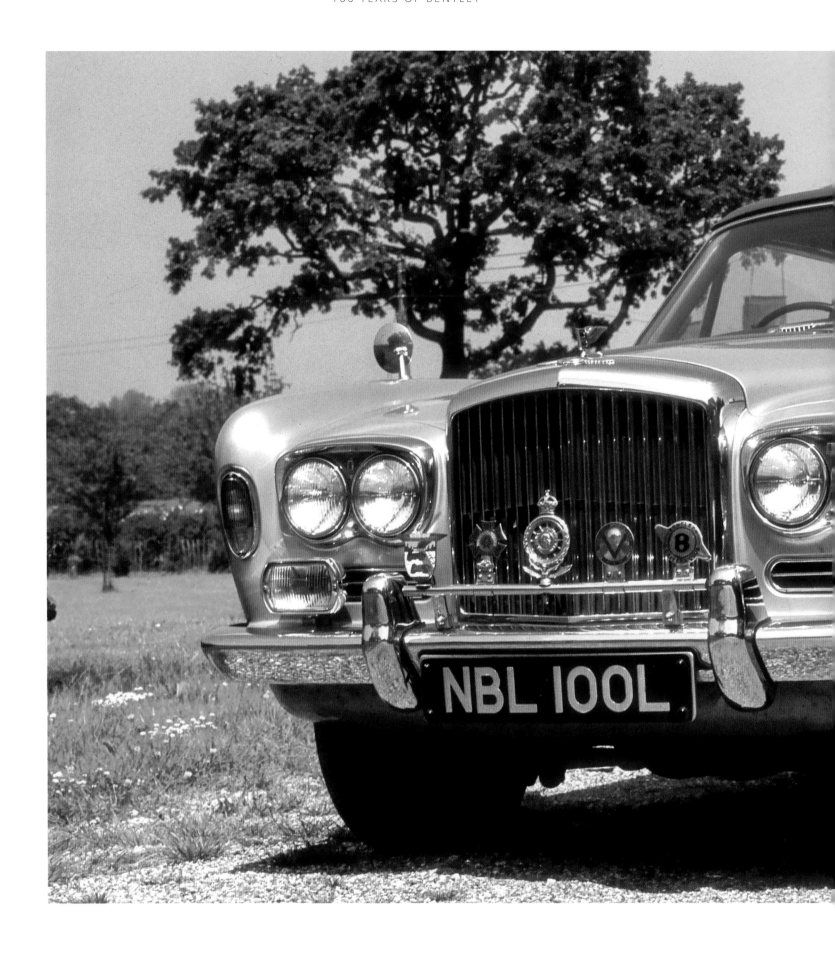

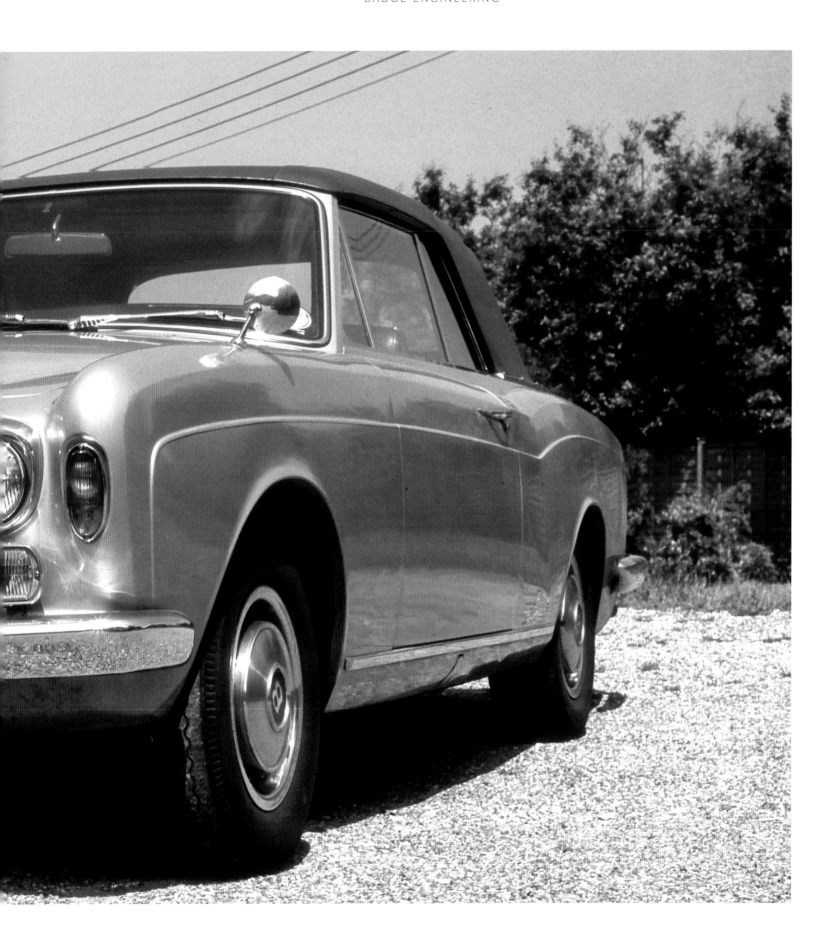

Because there was so much development work already in progress at Crewe the design of the new car was outsourced to Pininfarina. In 1968 the Turin styling house had created a one-off Bentley coupé based on a T-Series for industrialist James Hanson, hoping that Rolls-Royce might sanction a run of production cars. Shown at the Paris and London motor shows that year, it had a more angular style than the T-Series, with rectangular headlamps and a fastback rear roofline. It remained a one-off, but must have played a part in winning the contract for Pininfarina to design the car which became the Camargue.

Like the special T1 it was penned by Pininfarina's chief designer Paolo Martin, and the shape still causes controversy today. It was a vast two-door touring car, undeniably imposing and much more modern than the T-Series and Silver Shadow with which it shared a floorpan, but it lacked the grace of the big 130 Coupé that Martin had recently created for Fiat. A late decision to increase the size of the grille so as to underline the car's identity did it no favours. The most expensive production car in the world on its launch, it remained in production until 1986, and by then only 531 had been made – less than one a week. Only one of the production Camargues was built as a Bentley, in 1985, though an early prototype had carried a Bentley grille and at one stage a high-performance turbo version had been considered for production.

One feature of the Camargue which was universally praised was its sophisticated 'split level' air conditioning system which could deliver warm air to the foot wells while still providing fresh air at face level. Perfecting the system had taken eight years. It was, of course, designed with more than just the Camargue in mind, and was part of a package of revisions that turned the T-Series into the T2 in 1977 (when the earlier car became known as the T1). If it had not been for the disruption caused by Rolls-Royce going into receivership in 1971 the revised models would have been on sale much earlier.

Impact-absorbing bumpers had been added to cars destined for North America in 1973, and now big polyurethane-faced bumpers were made standard on all the cars. There was a new, tidier dashboard. Rack-and-pinion steering replaced the old steering box, finally giving the steering the precision it deserved, and there were fatter tyres on wider wheels. Shadows still outsold T2s by a factor of nine to one but there was some demand for a long-wheelbase Bentley, so a batch of ten cars was built in 1977 by Mulliner Park Ward alongside the long-wheelbase Shadow, which had acquired the name Silver Wraith.

Because it was a low-volume car built by hand it was easy to incorporate new features on the Corniche first, before they went into volume production on the four-door saloons. So the Mulliner Park Ward two-doors were the first to get a series of detail changes to the suspension as Crewe sought for improvements to the ride and handling, and the first to get the Camargue's split-level air conditioning. In 1979 the Corniche was given a revised rear suspension system that was intended for the Mulsanne and Silver Spirit – replacements for the T2 and Shadow which were still a year away. Electronic ignition, which made starting easier and reduced maintenance, was another first for the Mulliner Park Ward cars, along with ventilated front brake discs which were more resistant to fade.

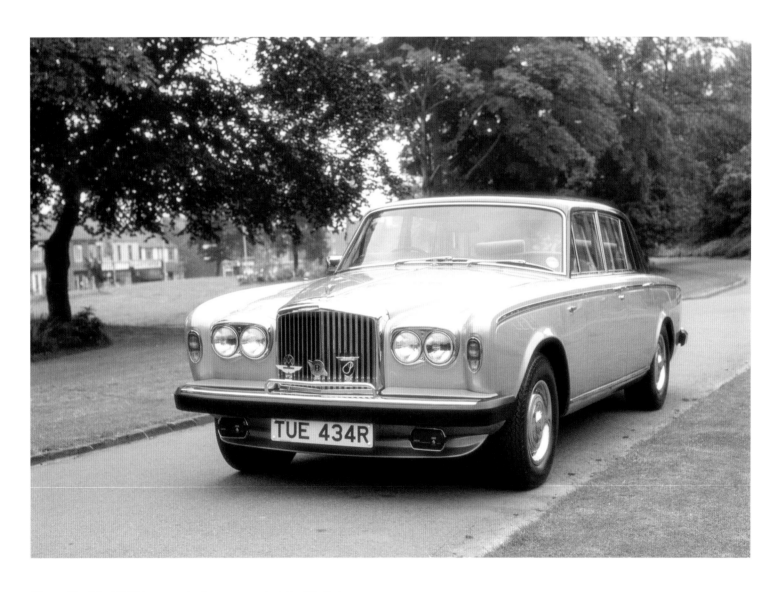

Above: The T2 of 1977 incorporated numerous changes. Obvious front-end differences included a sleeker nose, bigger bumpers and a chin spoiler.

In 1984 there was a change of name when Corniche was dropped and a favourite from the past, Continental, was reintroduced. Fuel injection was adopted, first for the US market and subsequently for all the cars, initially using the Bosch K-Jetronic system which was later upgraded to Bosch Motronic. Anti-lock brakes were added in 1987, and in 1993 there were engine tweaks which liberated 20 per cent more power. Customers who wanted higher performance could order their Continental with the turbocharged engine from the Mulsanne Turbo – though only eight Continental Turbos were ever made.

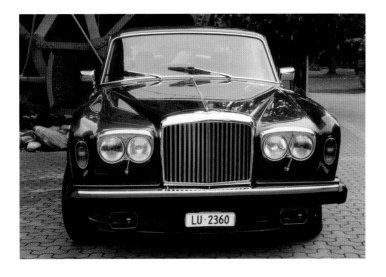

Above: The grille and bonnet were the only major features to differentiate the T-Series from the Rolls-Royce Silver Shadow.

Opposite: The Corniche kept on going, latterly reviving the name Continental. Eight were fitted with turbocharged engines.

Twice during its long production run the Corniche/Continental survived what appeared to be the end of the road. When the Mulsanne replaced the T2 (and the Spirit took over from the Shadow) it would have been reasonable to assume that the two-door cars would also be dropped. Production of the two-door saloon did end in 1980, but the drophead went on because there was no drophead version of the Mulsanne/Spirit saloon. And when the Mulliner Park Ward factories in London were closed down in 1991–2 once Phantom VI production ceased that could have spelled the end for the Continental – but demand was high enough to make it worth moving the production facilities up to Crewe. Continentals were manufactured there until 1995, even overlapping with the introduction of the new generation Continental R, the last of them being listed for £163,313. In all, the T-Series/Corniche/Continental drophead was in production for a remarkable 33 years during which time a total of 569 were made. The bulk of those – 429 of them – were the Continental model, even though it was in production for a much shorter period than the Corniche and was only available in the convertible body style.

By the time production of the Continental finally came to an end the future for the Bentley marque was looking a lot healthier than it had once been. Bentley production was increasing, and there were new models which were distinctly different in style and character to their Rolls-Royce brethren, and which had more of a focus on performance and driver appeal. It was no less than a re-emergence of the marque in its own right, and it began in 1980 with a new family of saloon cars.

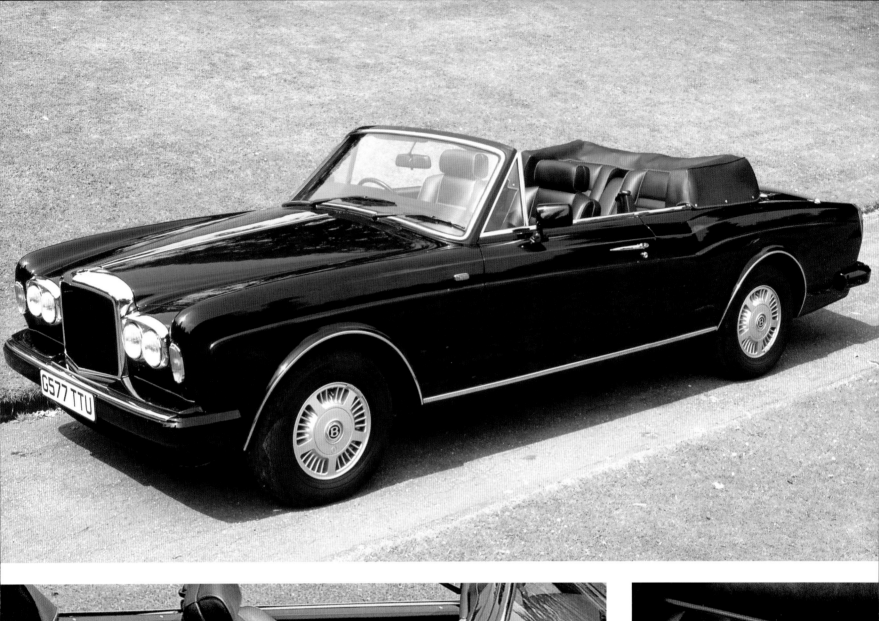
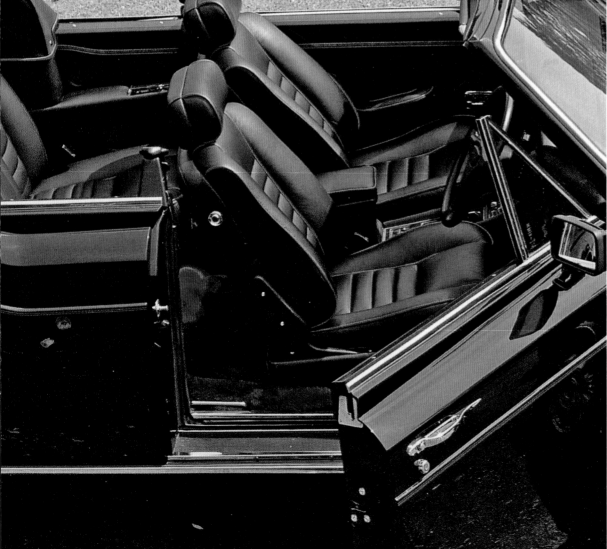
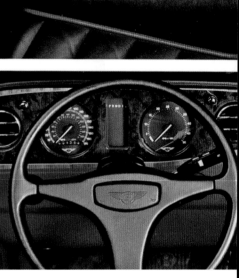
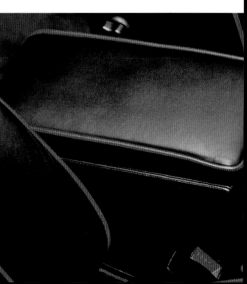

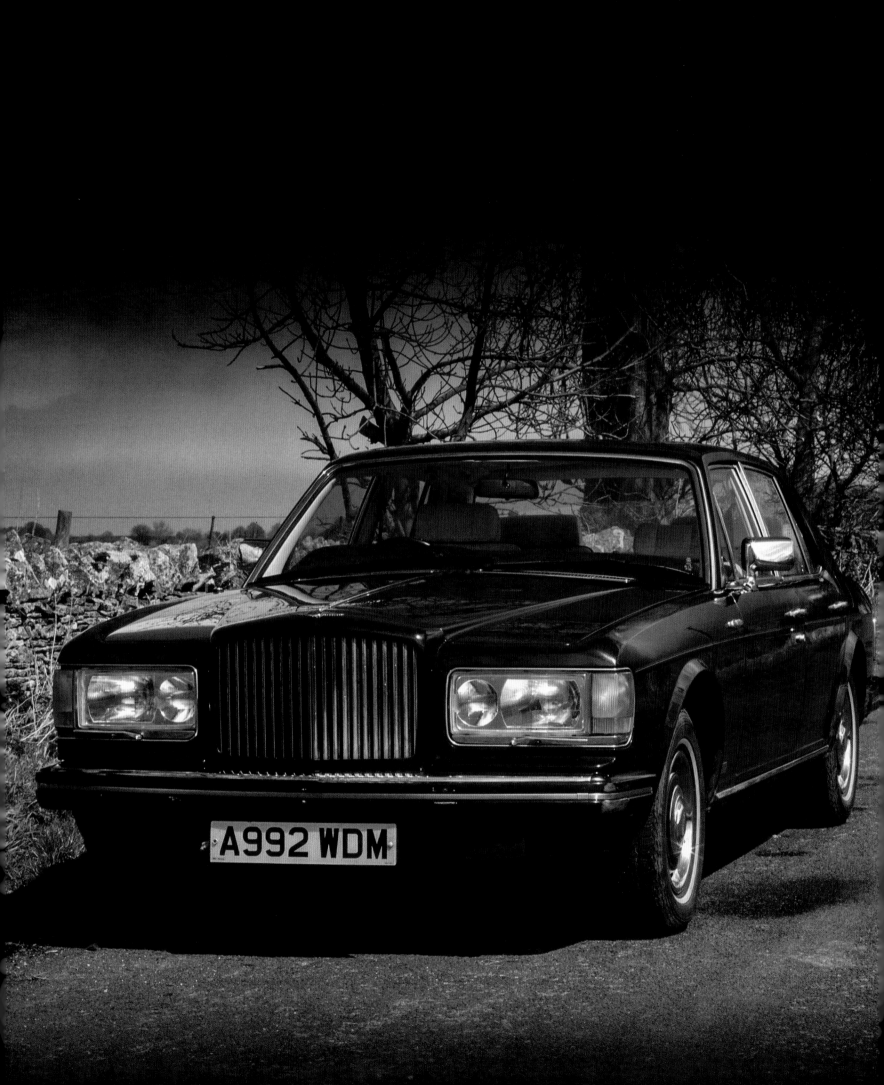

Chapter 6

R FOR REVIVAL

The T-Series Bentleys were fine machines, and they kept the Bentley name alive – just about – throughout the 1970s and 1980s. On the road, their more modern brakes and suspension made them clearly superior to the previous generation of cars. But they also perpetuated Rolls-Royce's 'rationalisation' of its car designs, with virtually no difference between Bentleys and their Rolls-Royce counterparts. For the vast majority of Crewe's customers there was simply no reason to buy a Bentley rather than a Rolls-Royce.

That began to change when a new generation of saloon cars, the Bentley Mulsanne and Rolls-Royce Silver Spirit, replaced the T-Series saloon and Silver Shadow in 1980. Known internally as Project SZ, they had been in development since the early 1970s, and were based on the same floor panel as the SY T-Series/Shadow. Retaining this major component was a huge cost saving, but even then the new car represented a £50 million investment.

The design team was now led by Austrian Fritz Feller, an engineer rather than a designer – but more importantly, someone who understood Crewe's clientele and could effectively lead the small team charged with creating the SY's successor. The aim was to improve the SZ's road presence in comparison to the SY, but without making the car substantially larger. Other constraints were the retention of the classic Bentley and Rolls-Royce grilles, the stainless steel side window frames, and the broad C-pillars that gave a sense of solidity and also provided a measure of privacy to the rear of the cabin. The new car had to have a more modern appearance, but with the same elegance of bearing as its predecessors. It also had to offer improvements in aerodynamic performance and occupant safety to bring Crewe's products up to the standards of its competitors.

The SZ was fractionally wider and longer than the SY, but also slightly lower, which gave it proportions that instantly looked more modern. The grilles were shorter and wider to match. The new car had 30 per cent more glass area than the old one, and for the first time the side windows were made from curved rather than flat glass. The windscreen rake was more pronounced, now 53 degrees from the vertical rather than 46, to aid aerodynamics. The SZ also penetrated the air more effectively thanks to a front end which was more rounded in plan than the bluff front of the T-Series and Shadow. Though Crewe declined to release any figures for the coefficient of drag or frontal area, it was said that the SZ was competitive with other big saloons, and the Bentley version with its rounded radiator was actually the better of the two. But the Bentley did have to make do with the Rolls bonnet, the profile of which did not quite match the grille shape, because there was no budget available for a Bentley-specific bonnet.

Safety was high on the agenda. The driver's-side wiper was given a pantograph linkage so that it wiped more of the screen, and deflectors and drainage channels were fitted to manage the water spill from the wipers, avoiding splashes onto the side windows and improving visibility in poor conditions. Flush door handles replaced the protruding handles of the previous car, and the doors now contained stout steel anti-intrusion beams to protect the occupants of the car from side impacts. The edges of the Rolls grille were slightly more rounded, and the Spirit of Ecstasy mascot was designed to retract into the grille in a fraction of a second

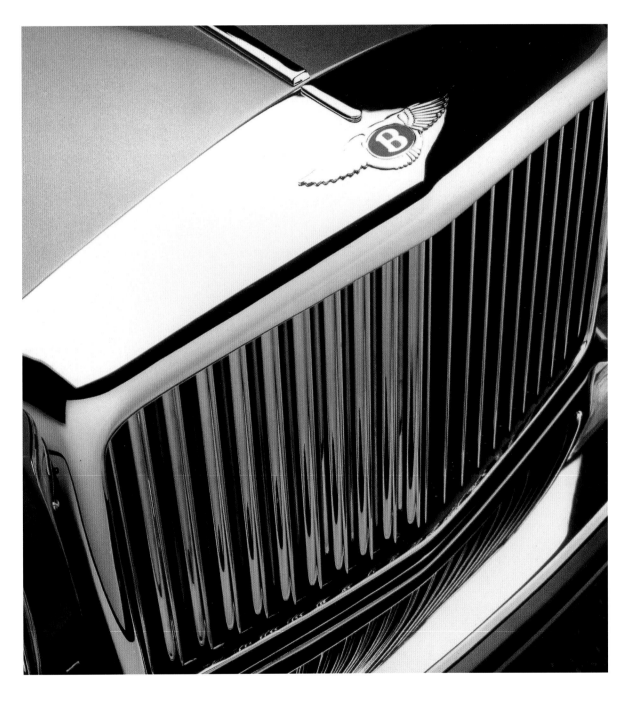

Above: The traditional Bentley radiator grille shape was retained by the
Mulsanne, and under the skin it shared a lot with the outgoing T2.

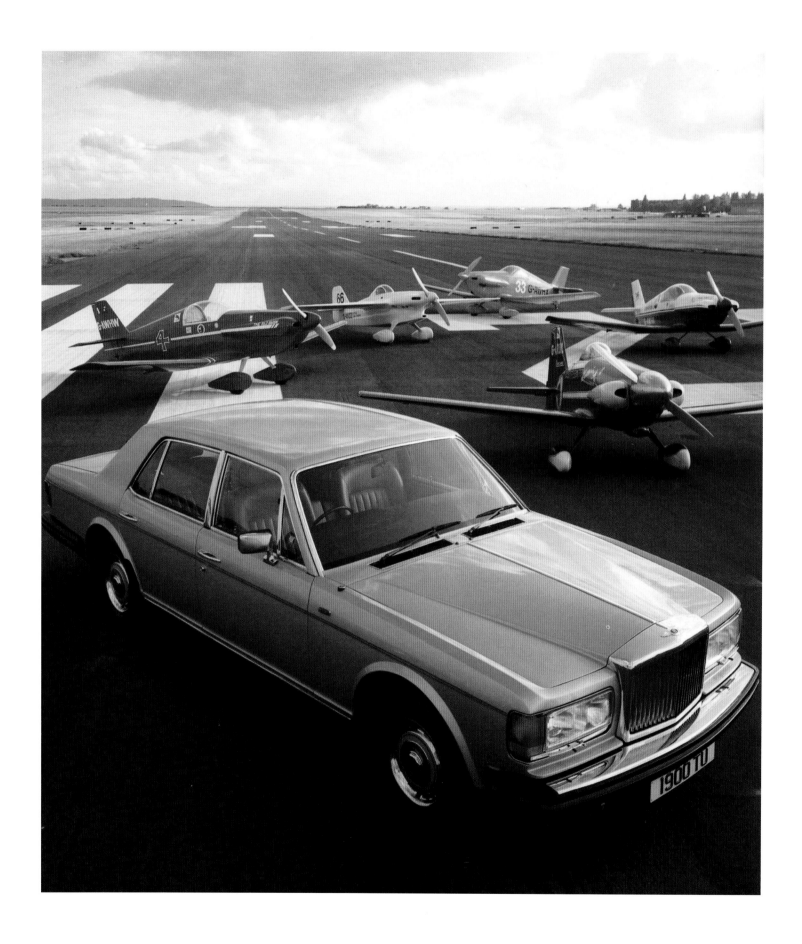

if it was struck. The Bentley needed no such elaborate mechanism because the winged B mascot was replaced by the flush-fitting badge.

Despite the lower roof, headroom inside remained the same, due to a slightly lower seat position and a recessed headlining. The dashboard and controls were largely carried over from the SY, though there was the addition of an LED digital display panel in the centre which showed the outside temperature, time and elapsed time. It was a system which had already been trialled on the Corniche. Chief engineer John Hollings had wanted the rest of the instruments to be digital, too: in response, Fritz Feller drew a cartoon of Big Ben with a digital clock face…

The SZ's boot was a usefully square shape, and big enough to swallow golf bags or piles of Samsonite suitcases. The lid was extended right down to the level of the bumper to make loading and unloading easy, though this meant that some of the rear lights had to be mounted on the boot lid. At first there were worries that repeated slamming of the lid would break the bulbs in the lights, but extensive testing proved that the fears were groundless. At the front end the lighting was equally innovative: the simple, round lamps of the SY were dropped in favour of much more modern rectangular lamps, with wrap-around indicators and bright trims.

The Pressed Steel company that had supplied the SY bodyshells to Crewe had now merged with Fisher & Ludlow to form Pressed Steel Fisher, and was engaged to build the bodies for the SZ. The shells were welded together from 176

Opposite: Mulsanne marked the beginning of a Bentley revival.

pressings. The lower parts of the body, including the sills, chassis rails and inner wheel-arches, were now galvanised to fight corrosion, and the doors, boot lid and bonnet were skinned in aluminium alloy to save weight.

Mechanically the SZ was much the same as the T-Series and Shadow before it, carrying over the 6.75-litre V8 engine and the GM-sourced three-speed automatic transmission. In the UK and many other markets the engine was still fed by a pair of SU HIF7 carburettors, while US cars adopted Bosch K-Jetronic fuel injection. There was a new, low-loss air cleaner and a quieter stainless steel exhaust with a tail pipe on each side of the car.

The coil and wishbone front suspension was carried over from the SY, while at the back the SZ adopted the new rear suspension which had already been tried out on the low-volume Corniche and Camargue. The new design had two main aims: to reduce the potential for oversteer, and to reduce a feeling that the rear end was losing grip, which was caused by the body moving outwards at the back relative to the wheels. There were changes to the geometry of the suspension, with the mountings for the semi-trailing arms now at a more oblique angle, which improved rear-end grip by keeping the more heavily loaded outer wheel more upright in cornering. The changes also raised the roll centre of the rear suspension, resulting in less cornering roll. Connecting the differential to the suspension cross-member using a system of tie rods helped to avoid the body movements which had given the impression of oversteer. The Citroën-style hydraulics which had proved successful on the SY again provided self-levelling for the rear suspension and power assistance for the brakes.

The Mulsanne, Spirit and long-wheelbase Silver Spur were warmly received, with particular praise being lavished on the quieter high-speed cruising which resulted from the more aerodynamically efficient body and careful use of rubber bushes to isolate the suspension from the body.

By the time the SZ was announced Rolls-Royce Motors was under new ownership, after Rolls chairman David Plastow brokered a deal to merge with the Vickers engineering group. Vickers had begun as a Sheffield steel foundry in the nineteenth century, and had grown steadily to become one of the largest engineering conglomerates in the UK. For a while it was in the motor industry as the owner of car maker Wolseley. In 1927 it merged with Armstrong-Whitworth to form Vickers-Armstrongs, and by the 1960s it had interests in a wide range of engineering and manufacturing sectors including steel, aircraft, railway rolling stock, ships, and military equipment.

It was government policy which prevented Vickers' further expansion. In 1968 the group's steelmaking interests were nationalised by Harold Wilson's Labour government. In 1977 there was further nationalisation by another Labour government, under James Callaghan: British Aerospace took over Vickers' aircraft manufacturing interests, and British Shipbuilders took over its marine engineering companies. The remainder, a disparate group of engineering firms, was reorganised as Vickers PLC.

As an independent car maker, Rolls-Royce Motors was too small to compete against large corporations like Daimler-Benz, and it was vulnerable to the kind of fluctuations in demand which it had seen throughout the 1970s. Vickers was cash rich, but the operating divisions it had been left with following nationalisation were not very profitable. Together the two companies could be more stable and make more money, and they had a greater chance of raising funds for future production development. Vickers bought Rolls-Royce Motor Cars for £38 million, and David Plastow – who was knighted in the Queen's 1986 Birthday Honours – took over as Vickers' chief executive. Vickers continued its policy of growth by acquisition, adding the automotive engineering business Cosworth Engineering to its portfolio in 1990. Cosworth would later collaborate with Crewe on new engine projects.

Plastow had been behind the 1970s preoccupation with the Rolls-Royce brand, at the expense of Bentley. After separation from the aero engine company in 1973, Rolls-Royce Motors needed stability. A decade with two global oil crises and considerable political upheaval in the UK, including entry to the EEC and several changes of government, was not the ideal background to achieve that. Plastow's strategy was to concentrate for the time being on the Rolls-Royce marque, which was already achieving the most sales and had the widest global reputation. But his long-term aim was a revival of Bentley, and he ensured that Bentley models continued to be built even when there were factions within the company suggesting that the brand should be dropped.

A revival in Bentley's fortunes had its roots in 1973, when Plastow suggested developing a turbocharged version of the 6.75-litre V8. John Hollings' engineering team was at full stretch and in any case had no experience of passenger car turbocharging – hardly anyone did in 1973 – so Crewe sought outside assistance. Ralph Broad's tuning company

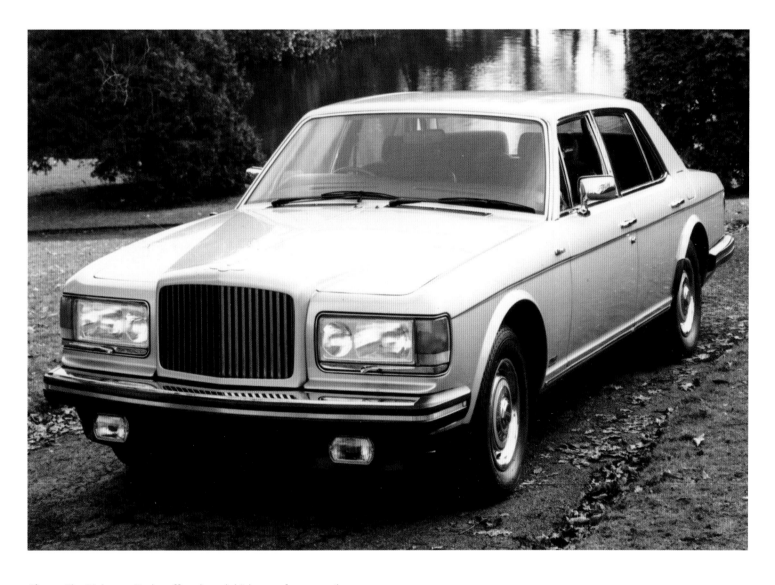

Above: The Mulsanne Turbo offered much higher performance than
the standard model, and was the first Bentley for decades that had
no direct Rolls-Royce equivalent.

Broadspeed, based at Southam in Warwickshire, had just announced a turbocharged version of the Ford Capri and was working on a turbocharged Opel Manta, so a well-used Shadow development car was sent to Southam. Broadspeed quickly put together a turbocharger installation for the L-Series V8 that proved the potential of the idea. Further work at Crewe, led by engineer Jack Read, refined the turbo engine, using a single Garrett turbo (a Holset was also tried) as there was no room in the engine bay to provide a turbo for each cylinder bank.

There were also other problems to address. The extra power provided by the turbo engine clearly fitted the persona of Bentley much better than Rolls-Royce, but it was possible that making a faster Bentley could simply be creating an in-house rival for Rolls-Royce that the company could well do without. There was also the question of how to price such a machine, and even what to call it.

Crewe got to grips with those issues in the early 1980s, once the SZ was safely in production. The result was the Bentley Mulsanne Turbo, unveiled to the press at the firm's Conduit Street showroom in London early in 1982, and first seen in public at the Geneva Motor Show that March. Six cars were available for journalists to drive at Le Mans in April. When deliveries began later that year the Mulsanne Turbo cost £61,744, positioning it between the Silver Spirit at £55,240 and the long-wheelbase Silver Spur at £62,778.

The turbo car could be distinguished from the existing Mulsanne not just by 'Turbo' badges on the sides and tail, but also by the radiator shell which was painted in body colour rather than chromed. The turbo engine was still fed by a Solex carburettor which was mounted in a plenum chamber, and had an extra air feed to the enrichment circuit to improve response under acceleration. A knock sensor which could trigger a retardation of the ignition timing was included as a safety measure. The normally-aspirated engines had recently been given higher compression ratios, up from 8:1 to 9:1, but the turbo remained at the lower figure. There were special pistons and an oil cooler to handle the extra heat generated, wider tyres (235/70VR15 Avons) and stronger half shafts in the rear axle to take the extra torque.

The engine developed about 50 per cent more power than the normally-aspirated unit, giving it around 300bhp. The turbo car was capable of a 0–60mph (97km/h) sprint in 7.4 seconds – extraordinary pace for a machine that still weighed the best part of two and a half tons. The Mulsanne Turbo was quite happy to accelerate beyond the end of its speedometer scale at 140mph (225km/h), representing a true maximum of about 135mph (217km/h). The turbo engine elevated the Mulsanne to the 'Interesting' section of CAR magazine's trenchant summary pages, The Good, The Bad and The Ugly: the Rolls-Royces were classed as 'Boring'. Reviewing the Turbo for CAR, L.J.K. Setright revealed that he could hear hushed conversation from his back-seat passengers while driving the Mulsanne Turbo at 120mph (193km/h), and said the Bentley had the best turbocharger installation he had ever encountered. He reserved some criticisms for the handling, suggesting that it was not up to the performance of the car, but predicted that Crewe would sell far more than the 50 a year they were predicting.

When Mike Dunn arrived at Crewe as the new engineering director in 1983, he found a programme of

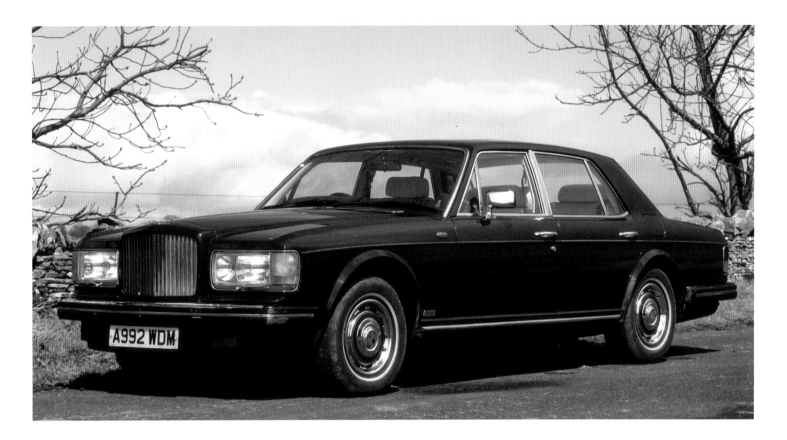

Above: The Mulsanne was slightly bigger than the previous T-Series, but its squarer shape gave it superior road presence.

suspension development already under way to address the criticisms of the Mulsanne Turbo. But for Dunn the proposed changes did not go far enough: instead of the 10 per cent increase in roll stiffness the engineers suggested, Dunn specified 50 per cent. The spring rates were left untouched in an effort to retain good ride quality, but the target for roll stiffness was achieved using new anti-roll bars, twice as stiff at the front and 60 per cent stiffer at the rear, and stiffening the dampers. There was also a further effort to stabilise the rear suspension subframe, with the addition of a Panhard rod.

The new model was called the Mulsanne Turbo R – the R stood for 'roadholding' – and it went on sale in 1985. The Mulsanne Turbo remained on offer for a while, but was soon dropped when it became obvious that virtually all Bentley customers would pick the Turbo R. The two cars looked very similar, except that the Turbo R had a rev counter on its dashboard and a small chin spoiler under the front bumper, and rode on alloy wheels – a first for a Bentley or Rolls-Royce production model.

The result was a transformation. The suspension tweaks made the Mulsanne a much more agile and responsive car, whose handling was now in keeping with the performance created by the turbocharged engine. The Turbo R would always be too big and heavy to be a sports car, but it did make a very effective fast, luxury saloon which could compete on level terms with top models from the likes of Jaguar, Mercedes-Benz and BMW.

As well as making a more attractive flagship Bentley, Crewe expanded the range in the opposite direction with the introduction of the Bentley Eight. Priced a fraction under the £50,000 mark, making it £6,000 cheaper than the Mulsanne, the Eight provided an entry-level model to Crewe's range. Cost was taken out of the car by fitting a wire-mesh grille in place of the grander Mulsanne's chromed slats, and simplifying the interior.

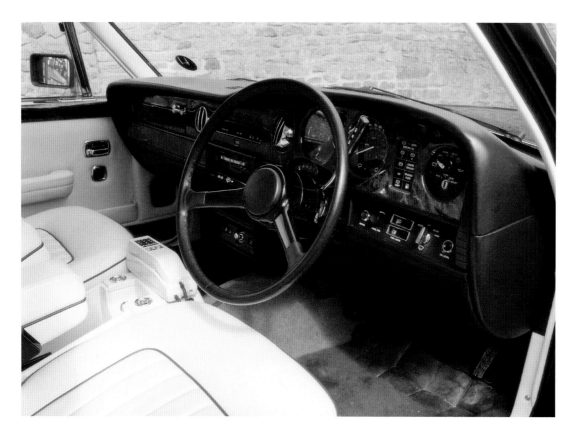

Left: The Mulsanne's interior, with its rich mix of wood and leather, contributed to what Bentley publicity described as the car's 'understated elegance'.

Below: The Turbo R had alloy wheels – a new departure for the company – and important suspension revisions.

Opposite: Later cars adopted the four-headlamp layout introduced on the Bentley Eight.

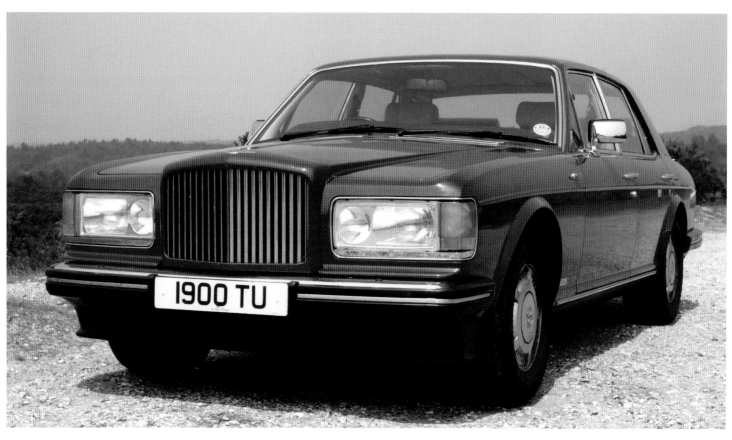

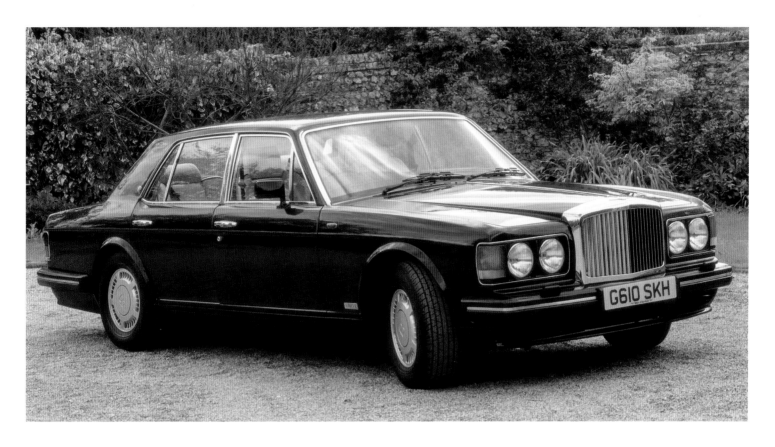

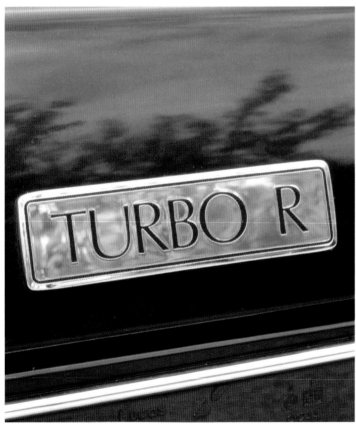

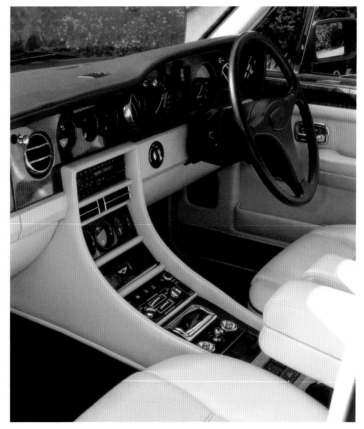

The seat facings were in cloth instead of leather and the veneers covering the interior woodwork were less expensive. The digital display in the centre of the dash was replaced by analogue gauges, and the lambswool rugs were deleted. The Eight was also aimed at a younger clientele, so it was offered with firmer suspension and weightier steering.

Fuel injection and anti-lock brakes were introduced across the range in 1986, and the Eight was upgraded the following year with leather upholstery and powered memory seats as standard to take the place of the base Mulsanne, which was discontinued. Instead there was a Mulsanne S, which still had the normally-aspirated engine but was dressed up with the Turbo R wheels and sports seats. For the 1989 model year the Bentleys switched back to quad circular headlamps and the Turbo R gained a bigger front spoiler. A new variable damping system called Automatic Ride Control was introduced. The Rolls-Royces were also revised and were renamed Silver Spirit II and Silver Spur II, but despite their updates, the Bentleys' names were not changed.

A new model replaced the Eight and Mulsanne S in 1992, but you would have been hard-pressed to see the difference. The Brooklands was essentially a non-turbo version of the Turbo R, featuring the more powerful car's alloy wheels, front spoiler and interior, but fitted with the non-turbo engine – and costing considerably less. The Brooklands was listed at £87,548, while the Turbo R now started at £119,427. Long-wheelbase versions of both were available, at £100,686 and £131,882 respectively.

By then the Bentley saloons had been joined by a new model that really did look new. Dubbed Continental R, it had started life with a two-door coupé concept called Project 90, designed by independent design consultants John Heffernan and Ken Greenley, who had recently designed Aston Martin's new Virage. A mock-up was built by IAD in Worthing for display at the Geneva show in 1985. Reaction was largely positive, and a drophead version was developed as a potential replacement for the ageing SY-based Continental, but as the Continental was still selling well the new car was then turned back into a coupé. Project Nepal, as it became known, gained the four-headlamp front end destined for the 1989 saloons – and to give it the wow factor expected of a coupé, it had much more of a 'Coke bottle' shape. This concentrated the visual weight of the car over its wheels, giving the shape more drama. Nepal also featured subtle box arches, which had been popularised by cars like the Audi Quattro and Lancia Delta Integrale, and doors cut into the roof – a first for a Bentley. The interior featured a bold centre console which split the cabin in half, making it a four-seater.

Nepal was based on the SZ saloon platform, and despite being only a two-door car it turned out slightly longer and even heavier than the saloons. But despite the coupé's extra length it had a surprisingly snug interior, with restricted legroom for rear-seat passengers. It carried over the Turbo R engine together with the four-speed automatic transmission that was now being introduced, with the gear selector on the centre console rather than the steering column (where it remained on Rolls-Royces). Crewe's styling team, under chief designer Graham Hull, fought for larger 16-inch alloy wheels which were more in proportion with the rest of the car, and that meant that bigger brakes could be fitted.

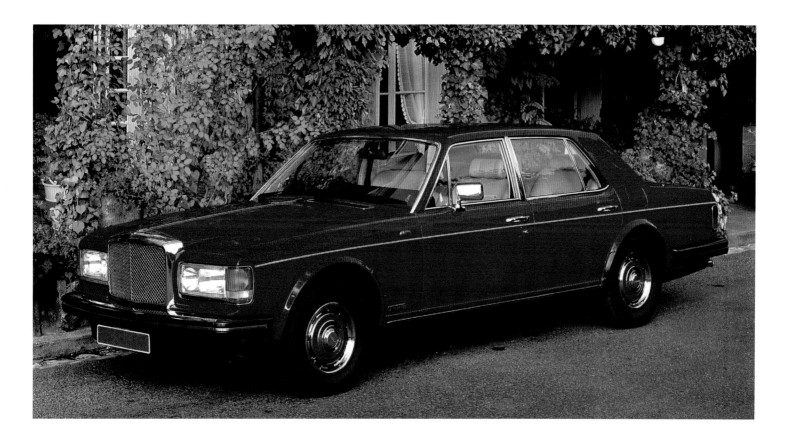

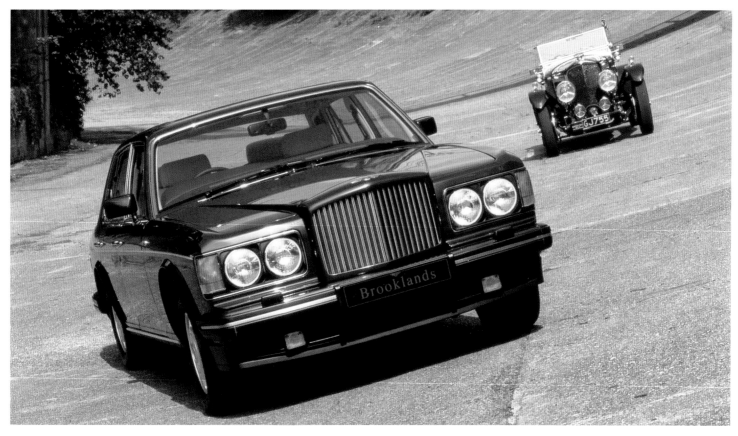

Top: The Bentley Eight was a Mulsanne aimed at younger drivers, with an entry-level specification and a lower price.

Above: A Bentley Brooklands at the racing track that inspired its name – on one of the remaining sections of banking there.

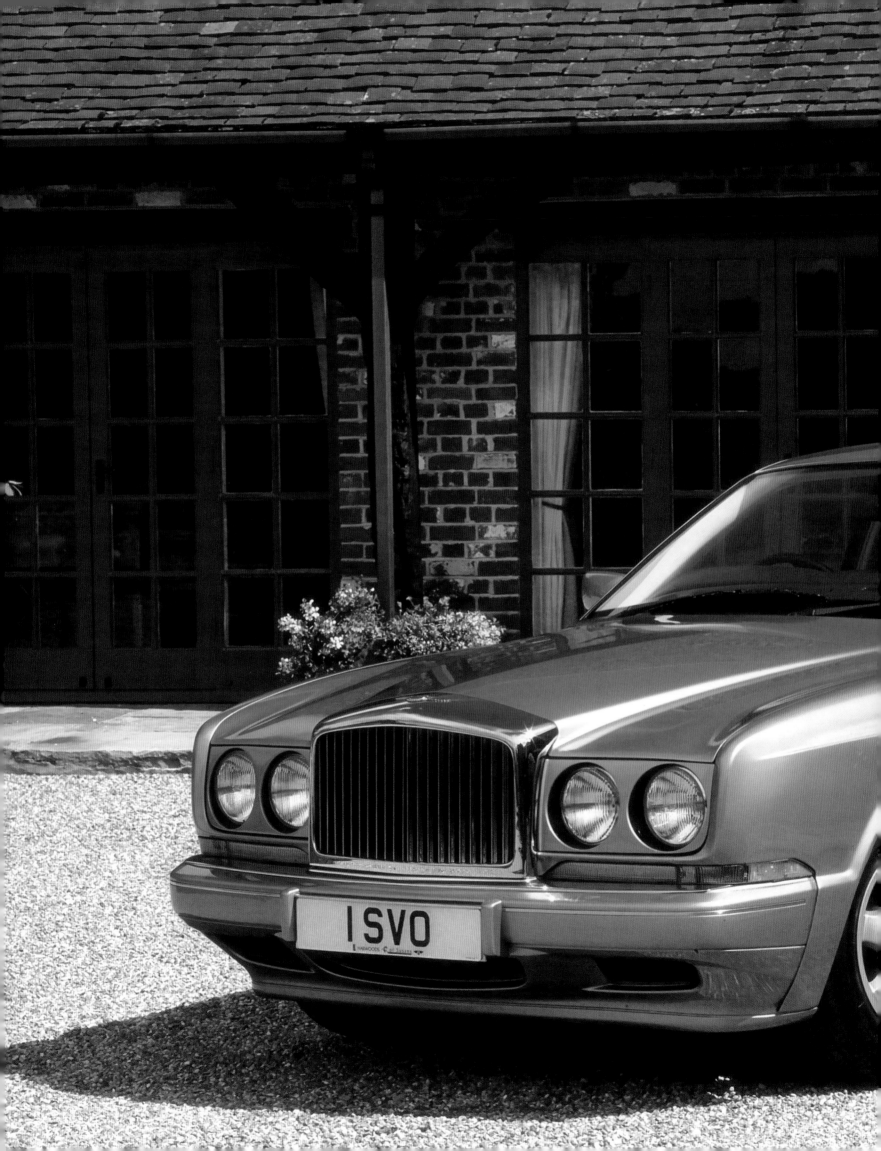

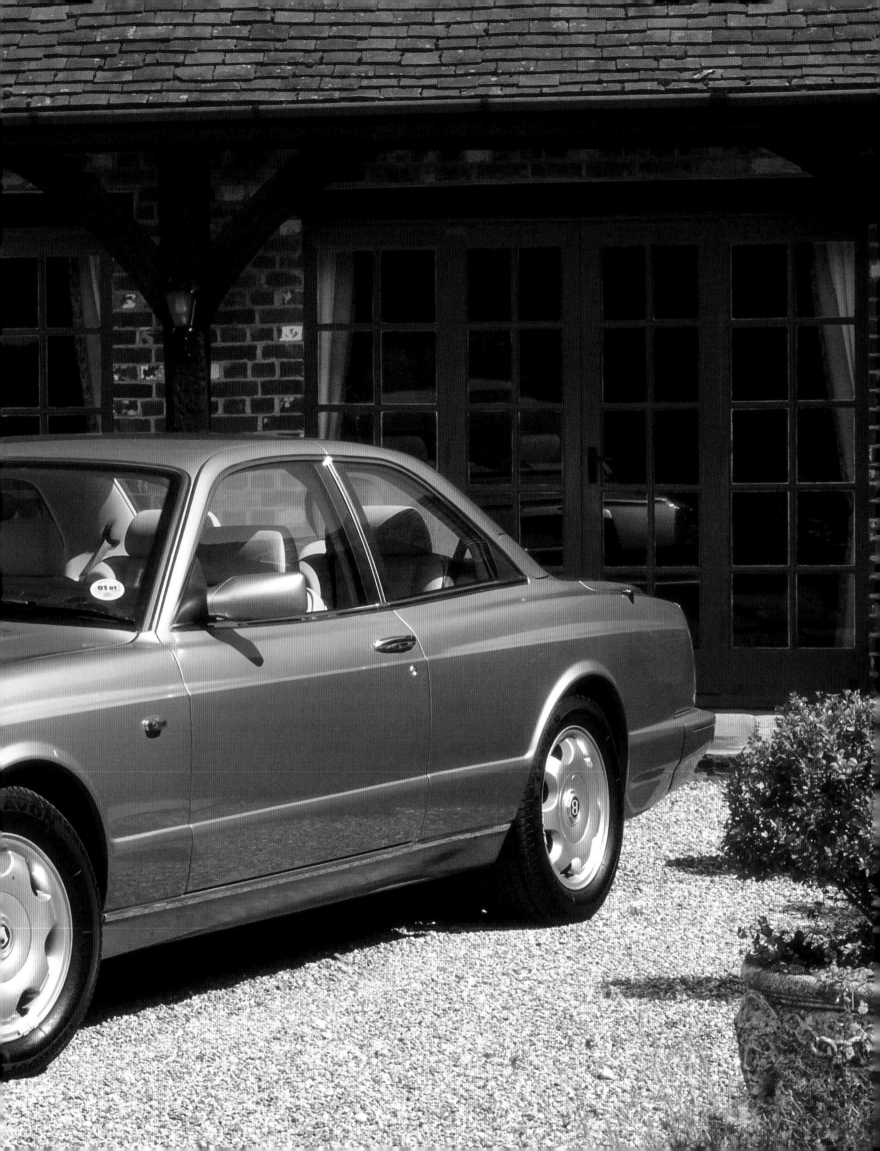

The production car was a surprise announcement at the Geneva Motor Show in 1991, and when it went on sale later that year it was the costliest new car in the world: at £146,094 it was £22,000 more than the next most expensive Bentley, the long-wheelbase Turbo R. The first, bright red show car was even pricier: the Sultan of Brunei paid Crewe handsomely for it while it was still on display in Geneva, and subsequently Brunei became a big market for the Continental R and ordered several special versions, including four-door saloons, estates and convertibles. The high price of the Continental R was turned into a benefit in an advert headlined 'Two cars for the price of four'. The copy gushed: 'The Continental R became a classic motor car the moment it swept onto the highways and by-ways, reintroducing connoisseurs to the meaning of "gran turismo"; a motor car that provides the epitome of comfort over long distances and, when requested, performs like a whole stable of thoroughbreds...You will find no single other car will ever capture the essence of the Continental R. No matter how many you buy.'

A revised turbo engine with Bosch Motronic engine management, a larger turbocharger and a big intercooler was developed in 1995. New rules obliged Crewe to quote power figures for the first time in decades, and this new engine developed a substantial 385bhp. At first it went into special, low-volume models – the Turbo S saloon (60 built) and Continental S (12 built), and there were also three Rolls Silver Spirit S saloons. To handle the extra power there were wider tyres, electronic traction control and a viscous-type limited slip differential. Four-wheel drive had been considered in the early 1990s but was not pursued.

The same year Bentley unveiled another new model, a convertible version of the Continental R called Azure. The conversion to a drophead was designed by Pininfarina and the Italians achieved much tidier stowage of the hood than had been possible in the long-running Corniche/Continental drophead. New seats with built-in seat belts were created for the Azure, and were later adopted on other models. The Azure was the first new convertible Bentley for nearly 30 years, and it marked the point at which the revival of the Bentley brand was very much complete. If the Azure was a high-water mark for Bentley's resurgence it also set a new record for the marque's prices: Pininfarina built the bodies and the folding roofs before sending them to Crewe for finishing, and this pushed up the Azure's price to a colossal £215,000.

Crewe had been considering a smaller car for some time, and a concept car called Bentley Project Java was unveiled in 1994. A short run of Javas – in drophead, coupé and five-door estate form – was built for the Brunei royal family on the BMW 5 Series platform. But, despite further development work, it never became a true production car.

A third Continental R derivative arrived in 1996. Originally created as a one-off for a special customer, the Continental T had four inches taken out of the wheelbase behind the doors to make the car lighter and give it more

Previous pages: The Continental R was based on the Turbo R's engine and running gear, but it boasted a spectacular new body.

Opposite: Priced at just over £146,000, this was the most expensive new car in the world when it was launched in 1991.

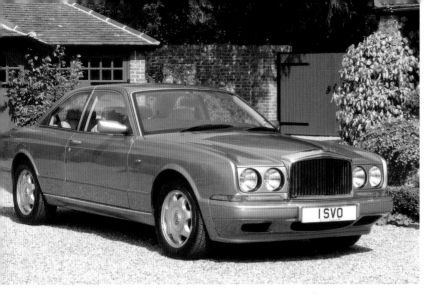

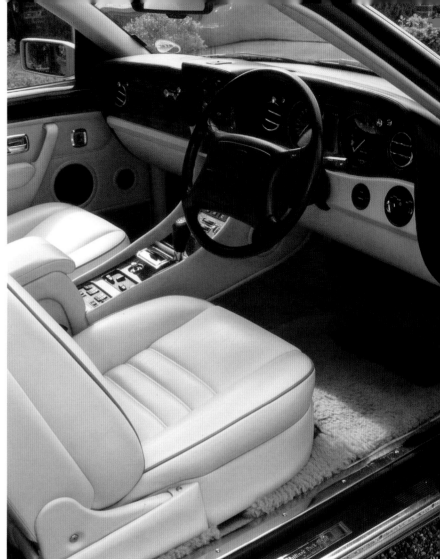

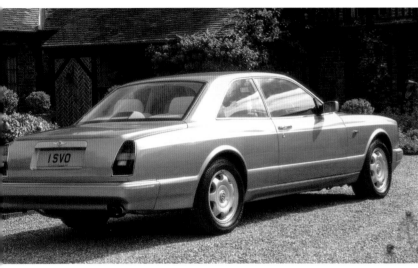

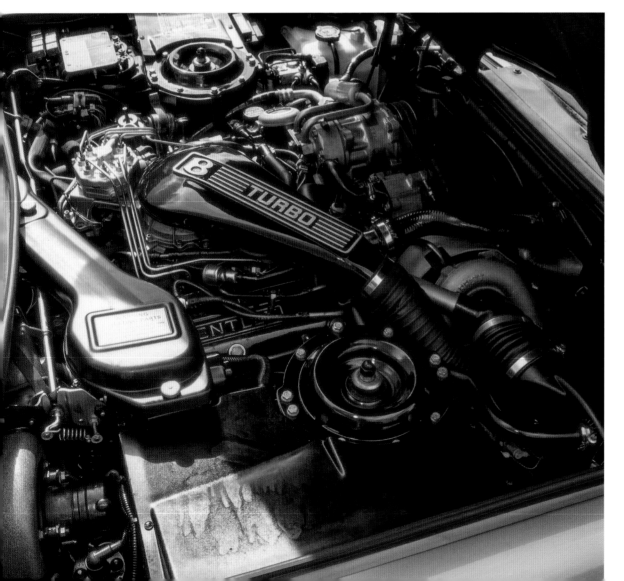

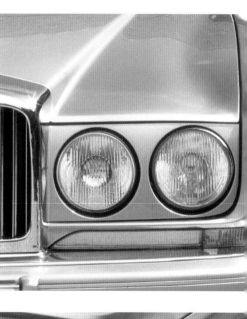

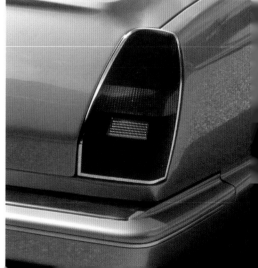

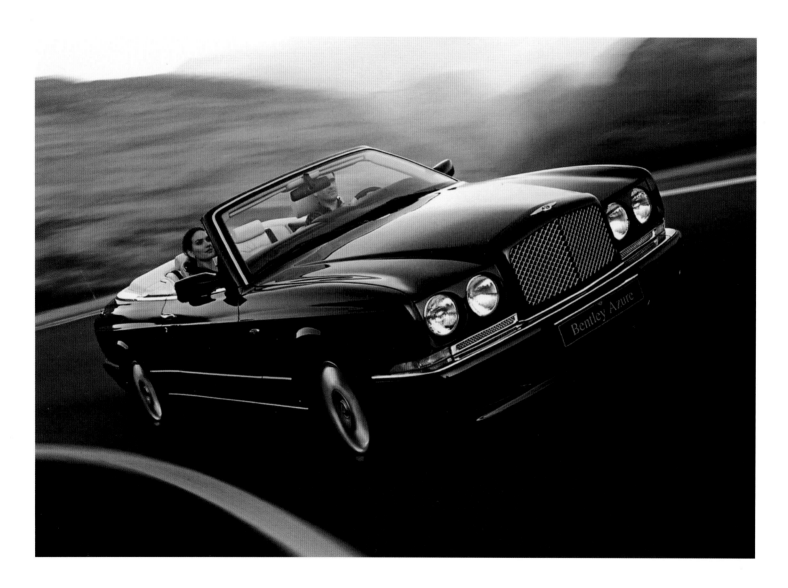

Above: The Azure was a drophead version of the Continental R,
providing the same performance with added glamour.

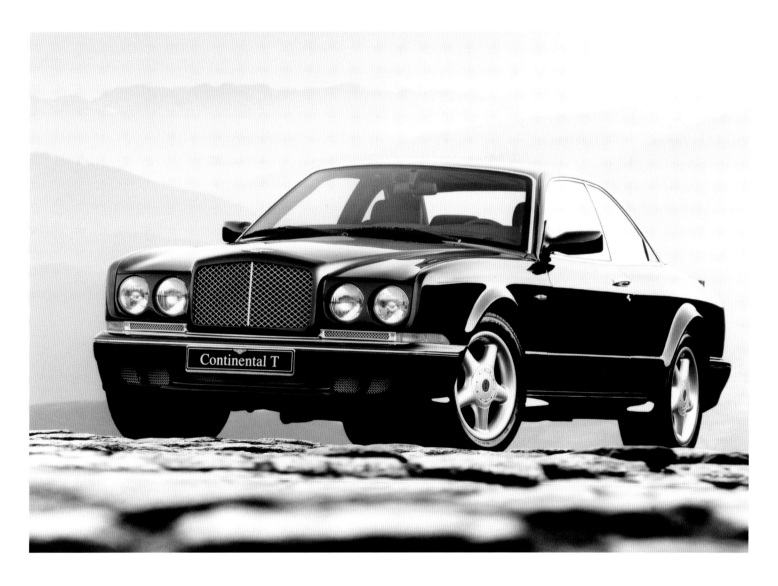

Above: A shorter wheelbase and an increase in power made the
Continental T the optimum mid-1990s Bentley for driving enthusiasts.

responsive handling, at the expense of rear legroom – which was already less than lavish in the Continental R, despite its vast length. The shortened body helped to emphasise the muscularity of the arches, giving the Continental T a more aggressive demeanour. Wider wheel-arches covered bigger wheels and tyres, and the engine was revised with Zytek engine management to provide an extra 15bhp, taking the total to 400 (raised again to 420bhp a couple of years later). Inside, you knew you were in a Continental T because of the engine-turned aluminium panels facing the dashboard and centre console, and for the first time in several decades there was a push-button starter. A rare derivative was the Sedanca Coupé, which had a lift-off roof panel and wider wings. Just 79 were built in 1999.

The SZ saloons continued with regular updates, notably the deletion of the front door quarter-lights to smooth out and modernise the appearance while also reducing the potential for wind noise. The wire-mesh grille introduced on the Bentley Eight was now adopted right across the range, not because it was cheaper but because it looked better. Bumpers were colour-matched to the body and grew larger, so the grilles were reduced in height to suit. All the Turbo Rs gained the long-wheelbase body of what had been known as the Turbo RL from 1996, and in 1998 there was a new Turbo RT using the Continental T's 400bhp engine. The 420bhp was available in a special-order Turbo RT Mulliner, of which 56 were made. At the other end of the range the Brooklands was given a light-pressure turbo engine developing 300bhp, together with Turbo R suspension, a mesh grille and new bumpers to become the Brooklands R. This retained the original wheelbase, so it was now

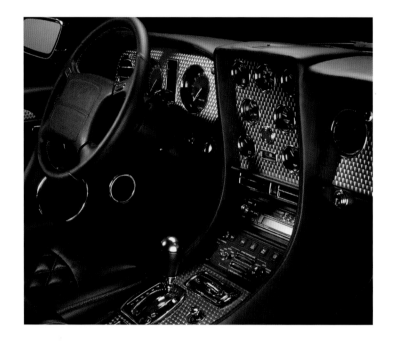

Above: Engine-turned aluminium was a feature of the Continental T interior.

four inches shorter than the Turbo R. There were several limited-edition versions of the Continental R – Concours, Special Edition, Mulliner, Millennium, 420, Le Mans – and several more dealer-sponsored specials. Eventually there was a Final Edition when production ended in 2003.

A new range of saloon cars was already in place by then, and that was not the only big change there had been at Crewe. Bentley was under new ownership: it had been separated from Rolls-Royce after a rather unseemly battle for control between two potential purchasers, and it now had the backing of one of the world's largest and richest car makers. A whole new era was beginning.

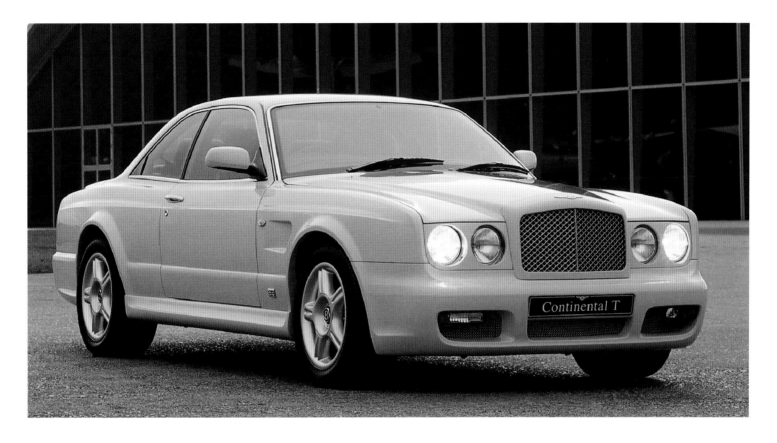

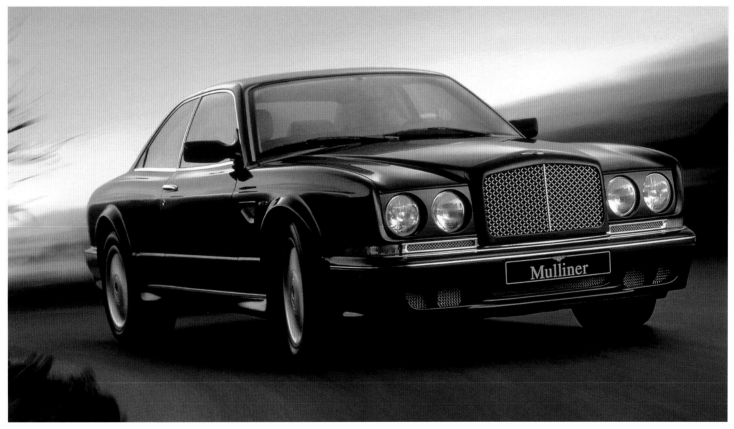

Top: Most Continentals were finished in sober colours – but there were some exceptions.

Above: Mulliner Edition was one of several limited-run versions of the Continental R, ending with the Final Edition of 2003.

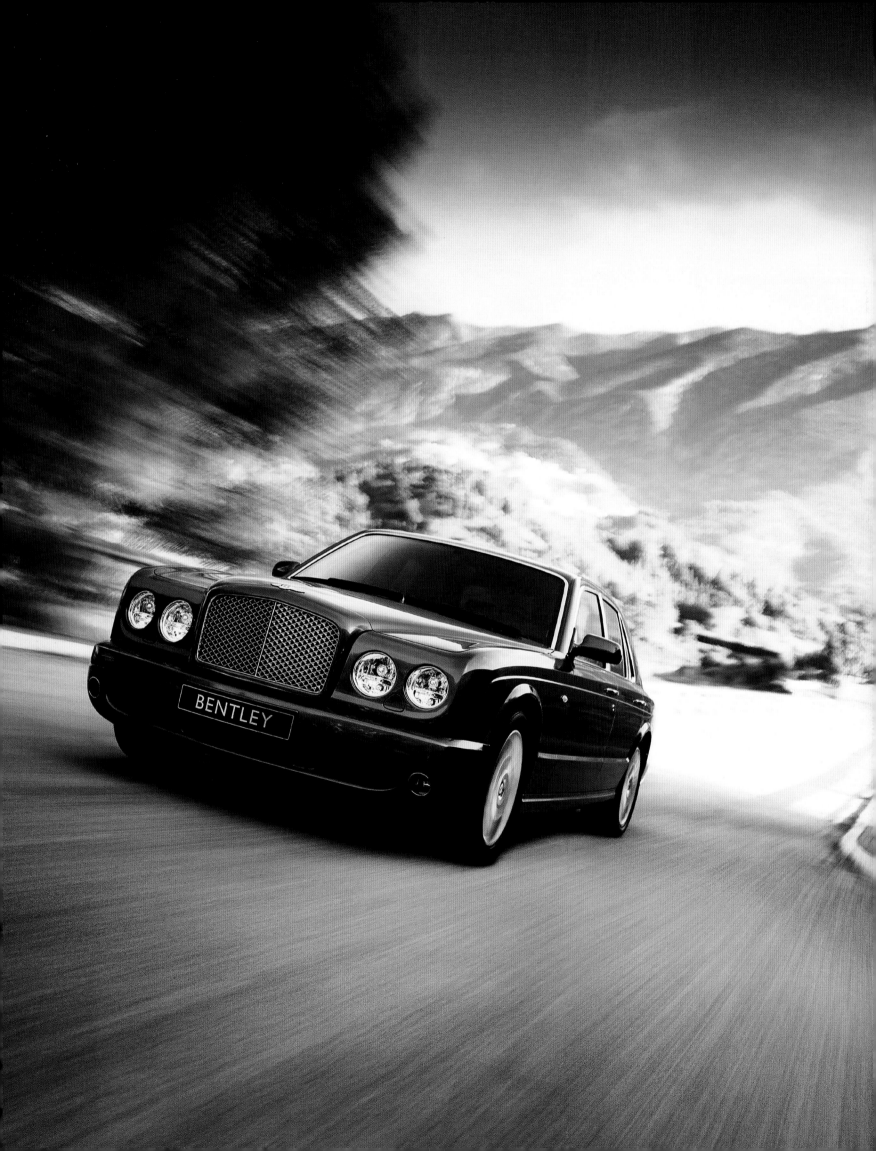

Chapter 7

FROM VICKERS TO VOLKSWAGEN

Late in 1997, Vickers announced its intention to refocus on its core activities in military and marine engineering and offer Rolls-Royce Motors for sale. The decision kicked off a six-month auction which would find a new owner for two of motoring's most famous marques. A couple of industry giants, BMW and Volkswagen, quickly emerged as the main contenders, alongside a consortium of Rolls-Royce enthusiasts, and British venture capital group Doughty Hanson. Others linked with the sale included Toyota, Ford and Daimler-Benz.

The Munich-based BMW group had been formed from an aircraft manufacturer and an aero engine company at around the time W.O. Bentley was beginning to tune his DFP engines for more power. BMW diversified into motorcycles, then bought the Eisenach car factory which made the Dixi, a licence-built Austin 7. After the Second World War BMW built the impressive 'Baroque Angels' as well as tiny bubble cars, but nearly folded in 1959. After its rescue by the Quandt family BMW reinvented itself making high-quality mid-range cars, gradually expanding its brand into the high performance and luxury market sectors. In 1994 it bought the Rover Group and invested millions of pounds in new production facilities and new model programmes.

Until the Rover deal BMW had always focused on a single brand, but its rival Volkswagen had a very different policy. After years of concentrating on the famous Beetle and derivatives from it, Volkswagen diversified by buying Auto Union (which owned the Audi brand) in 1965, and NSU in 1969. It reinvented itself with the front-wheel drive Polo, Golf and Passat in the 1970s, and then bought SEAT in 1986 and Skoda in 1994. By 1998 it was also investigating the purchase of Lamborghini and Bugatti.

Before the ownership of Rolls-Royce and Bentley could be settled a new family of cars was announced. The Bentley version, called the Arnage after a corner at Le Mans, was unveiled in April 1998 – three months after the Rolls-Royce equivalent, called the Silver Seraph. Though the SZ had been thought of as something of a stop-gap that was not expected to match the SY's fifteen years in production, it had in fact lasted three years longer. That gave Crewe's styling department, and a host of external collaborators, plenty of time to refine the style of its replacement. The basic theme came from chief stylist Graham Hull, who analysed the shape of the much-revered 1950s Silver Cloud and came up with the idea of 'yacht aesthetics'. The Cloud, he said, had the visual language of a yacht, with the flowing wings as waves. The front end was tall, the rear low. Unfortunately, the prevailing automotive style was a wedge shape with a high tail. The two conflicting styles were resolved by incorporating a substantial shoulder along the side of the car which sloped downwards towards the rear, to give the feeling of a low tail. At one stage there had been a plan to provide the two cars with different bodies, based on the same new platform, but in the end Crewe took the same approach as with the SY and SZ projects, and built Bentley and Rolls versions using the same body, with modifications to the front end to suit the Bentley grille.

Rather than continue with the now-venerable L-Series V8, which was increasingly difficult to get through tightening global emissions regulations, it was decided to buy in a more modern engine. After examining a number of

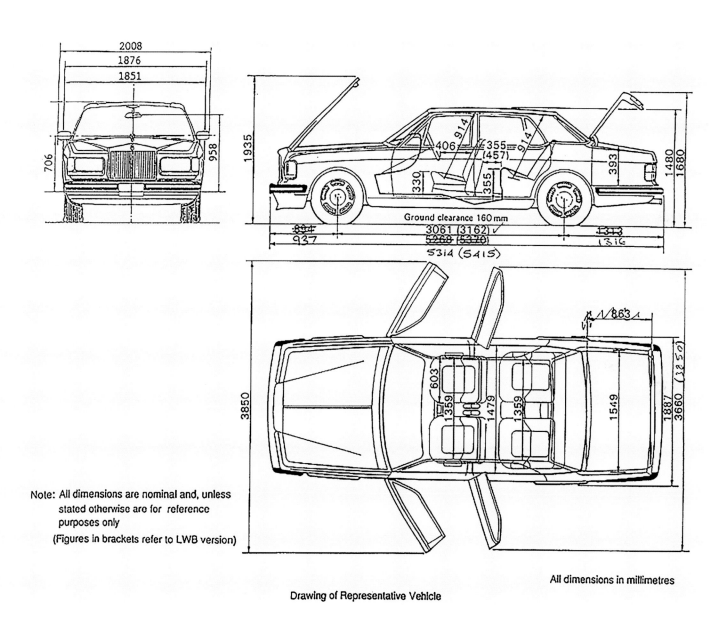

Note: All dimensions are nominal and, unless
stated otherwise are for reference
purposes only
(Figures in brackets refer to LWB version)

All dimensions in millimetres

Drawing of Representative Vehicle

Above: Dimensions of the Bentley Mulsanne submitted for
homologation, the process of obtaining certification from official
regulators. Note that one drawing clearly shows a Rolls-Royce!

alternatives, including GM's Northstar V8 and a Mercedes-Benz V8, Crewe settled on a pair of BMW engines. The Seraph used the 322bhp M73 5.4-litre naturally-aspirated V12 from the BMW 7 Series and 8 Series, but the Bentley's more sporting character was underlined by the choice of a 349bhp twin-turbo version of the M62 4.4-litre V8 developed by Cosworth Engineering, a Vickers stablemate since 1990. It was launched at Le Mans, where 1992 Formula 1 world champion Nigel Mansell was on hand to give journalists rapid passenger rides.

When the auction period came to an end Vickers declared that the winning bid of £340 million had come from BMW. The chairman of BMW, Bernd Pischetsrieder, announced a £1 billion investment plan which would double the workforce at Crewe and push car production from 2,000 a year to 6,000 or more by introducing two new model lines. There were few details, but the speculation was that the new models would be a smaller Rolls-Royce and a Bentley sports car. In the normal course of events that would have been the end of the story, but this was to be a far from normal transaction.

The Rolls-Royce enthusiasts had split into two factions, both of whom vowed to fight on to save the company from falling into foreign hands. Then Rolls-Royce revealed that an improved offer had been received from Volkswagen, as reports in German media said Volkswagen chairman Ferdinand Piëch was willing to pay 'almost any price' for the company. Vickers gave BMW four weeks to finalise the terms of the deal, during which it would not entertain any other bids, though if a higher bid was received it would expect that to be reflected in BMW's final offer. BMW

chairman Pischetsrieder responded by saying he had made his one and only offer for the company but could not rule out a higher bid from a rival. By the time Vickers shareholders were asked to vote on the deal a higher offer of £430 million had been received from Volkswagen. In addition, Volkswagen subsidiary Audi offered Vickers £120 million for Cosworth Engineering, which had now taken over production of Crewe's old V8 engine, conditional on the Volkswagen offer being accepted. True to his word, Pischetsrieder did not make a counter-offer on BMW's behalf. Vickers recommended to shareholders that they accept the Volkswagen offer, which they did by a huge majority. But even that wasn't the end of the story.

Rolls-Royce PLC – the aero engine manufacturer from which Rolls-Royce Motors was divested in 1973 – suggested that it would rather see the car company sold to BMW. That view was coloured by the fact that Rolls-Royce PLC had entered into a joint venture with BMW, called BMW Rolls-Royce AeroEngines GmbH, to build the BR700 family of twin-shaft turbofan jet engines in Germany. BMW, of course, not only had connections with Rolls-Royce PLC – it was also now a supplier of engines and many other parts to the car company. The contract stated that if the company was sold to a rival, BMW could pull the plug on the supply of engines for Crewe's cars within twelve months. Volkswagen was defiant, saying it would use British-built engines.

There was also a suggestion that BMW was in a position to raise the £1 billion or so it would need to buy the whole of Vickers, heading off the Volkswagen bid for Rolls-Royce Motors. BMW could then sell off the engineering side of Vickers and retain the car company.

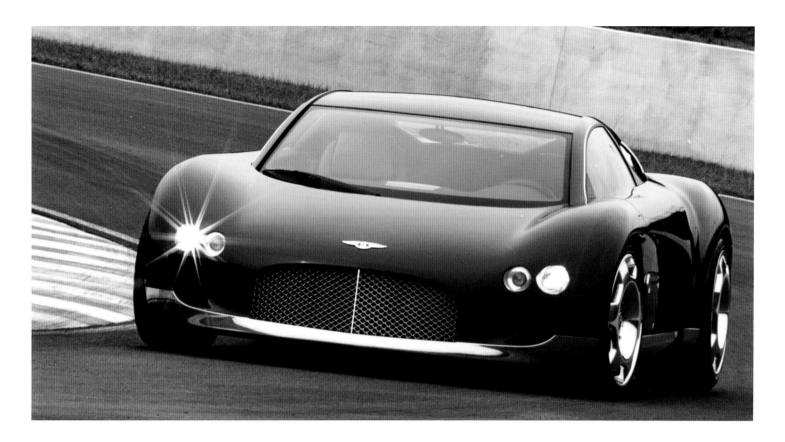

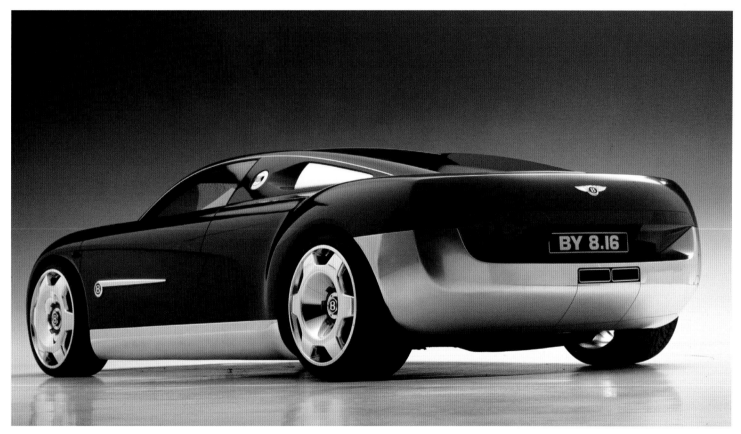

Above: The Hunaudières concept car of 1999 was developed in just six

months. It was based on the Lamborghini Diablo VT.

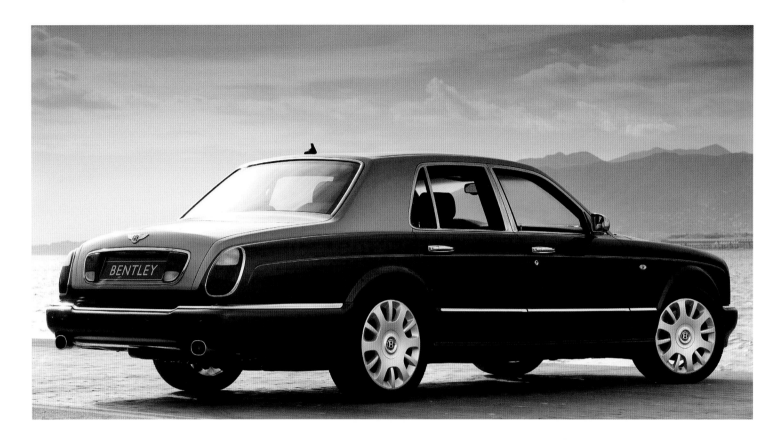

Above: The styling of the Arnage and its Rolls-Royce stablemate, the Silver Seraph were influenced by yacht design.

Right: Eight decades on from the birth of the Bentley marque, the Arnage still featured the firm's distinctive radiator grille shape.

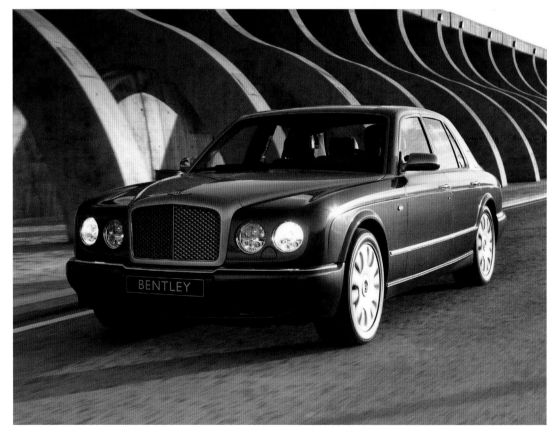

That was not the only twist to an increasingly complex situation. Volkswagen's deal bought them the car company, including the Crewe facility and the trademarks the car company owned – including the Bentley name and logos, the Rolls-Royce grille and the Spirit of Ecstasy mascot. But the rights to the Rolls-Royce name and the RR logo were still owned by Rolls-Royce PLC, a firm which already had a strong relationship with BMW and was on record as preferring BMW as the new owners of the car company. Volkswagen either did not realise this, or underestimated the challenge of negotiating for the rights with Rolls-Royce PLC. Entitlements to use the Rolls-Royce name and logo were considered by some analysts to be the most valuable assets under discussion, and without them Volkswagen owned Bentley and Crewe, but couldn't make Rolls-Royces.

Piëch and Pischetsrieder met for personal negotiations, and finally a deal was thrashed out which many saw as delivering a big win for BMW. In July 1998 a three-way agreement was announced between BMW, Volkswagen and Rolls-Royce PLC. BMW would pay £40 million to the aero engine company for the licence to use the Rolls-Royce trademarks on cars. It would allow Volkswagen to exploit those trademarks until the end of 2002, and would agree to continue supplying engines and other parts to Crewe for the Arnage and Seraph. In the meantime, BMW's plan was to set up a new Rolls-Royce factory which would produce a new generation of cars. That new factory was established at Goodwood in Sussex, and BMW took over the Rolls-Royce brand from 1 January 2003.

Meanwhile, Volkswagen took over at Crewe and set about two tasks: organising a transition to a BMW-free range of Bentley and Rolls-Royce cars in the short term, and then establishing a whole new generation of Bentleys for the future. But before Volkswagen sanctioned any new production cars it announced that it meant business with Bentley by unveiling a concept car, named Hunaudières after the straight at Le Mans that most of us call Mulsanne. It was unquestionably one of the stars of the Geneva Motor Show when it appeared there in 1999.

A smooth, low, dark green form hunched over enormous six-spoke alloy wheels, the Hunaudières was a break from virtually every Bentley tradition. It was Bentley's first mid-engined car: Crewe's styling team had formulated a plan in 1996 for a '110 per cent scale' supercar, but it had never got beyond the scale model stage. Hunaudières was created by an Anglo-German team working at Volkswagen's Wolfsburg HQ. The show car was developed in just six months and was based on a Lamborghini Diablo VT, the Automobili Lamborghini company having been another Volkswagen Group purchase in 1998. Hunaudières was fractionally shorter and wider than the Diablo, but substantially taller so that headroom was improved and it was much easier to get in and out. Power came from a brand-new engine, an 8.0-litre, 600bhp W16 which had been developed centrally by Volkswagen. The unusual W layout had two banks of cylinders at a 72-degree angle, each of which had its cylinders arranged as a narrow-angle (15-degree) V – technology Volkswagen had developed with its VR6 and VR5 engines. W16 and W18 engines had already been seen, but the W16 was new. At one stage Hunaudières was to have been powered by an Audi V8, but it was decided that it needed a motor providing relaxed performance.

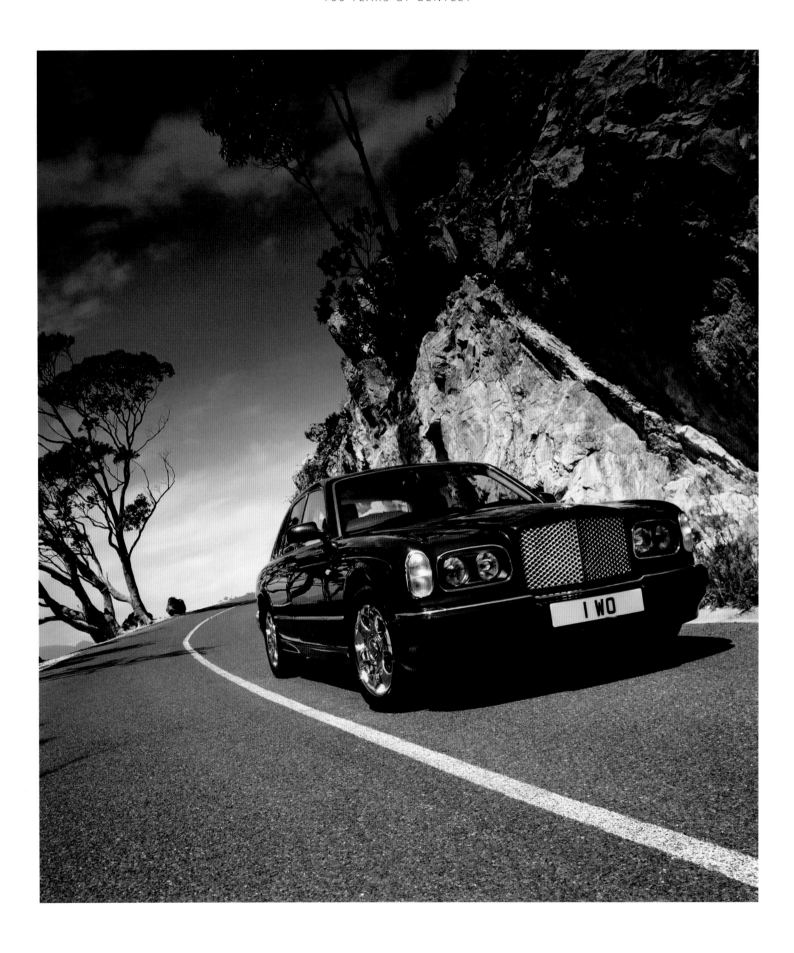

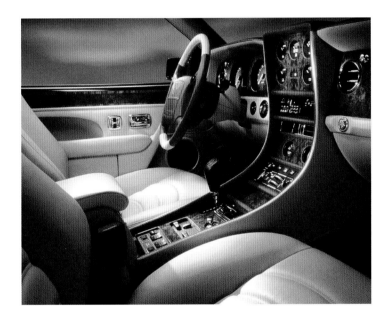

Above: The Arnage's interior blended fine craftsmanship, sumptuous luxury, and the latest and most sophisticated modern technology.

Opposite: The Arnage R had a heavily revised version of Bentley's long-running V8 engine. The 'WO' registration is a nod to the firm's founder.

Officially the car was a technology demonstrator, though there was talk of a production run within a couple of years, with a price around £250,000, if enough customers could be found. But Hunaudières never went into production, and instead its ideas were fed into the development of a new car for another marque Volkswagen purchased in 1998: Bugatti. The Hunaudières interior, in particular, strongly influenced the Bugatti Veyron's, and the W12 engine – in quad-turbo form – would power what became the world's fastest car.

Crewe's Rolls-Royces, living on borrowed time as they were, now started to become secondary to the Bentleys. The Silver Seraph continued virtually unchanged until production ended in 2002, and the last Rolls design to enter production was the new Corniche, a blend of the Azure drophead and Seraph saloon. Volkswagen wanted to sever the connection between Bentley and BMW as quickly as possible, and the Arnage was hastily re-engineered to replace the BMW V8 with the old L-Series V8 in what became the Arnage Red Label. The BMW-powered Arnage was renamed the Arnage Green Label and production ended in 2001 with a special edition called Birkin, after the 1920s Bentley racer. Arguably the pushrod Bentley V8 had a character which was more appropriate to these cars than the high-revving BMW engine, with lots of low-speed torque for effortless performance. But it was an old engine, fitted to an outdated gearbox. The Red Label weighed 600lb more than the Green Label, so even though power increased there was little performance advantage. Handling and fuel economy worsened.

A heavily reworked version of the V8 appeared for 2001. The big single Garrett T4 turbocharger was dropped in favour of two smaller T3 units, and there was a modern Bosch Motronic engine management system. Half of the engine components were said to be brand-new. The new engine developed 399bhp and went into a long-wheelbased Arnage RL, followed by a replacement for the Red Label, the Arnage R. In 2002 there was an Arnage T, said to be the most powerful road-going Bentley ever when it was unveiled at that year's Detroit Motor Show, with a 459bhp version of the same engine.

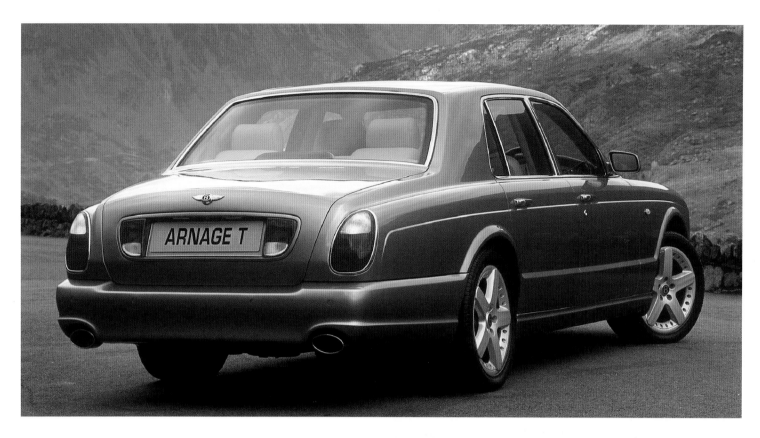

Above and opposite: The Arnage T had more than 450bhp, and offered an extraordinary level of performance from such a large and comfortable car.

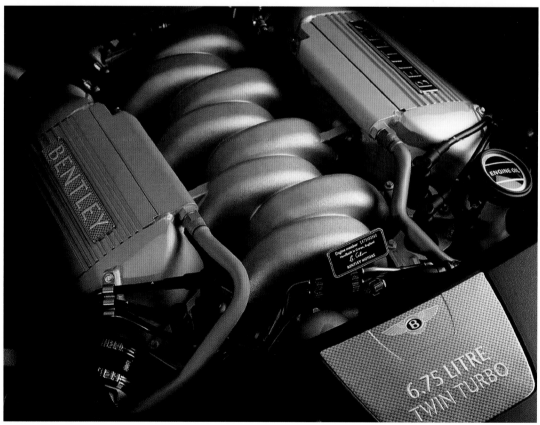

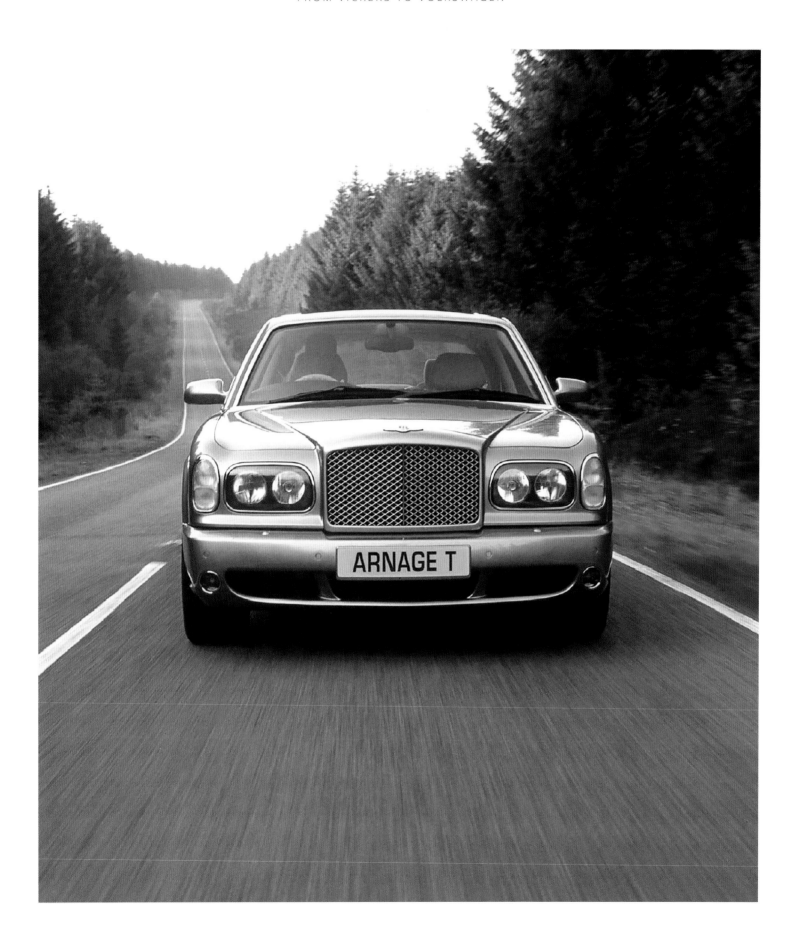

The reworked V8 also went into two state limousines, built by Bentley for Queen Elizabeth II's Golden Jubilee in 2002. The limousines were longer and taller than the Arnage, armoured, and included special features such as blue flashing lights, a roof mounting for a coat of arms, and interchangeable radiator grille mascots. The rear seats were trimmed in cloth, which has always been Her Majesty's personal preference. There were other special cars too, though fewer than in their 1990s heyday – when the Brunei royal family, in particular, kept Crewe's 'Blackpool projects' team very busy.

The Azure convertible continued until 2003 before being dropped, but was not immediately replaced. It took until 2006 for a second-generation Azure to arrive, now based on the Arnage platform and powered by a 456bhp version of the recently refreshed V8 engine. From 2008 there was also a fixed-head version, which revived the Brooklands name and went some way towards filling the gap left by the demise of the Continental R in 2003.

After the arrival of the Continental GT the Arnages were given a GT-style front-end facelift, and in 2007 there were further mechanical changes. The Garrett turbos were swapped for low-inertia Mitsubishi units to improve response, and the engines retuned to give 454bhp in the Arnage R and 493bhp in the Arnage T. A more modern six-speed ZF automatic transmission, another innovation from the Continental GT, was also fitted.

Arnage production was brought to a close in 2009 with the Final Series, which had the Arnage T's 493bhp engine, plus 20-inch alloy wheels, front wing vents and a traditional-style winged B mascot. Inside there was a cocktail cabinet and picnic tables and a Naim 1000-watt audio system. The Azure T, with the same engine, also finished its production run in 2009.

That left the way clear for a new grand Bentley to be built alongside the new Continental GT, which was already being made in greater numbers than any Bentley before it, and would be Crewe's mainstay for years to come.

Opposite: Arnages in production at Crewe around the turn of the millennium. The Arnage Final Series featured front wing vents.

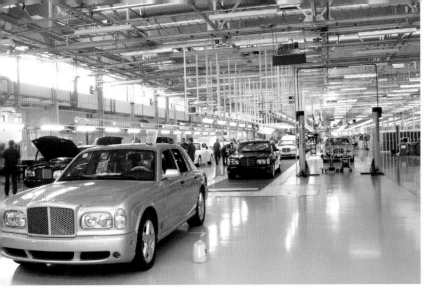
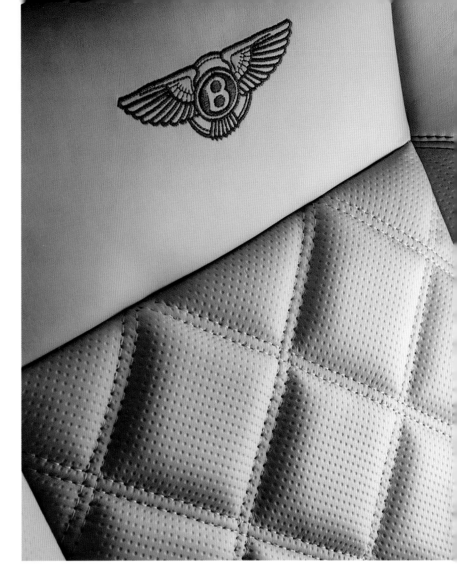
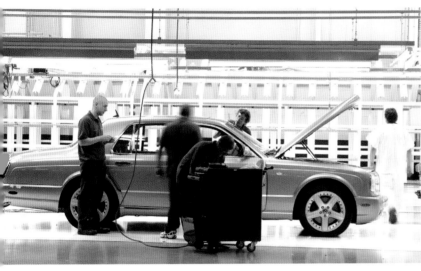
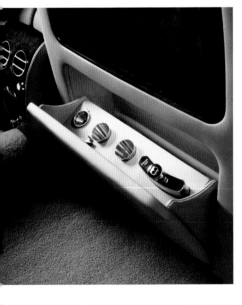
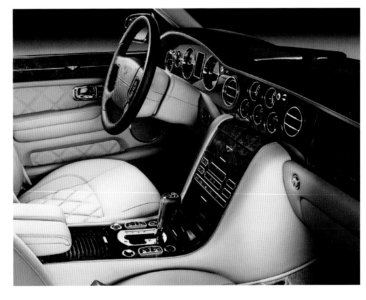
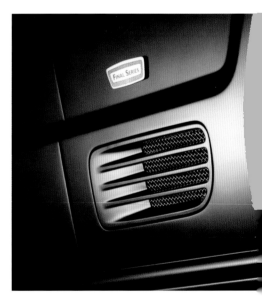
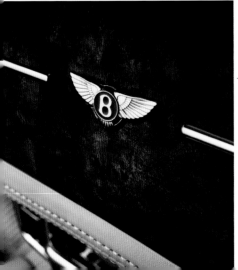
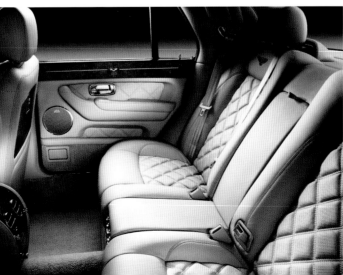
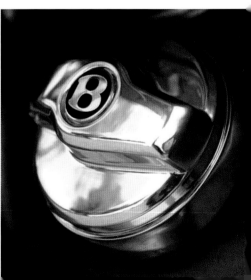

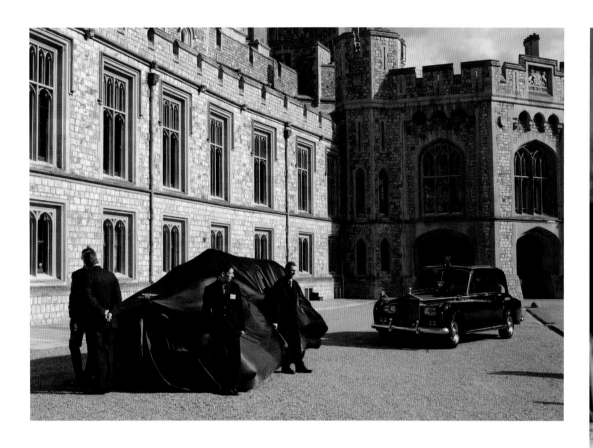

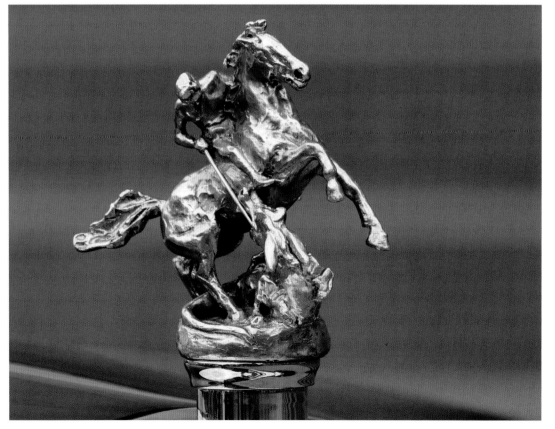

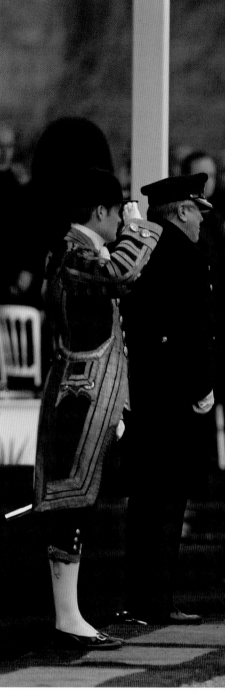

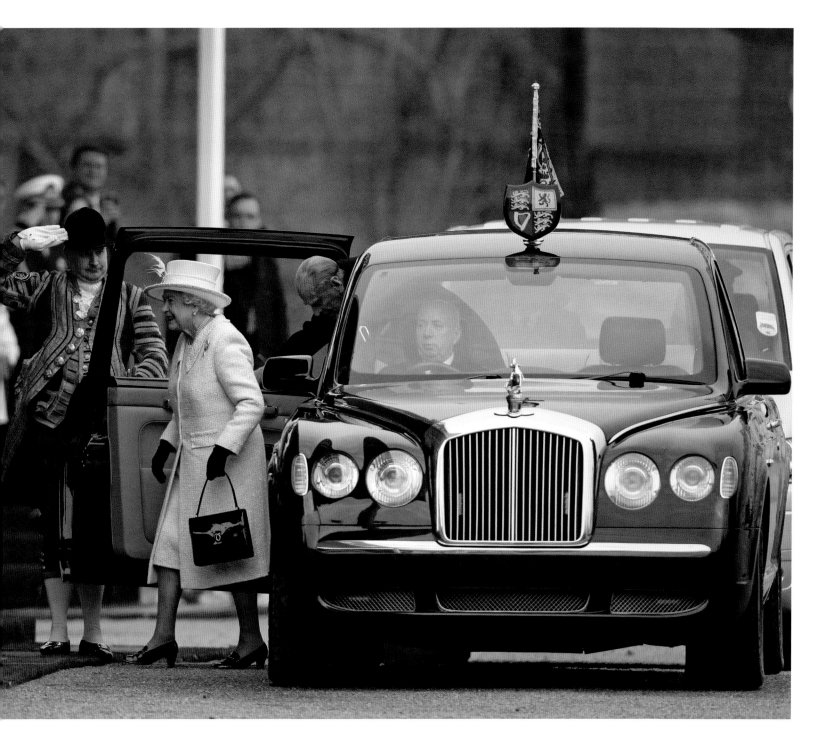

Opposite above: The Bentley State Limousine under wraps at Windsor Castle on 29 May 2002, alongside one of the Royal Family's Rolls-Royces.

Opposite below: The State Limousine features this bonnet mascot, designed by British artist Edward Seago, depicting St George slaying the Dragon.

Above: Her Majesty the Queen alights from the Bentley State Limousine at the start of an official engagement. Like all State Cars, it has Royal Claret livery and does not have to display a registration number.

Following pages: The Azure Final Series brought Azure production to a close in 2009.

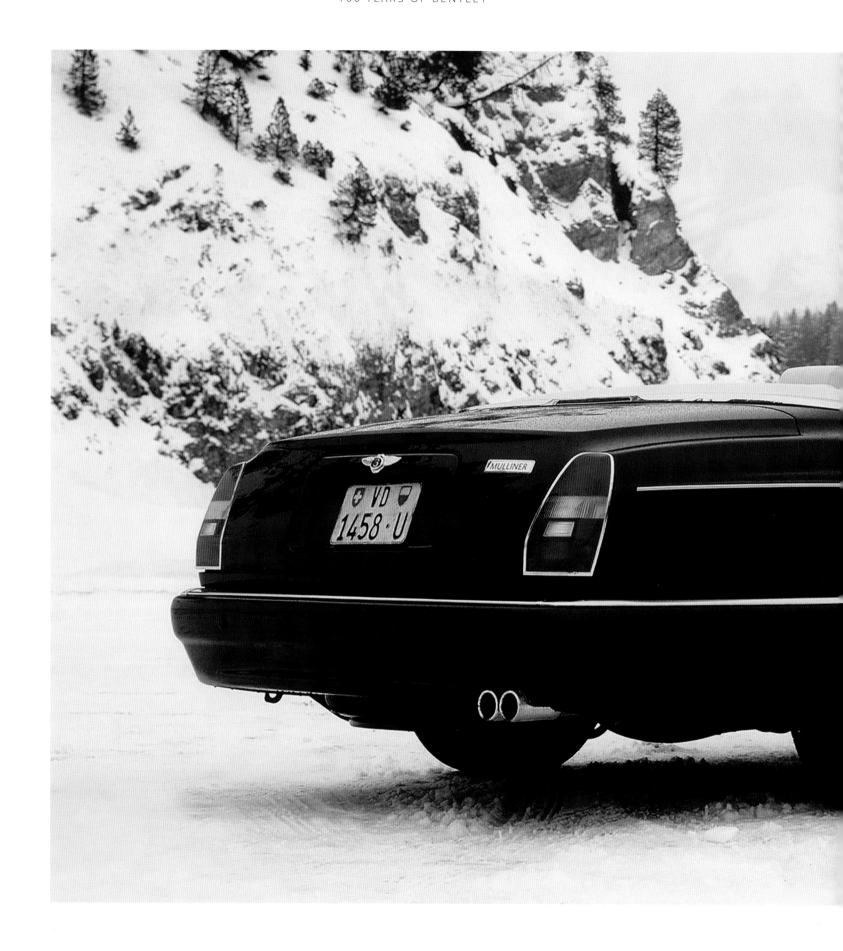

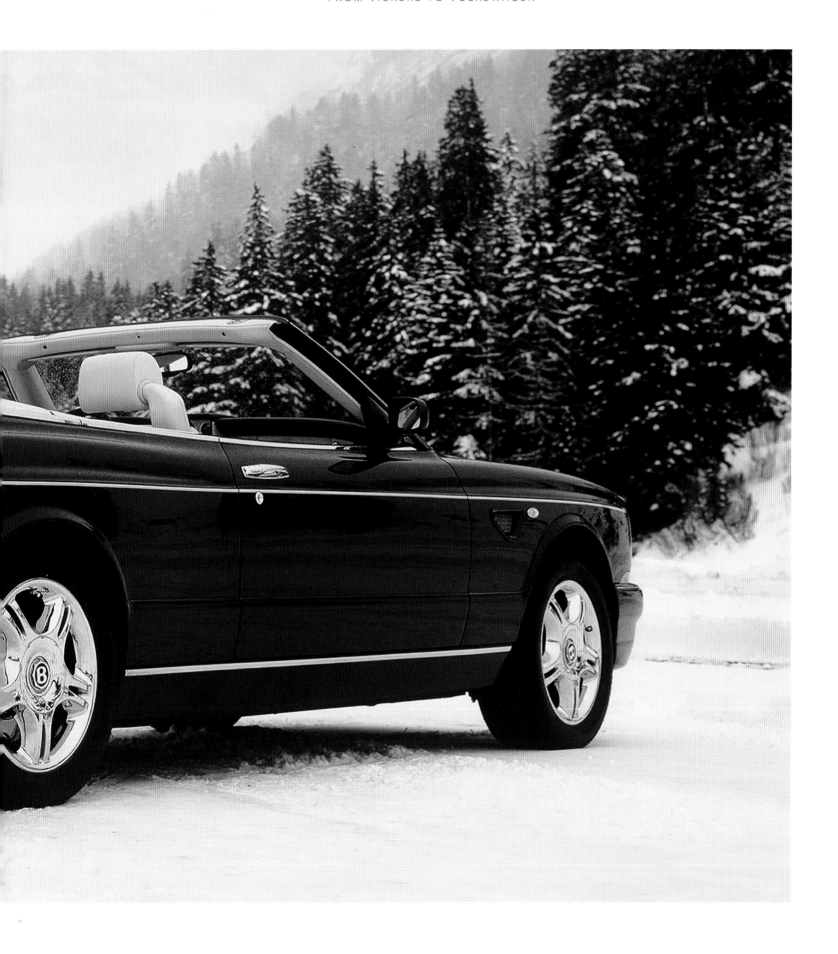

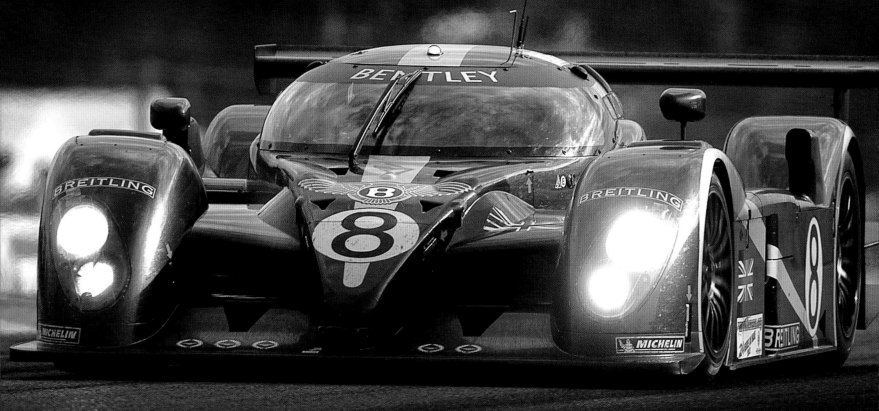

Chapter 8

BACK TO
LE MANS

Despite W.O. Bentley's initial objections to the idea of racing for 24 hours, much of Bentley Motors' early success was based on its string of victories at Le Mans between 1924 and 1930. The exploits of the Bentley Boys and their five wins in the early days of one of the world's toughest races became the stuff of legend. But by the time the dust finally settled on Volkswagen's takeover at Crewe in 1998, leaving the Wolfsburg group in charge of Bentley and setting a timetable for Rolls-Royce to be taken over by BMW, Bentley had not had an official racing presence for nearly 70 years.

The management at Crewe wanted to change that, and had a valuable ally in Volkswagen's chief executive, Dr Ferdinand Piëch. Piëch was a racer at heart: he was the grandson of Ferdinand Porsche, and had gone to work for the Porsche car company as an engineer in 1963. He was involved in the development of the 906 and 917 racing cars, and later moved to Audi where he was responsible for initiating the Quattro rally car project. Piëch was keen for Bentley to return to sports car racing, despite its Volkswagen stablemate Audi also competing in the same discipline. Audi's racing sports cars were to provide some of the technology behind Bentley's entry to the sport.

Audi's sports car challenge had begun in 1997 with the R8R programme. The car had a Dallara-built chassis and a bespoke 3.6-litre V8 turbo race engine. The R8R ran for the first time at Audi's own test track near Ingolstadt in August 1998 and was revealed to the public that December. It then tested again at Most in the Czech Republic and at the Paul Ricard circuit in France prior to a race debut at Sebring in March 1999. The two cars finished a promising third and

fifth, though they were well off the pace of the winning BMW V12 LMR.

Sports car racing regulations had evolved to allow two different classes of purpose-built racing prototypes: the LMP class for open-topped cars like the R8R and the LMGTP class for closed cars. Which of the two cars was better was the subject of hot debate. In theory the LMGTP cars were faster in a straight line because their closed roofs generated less drag, so tyre widths were restricted in an effort to equalise overall performance between the two classes. Open-top cars allowed faster driver changes, which was significant in a long race like Le Mans where there were numerous pit stops. The windscreen, wiper and doors of a closed car were all extra components that had to be designed and made to work correctly, and their weight raised the centre of gravity of the car. Drivers, meanwhile, often complained about the hot cockpit.

But Audi's management, clearly taking its Le Mans challenge very seriously, was concerned that the LMGTP cars might be more competitive at Le Mans, where their higher speeds on the long Mulsanne straight might count for more than the LMP cars' superior cornering grip. In September 1998 racing car designer Tony Southgate, who had been brought in as a consultant on the R8R, was engaged to create an LMGTP car using the same engine. The closed-roof R8C was designed by Southgate and Peter Elleray, built by Racing Technology Norfolk and tested at Snetterton and Hockenheim early in 1999, before running alongside the R8R at the Le Mans test day. It proved faster in a straight line than the open car, though not as fast as had been hoped.

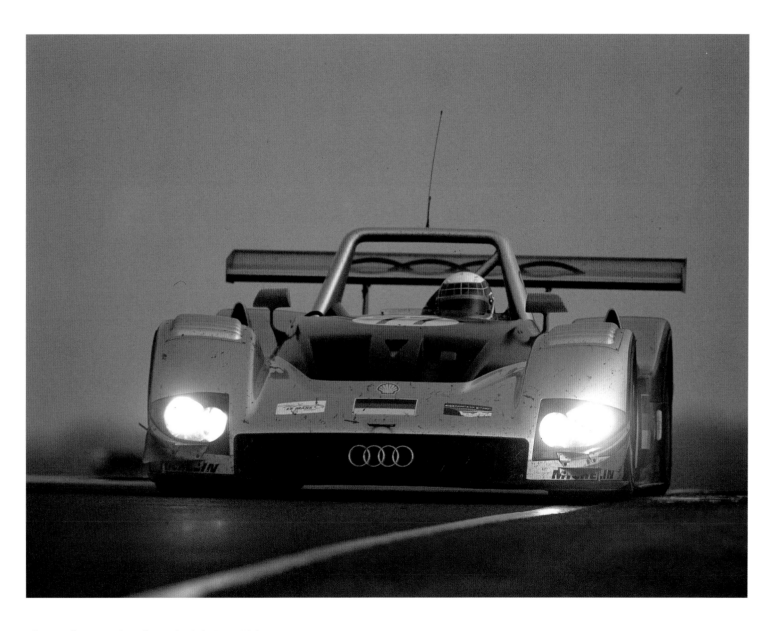

Above: Allan McNish in the Audi R8 during a 98-lap race at Silverstone in May 2000. McNish and his co-driver Rinaldo Capello went on to take third place.

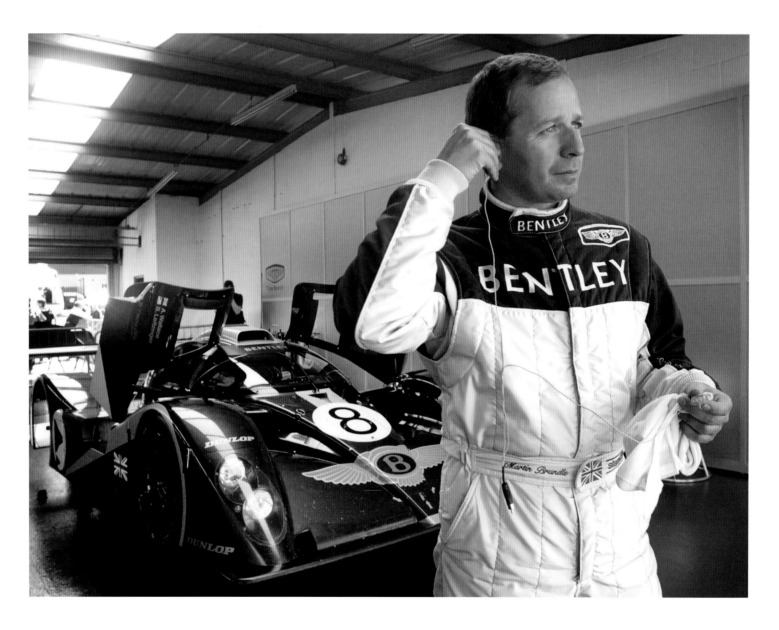

Above: Ex-F1 driver and 1988 World Sportscar champion Martin Brundle
was one of the experienced hands signed up for the Team Bentley racing
programme. His fellow drivers included Stéphane Ortelli and Guy Smith.

For the Le Mans race the R8Rs were fitted with new pneumatic paddle-shift gearchanges, while the R8Cs raced with manual gearboxes, and also had unassisted steering to save weight. The R8Cs proved to be harder on their gearboxes, and both retired with transmission trouble while the R8Rs finished third and fourth – a creditable result, but not what Audi was hoping for. By the end of the year Audi was testing a new open car, the R8, which carried over nothing except the V8 engine. That car would go on to dominate sports car racing until replaced by the diesel R10 in 2006.

Bentley's Le Mans challenge began late in 1999. Very quickly the decision was made to go for a closed-roof LMGTP car – perhaps to be seen as different to the Audis, but also because there were still suggestions in some quarters that the closed cars should be faster at Le Mans. Like the Audi – and most other Le Mans cars – the new Bentley was based around a composite monocoque tub with a mid-mounted engine and gearbox at the rear. Like the R8C the Bentley was built by Racing Technology Norfolk, but virtually nothing was carried over from the Audis except the experience designer Peter Elleray had gained, particularly with the aerodynamics. Extensive wind tunnel testing in Switzerland with a 40 per cent scale model fixed the basic shape of the car, but what had not been decided was the engine that would power it.

The LMGTP rules permitted either a turbocharged engine, as in the Audis, of up to 4,000cc, or a normally-aspirated engine of up to 6,000cc. Originally the Bentley was intended to use a normally-aspirated engine – possibly a version of the Continental GT's W12, or the normally-aspirated W16 that had been fitted in the Hunaudières

concept car, both of which could be tuned to produce the required 600+bhp. But as the project was developed in strict secrecy during 2000 it became clear that a turbo engine was a better solution. The car was re-engineered to take the V8 engine from the Audi R8C, but using a new Xtrac gearbox in place of the Ricardo transmissions fitted to the Audis. At the same time substantial changes were made to the two-piece monocoque, which was slimmed down at the rear and now had a composite rather than steel roll hoop.

The Bentley Le Mans project was revealed to the public at the end of 2000, and the new car, called EXP Speed 8, was testing by the end of the year. The Audi V8 engines were not yet available, so for the first runs at Silverstone with experienced sports car and touring car racer James Weaver behind the wheel, the EXP Speed 8 was powered by a Ford DFR race engine. This allowed the team to carry out initial suspension testing and to evaluate their Dunlop tyres – a change from the Michelins used by Audi. It was not until March, just three months before the Le Mans race, that the car ran for the first time with its Audi power unit. There proved to be problems replicating on track the performance that had been predicted in the wind tunnel. Front downforce was lacking, so a single-element rear wing was fitted to maintain the front-to-rear balance. Aero updates were created to solve some of the problems, but they would not be ready before the big race.

Richard Lloyd's Apex Motorsport team was retained to run the cars. Based in Buckingham, they had been behind Audi's British Touring Car Championship challenge in 1997, which netted seven race wins and second place in both the Drivers' and Manufacturers' Championships, and

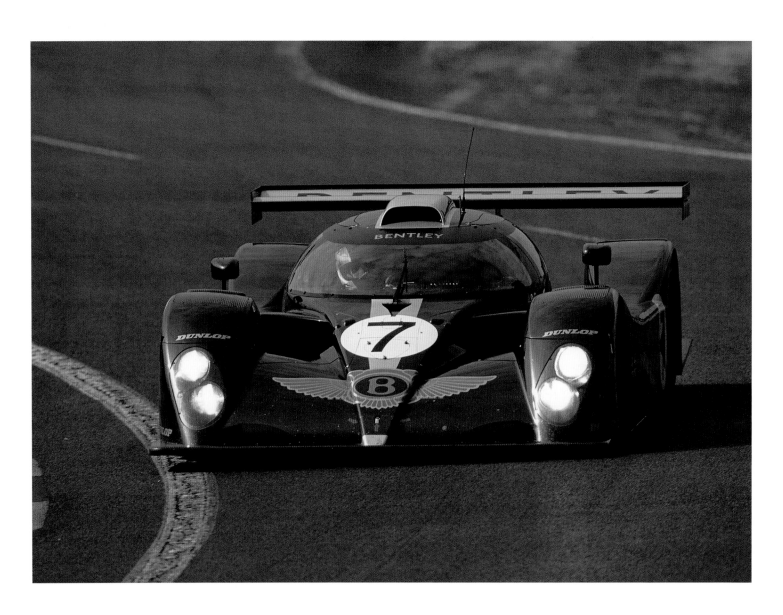

Above: The Brundle/Ortelli/Smith EXP Speed 8 during practice for the
2001 Le Mans race. It had been 68 years since a full works Bentley team
had last participated in the famous 24-hour event.

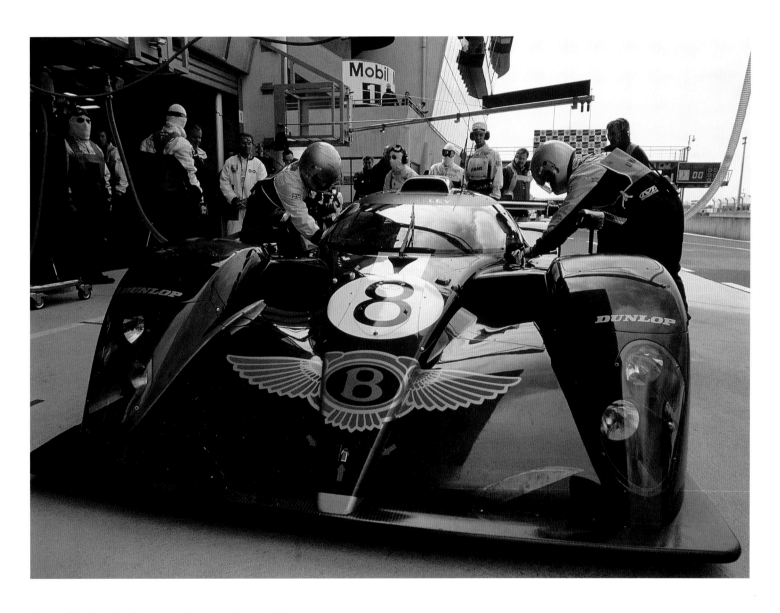

Above: Bentley's No. 8 car at a pit stop during a Le Mans practice session. These 'trial runs' provide valuable experience for drivers and crews.

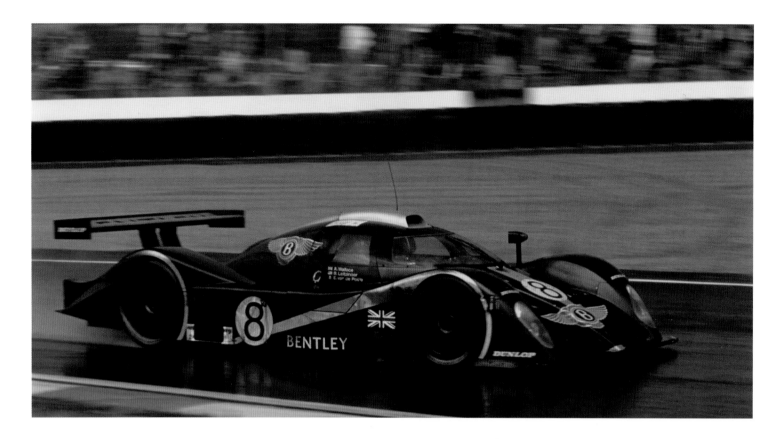

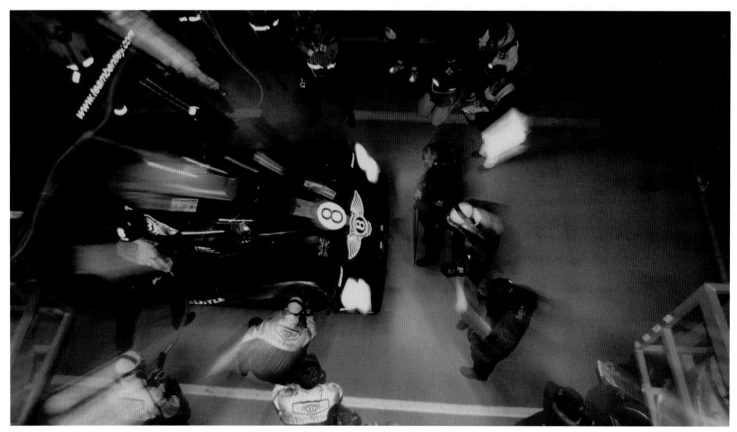

Top: During the 2001 Le Mans race, the Bentleys survived rainy conditions which put paid to the hopes of several high-profile rivals.

Above: Bentley's number 8 EXP Speed 8 – driven by Andy Wallace, Eric van de Poele and Butch Leitzinger – stops for a tyre change.

ran the Audi R8Cs at Le Mans in 1999. Two EXP Speed 8s were entered for the race, with some very experienced drivers among the crews. James Weaver was lined up to compete alongside Andy Wallace, winner of the Le Mans in 1988, and 1999 Rolex Sports Car champion Butch Leitzinger. The three had been part of a seven-man driving squad that had won the 1997 Daytona 24-hours in a Riley & Scott Mk III. The sister car was to be driven by former F1 driver and 1990 Le Mans winner Martin Brundle, 1998 Le Mans winner Stéphane Ortelli and 1998 Indy Lights Rookie of the Year Guy Smith. Five-time Le Mans winner Derek Bell was brought in as a consultant.

Top-level opposition came from the Audi R8s run by Reinhold Joest's experienced team, and from Chrysler, Cadillac, Panoz and a gaggle of smaller teams. By the time of the Le Mans test Weaver and Bentley had parted company, and in had come Belgian ex-F1 driver and two-time 12 Hours of Sebring winner Eric van de Poele. Martin Brundle raised plenty of eyebrows with a lap time fast enough for third place behind two of the Audi R8s, but in race qualifying the following month the Bentleys could do no better than seventh and ninth.

The Bentleys survived a rain shower at the start that claimed several rivals, even though the team had done very little wet-weather running, and Dunlop's rain tyres were an unknown quantity. An opportunist switch to intermediate tyres helped Brundle into the lead after the first hour in number 7, but as the race progressed the rain got into the cockpit and caused the windscreen to mist up, and more water got into the gearbox electrics, causing them to malfunction. Six hours in, Guy Smith had to retire the car

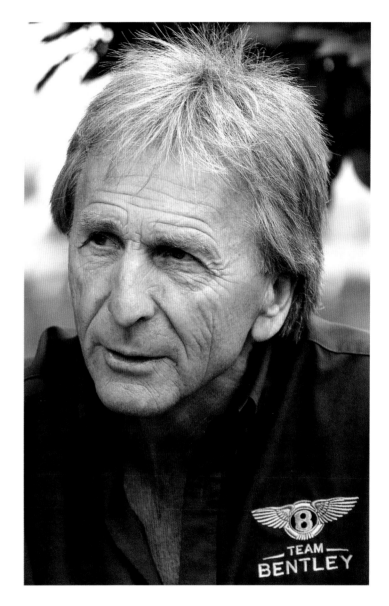

Above: Derek Bell MBE was brought in as a consultant to Team Bentley, and was able to provide a wealth of experience as a five-time Le Mans winner and twice World Sportscar champion.

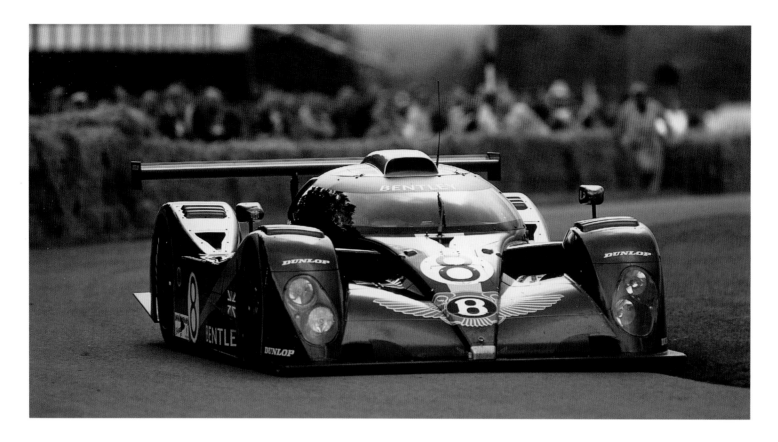

after it became stuck in sixth gear and the engine stalled, despite a valiant attempt to get the Bentley back to the pits on the starter. The number 8 Bentley suffered a similar problem but stuck in fourth gear, and Leitzinger managed to limp back to the pits for repairs. The compressor for the pneumatic gearchange was later changed after it failed, and when the radio went on the blink a walkie-talkie was stuffed in a plastic bag and tank-taped to the car. Despite a four-minute stop-go penalty for overtaking under a yellow flag, and a failing clutch, the Bentley finished third, a substantial 14 laps down on the two Audis ahead – but a podium finish on debut was a massive achievement. The three drivers donned vintage-style white overalls, flying helmets and goggles for the podium ceremony to evoke memories of Bentley's previous success at Le Mans so many years before.

For 2002 the EXP Speed 8s were extensively modified, with a new aero package and a 4.0-litre version of the Audi V8 engine which now had direct fuel injection – as used by the works Audis. The new injection system provided better fuel efficiency and faster restarting after pit stops. The bigger engine was no more powerful because the regulations dictated that it had to run with a smaller intake air restrictor, but it produced more torque. That cut down on gearchanges, which in turn reduced driver fatigue. The new body shape proved to work much better than the 2001 car's in some circumstances but not in others, so once again the team was resigned to tackling Le Mans with a vehicle which, aerodynamically, was less than ideal.

Van de Poele escaped unharmed from a terrifying testing accident at Paul Ricard when the car flipped and landed upside down on a crash barrier. A single car was entered for Le Mans, driven by Wallace, van de Poele and Leitzinger, with Smith as reserve. In practice, using an experimental ultra-low drag set-up, the car achieved nearly 210mph (338km/h) on the Mulsanne straight, but the team opted to use a higher-downforce aero package for the race.

At the Le Mans test sixth-fastest was the best the team had achieved, and they qualified for the race in eleventh. At one stage van de Poele had another scare when a

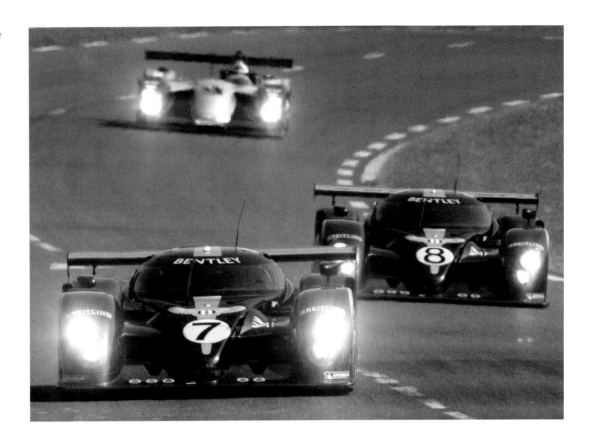

Opposite: Andy Wallace guns the EXP Speed 8 up the Goodwood hill at the 2002 Festival of Speed.

Right: The Bentleys were the class of the field at Le Mans in 2003. Here, number 7, the eventual winner, runs ahead of the number 8 car – which took second place, but recorded that year's fastest lap time.

backmarker moved on him as he tried to overtake and he slid into the gravel in avoidance, but the Bentley made it to the end in fourth place behind three Audi R8s.

Work on the 2003 car had already begun, with a series of wind tunnel tests to prove the aerodynamic concept of the car and to develop a sprint race set-up – because the Bentley would run at more than one race. A key improvement was to reduce the sensitivity of the aero package to pitch – the nose-up or -down attitude of the car. This made the car more drivable, and because the body no longer needed to be so tightly controlled the team was able to fit softer suspension springs which were kinder to the tyres, now supplied by Michelin. The engine and the gearbox internals were carried over – as were the wheels and hubs, and the basic layouts for the cooling system and fuel system. Much of the front suspension was unchanged, but the rear suspension was a new design with torsion-bar springs instead of coils. The design of the monocoque was new, too: instead of a two-piece design with a tongue-and-groove joint at hip level the

new monocoque came up to the driver's shoulders, with a separate composite roll hoop on top and a 360-degree hoop at the front forming the A-pillars.

For the first time Team Bentley contested more than just the Le Mans race, taking two cars – now known simply as Speed 8s – to the US for the 12 Hours of Sebring in March. The biggest name on the car was still that of the manufacturer, but there was also some new sponsorship from Breitling. Only Guy Smith remained from the previous group of drivers, sharing his Speed 8 with two experienced competitors, Italian Dindo Capello and Dane Tom Kristensen, while the sister car was driven by Johnny Herbert, David Brabham and Mark Blundell. Capello had won the 2001 and 2002 Sebring races for Audi, and had finished second at Le Mans the previous year in an R8. Kristensen had won Sebring in 1997, and had recorded four victories at Le Mans, winning the 2002 race in a Joest Audi. Herbert, Brabham and Blundell were three former F1 drivers, Herbert also taking first place at Le Mans in 1991 for Mazda and Blundell in 1992 for Peugeot.

The Bentleys were fast at Sebring, and Johnny Herbert thought he had put the number 7 car on pole position – but after the session the scrutineers deemed the Speed 8s to have illegal rear diffusers. They were sent to the back of the grid and spent the race carving through the field, recording fastest lap along the way and eventually finishing in third and fourth places behind a pair of Audi R8s. Without the grid penalty they might have won the race.

Herbert had destroyed the first Speed 8, chassis 004/1, in a massive testing accident at Jerez in Spain. Chassis 004/2 had done thousands of miles of testing, plus Sebring. A manufacturing fault sidelined 004/4, so the two Le Mans cars were the second Sebring chassis, 004/3, and the brand-new 004/5. The Sebring driver line-up was again employed at Le Mans. After winning the race three years in a row Audi did not field a works team, so the biggest rivals for the Speed 8s were privateer R8s. The Joest team, which had run Audi's official works sports car campaign, lent a hand with the Bentley effort.

In qualifying for the race the Bentleys were unmatched, with Kristensen fastest in 004/5, wearing race number 7. But both Bentleys had exhibited a strange phenomenon where the suspension would settle between static set-up in the garage and running on the track, and resetting the suspension again on the number 7 car saw it leave it very late for its grid slot. But after that early drama the Bentleys had what by Le Mans standards was an untroubled run, using their speed advantage over the R8s to build up a 25-mile advantage by the end.

After three years of trying Bentley finally recorded the Le Mans victory Crewe wanted, with the number 7 car of Capello, Kristensen and Smith winning the race. And not just a win, but a one-two finish as the number 8 car of Blundell, Brabham and Herbert was in second place. Kristensen racked up his fourth triumph in a row, and would go on to make that a run of six in the next two years.

The day after the race a convoy of Bentleys drove through Paris, from the Arc de Triomphe, down the Champs-Élysées to the Place de la Concorde. Derek Bell was at the wheel of the winning Speed 8, while the drivers were driven in a pair of vintage Speed Sixes, the winning crew chauffeured by Bentley chief executive Franz-Josef Paefgen. Two days later there was another celebration, this time in London, where the victorious car and team gathered for a dinner at the Savoy Hotel – just as in 1927. It took three hours to get the car inside, a process which involved removing the Savoy's revolving door and at one point tipping the car on its side, but it meant the Speed 8 could take its rightful place at the centre of the celebrations.

Its mission accomplished, Team Bentley was wound up. Bentley retained all but one of the race cars: one of the 2001 EXP Speed 8s went into private ownership and was last sold at an RM Sotheby's auction in 2012 for $2.5 million.

Opposite: Team Bentley celebrates a famous win in 2003 with a parade through Le Mans and a dinner at the Savoy Hotel in London.

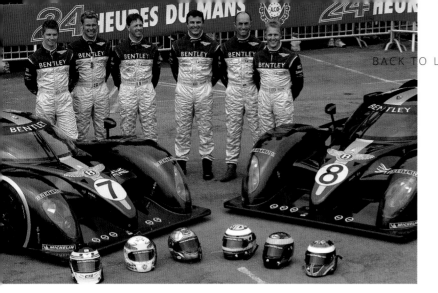

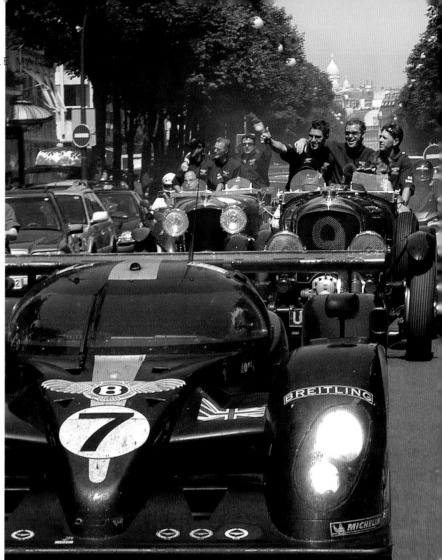

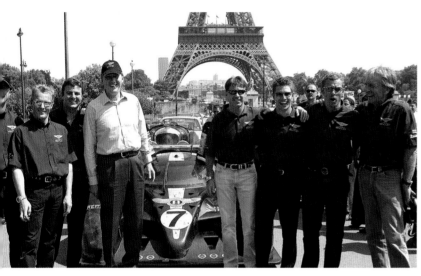

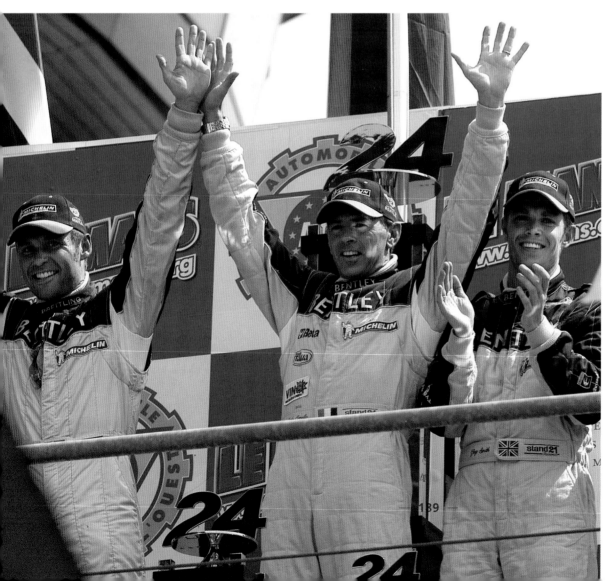

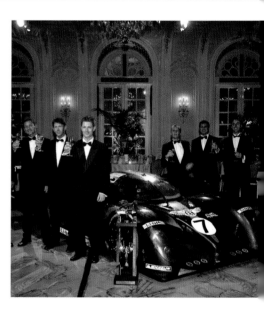

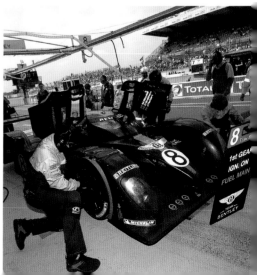

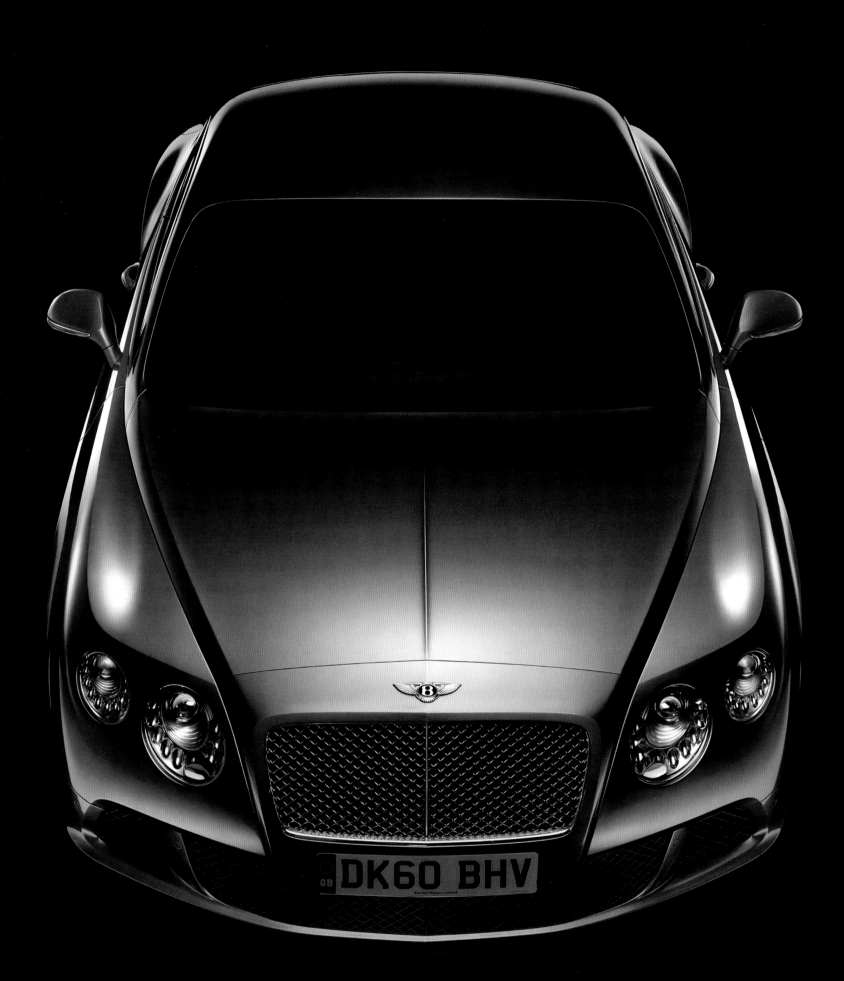

Chapter 9

BUILDING THE BENTLEY BRAND

Volkswagen's ownership of Bentley could not succeed by maintaining the status quo. Under new management, Bentley needed to reinvent itself for the new millennium, with new models and new technology.

Ever since the 1970s the design teams at Crewe had been talking about building a smaller, cheaper Bentley, and Volkswagen's plan for the expansion of the company was based around a similar idea. The new car had to be quicker, easier and cheaper to make than Bentleys had ever been before, while retaining the performance and the quality of fixtures and fittings that attracted people to the marque in the first place.

Bentley design was now in the hands of Belgian-born Dirk van Braeckel, who had come to Crewe from Skoda in 1999. By August that year he was working with designer Raul Pires on what would become the Continental GT, based on the broad themes of understatement, sportiness and heritage. Van Brackel says he was keen to avoid the 'retro design trap', so the new car had to have a flavour of Bentley's long heritage without being a direct copy of an old design. He cites the R-type Continental as a particular inspiration. The four-headlamp front, the shape of the radiator grille and the mesh grille itself were considered to be vital elements. Two scale models were made, exploring these themes further, and by the end of the year a decision had been made on the exterior shape.

Modern proportions, with a short front overhang and a long bonnet, made sure the Continental GT looked unique and fresh, while the curves of the front and rear wings, with their echoes of the 1950s Continental, grounded the car in Bentley heritage. The body was mostly steel, but the bonnet, boot and doors were aluminium and the front wings were made from a composite material. Inside, the wood and leather expected of a Bentley were retained, and there was a stylish symmetrical dashboard which made both driver and passenger feel welcome, with a Breitling analogue clock in the centre. A particular emphasis was placed on using high-quality materials to ensure the cabin felt, as well as looked, special.

The Continental shared a platform with the VW Phaeton, and under the long bonnet was a modified version of a W12 engine developed by Volkswagen. The first Volkswagen group W12 had never been anything more than a wooden mock-up in the back of the 1991 Audi Avus concept car. That engine was described as having three banks of four cylinders, giving it a 'broad arrow' layout like the famous Napier Lion aero engine. A more serious W12 design, related to the W16 that would be seen in the Bentley Hunaudières concept in 1999, was unveiled in the VW W12 Synchro concept, a mid-engined supercar introduced at the 1997 Tokyo Motor Show. This had two main cylinder banks, each of which was effectively one of Volkswagen's VR6 engines – a narrow-angle V6. This engine went into the Audi A8 W12 production car in 2001. For Bentley's use the W12 was given two turbochargers, one for each of the main banks of six cylinders, boosting at a relatively gentle 0.7 bar to ensure throttle response remained sharp. A bypass valve allowed the turbos to keep spinning when the throttle was closed, reducing lag when it was reopened.

Opposite: The Continental GT unveiled at the Paris show in 2002 was a new departure, introducing four-wheel drive and a new W12 engine.

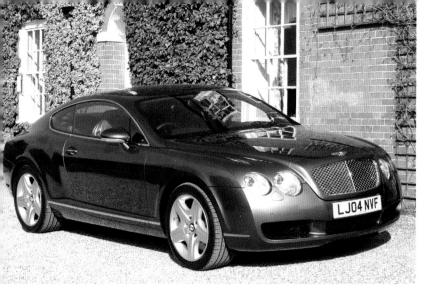
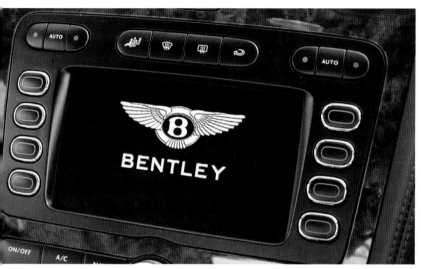
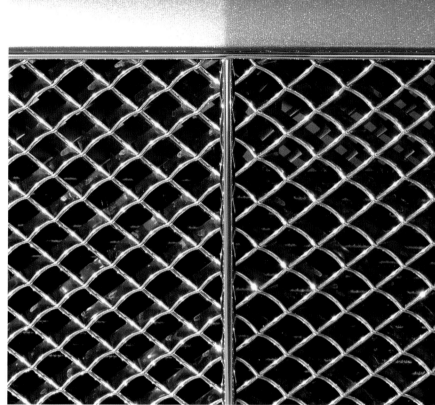
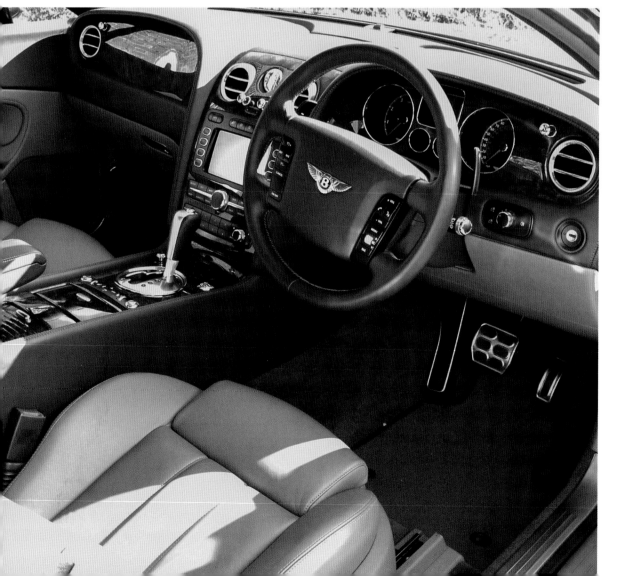
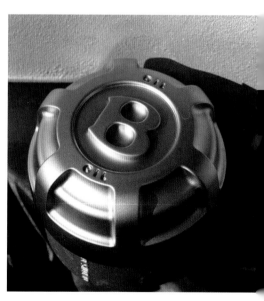
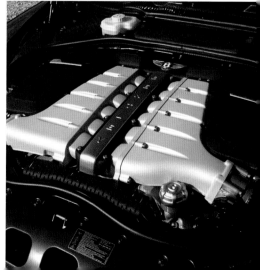

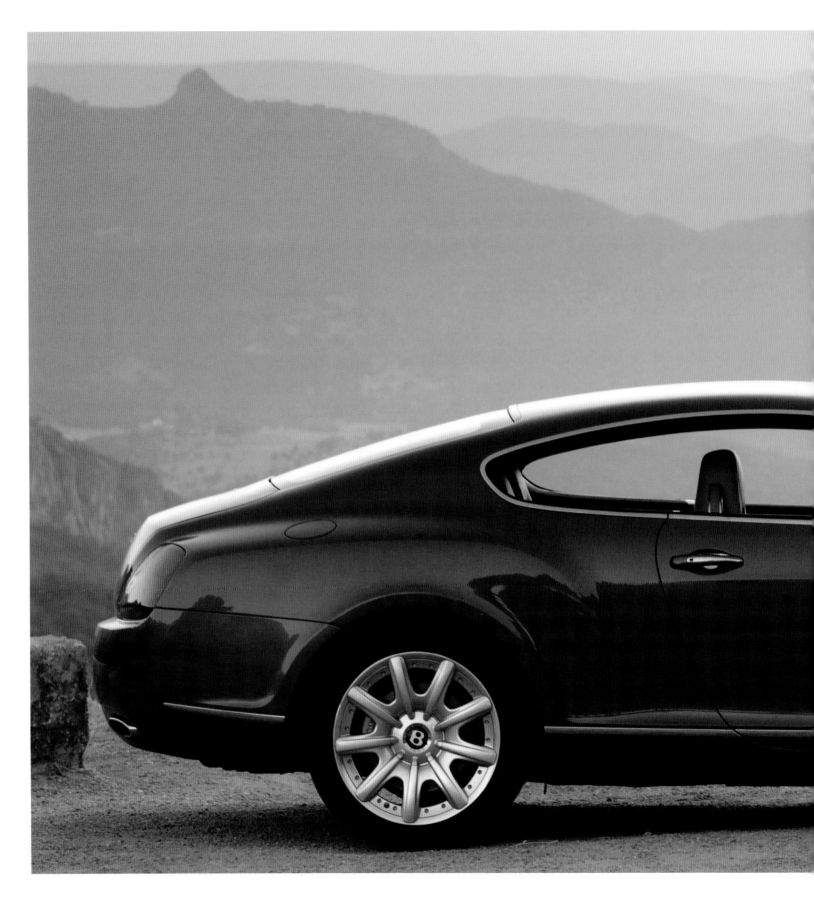

Above: The Continental GT became Bentley's most successful model
ever in sales terms, and put the company on a sound financial footing.

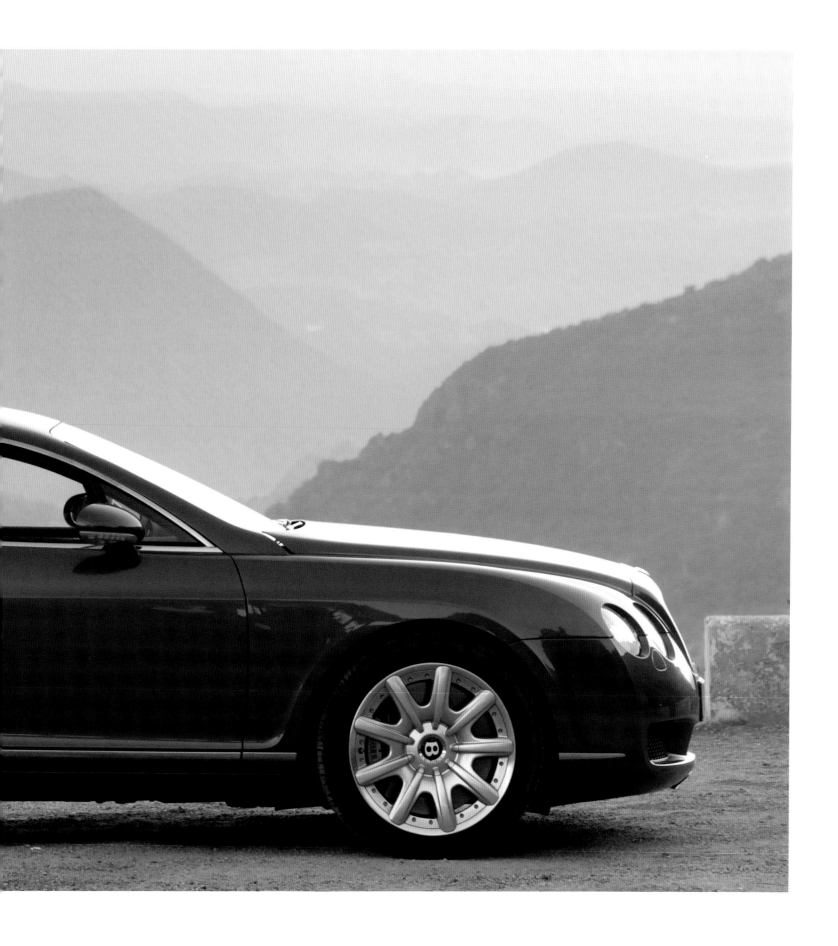

The engine developed a hefty 552bhp, more than any of the Arnage derivatives could muster – more in fact than any previous Bentley production car. It also reached its peak torque at just 1,600rpm and maintained it to 6,000rpm, giving effortless performance.

Power was delivered to all four wheels via a ZF six-speed automatic transmission and Torsen centre differential, with torque apportioned equally to front and rear unless one of the axles started to slip. Aluminium multilink suspension at both ends used air springs to give a good ride and a self-levelling capability. Above 75mph (121km/h) the system automatically dropped the car 25mm (1in) to reduce drag.

The Continental GT was a lot lighter than any recent Crewe car, and though it still weighed in excess of two tonnes its prodigious power and four-wheel drive traction meant it could reach 60mph (97km/h) from rest in less than five seconds, going on to a top speed of nearly 200mph (322km/h). It was fast, but just as important, it was a forgiving car that flattered its driver. Unveiled at the Paris show in September 2002, it went on sale the following spring at £110,000, less than half the price of a Continental T and good value compared to rivals – a Ferrari 456, for instance, was over £170,000. The Continental GT quickly became Crewe's biggest seller.

The first derivative of the main Continental GT theme was the four-door Flying Spur, which followed in 2005. The Arnage was still available, but the Flying Spur showed how old its design was: the new four-door was more powerful and faster, while still offering lots of space for passengers, and the grace and prestige synonymous with Bentley. It carried over the coupé's 6.0-litre W12 engine, automatic transmission and four-wheel drive system – but in a body 498mm longer, of which 320mm was added into the wheelbase to give palatial rear seat accommodation. The Crewe factory was already working at capacity, so for the first year or so the Flying Spurs built for some markets were made not in Cheshire but in Germany, at the Volkswagen Transparent Factory that also produced the Phaeton.

In 2006 Crewe announced a Mulliner Driving Specification for the Continental which added even bigger, 20-inch wheels and a special interior with quilted leather trim, drilled alloy pedals and a gear lever with a knurled top. There was also a Diamond Series special edition celebrating 60 years of car production at Crewe, which was based on the Mulliner but with the addition of carbon ceramic brakes, a first for a production Bentley. The 420mm (16.5in) discs were even bigger than those on the standard car, yet they were 23kg (51lb) lighter and provided fade-free stopping power.

A convertible version of the Continental, called the GTC, was unveiled at the New York International Auto Show in April 2006 and went on sale later that year. The design team aimed for simplicity and elegance, giving the GTC a longer rear deck than the coupé and ensuring that the hood folded away out of sight. To make room for it the rear suspension was redesigned to take up less space. Crewe aimed to make the GTC drive exactly like the coupé, which meant restoring the structural stiffness lost when the roof was removed. The sills, A-pillars and windscreen surround were reinforced, and additional cross-braces were added beneath the cabin. Two reinforced steel roll hoops were fitted in the rear headrests; they popped up to protect the

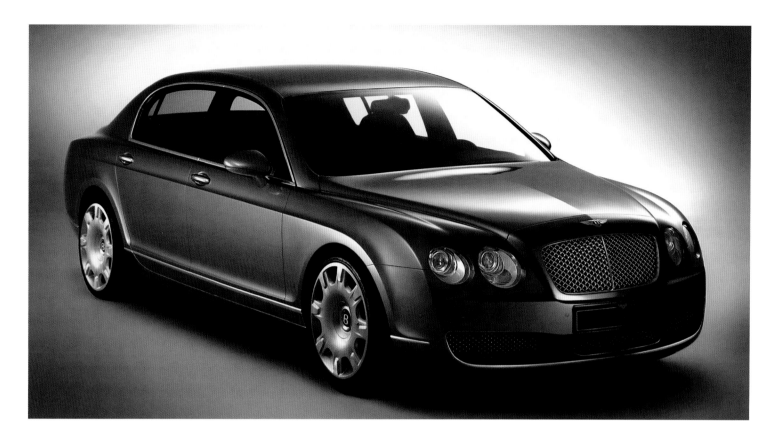

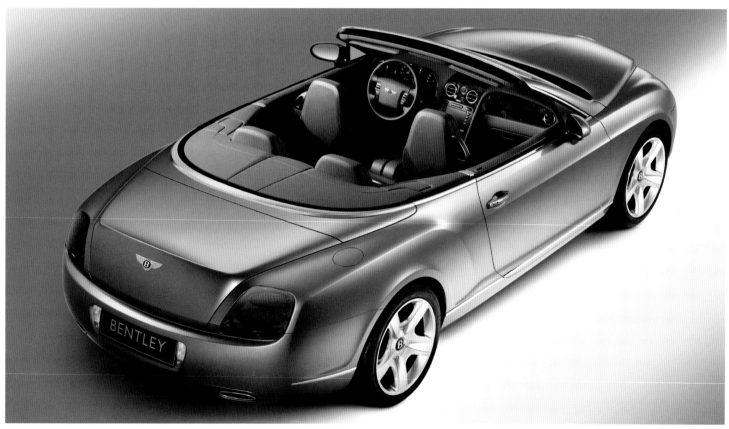

Top: The four-door Continental Flying Spur which augmented the range in 2005 provided extra comfort and convenience for passengers.

Above: A convertible Continental GTC, whose hood folded out of sight for the last word in elegance, was introduced in 2006.

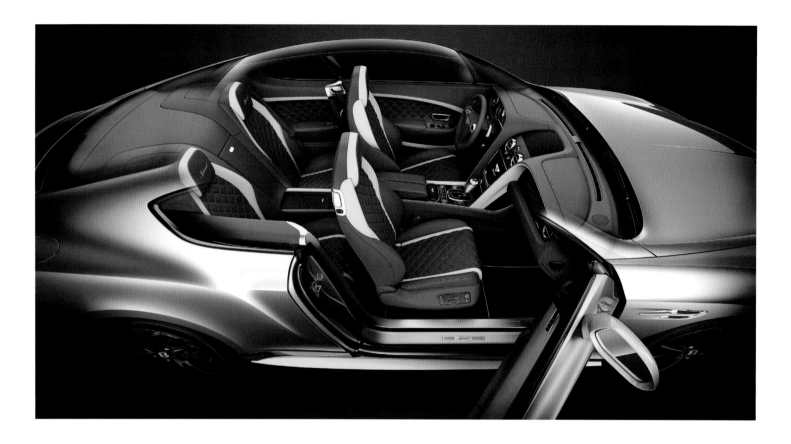

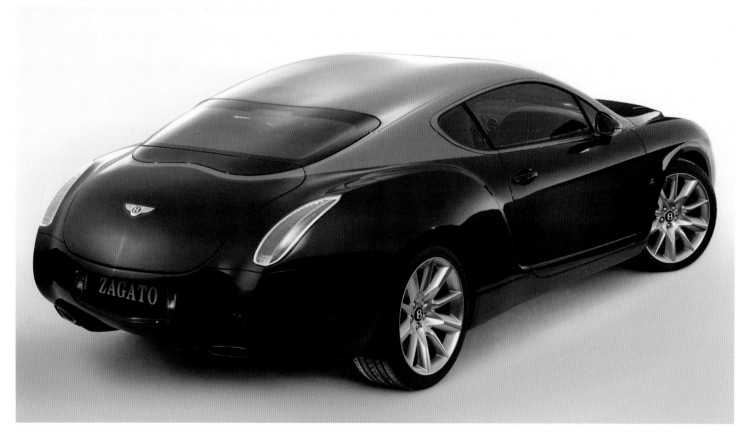

Top and following pages: The Continental GT Speed had even more brake horsepower, giving a top speed in excess of 200mph (320km/h).

Above: Zagato's take on the Continental was lighter than the standard car, but enormously expensive. Only nine were made.

passengers if the car was about to roll over. The roof had a three-layer construction with, Bentley said, a thicker and more padded outer layer than any other convertible. It had a heated, glass rear window and could fold down – electro-hydraulically, of course – in just 25 seconds. The GTC shared the GT's powertrain and could sprint to 60mph (97km/h) from rest in 4.8 seconds, on the way to a top speed, with the roof raised, of 195mph (314km/h). With the roof down it was 'only' capable of 190mph (306km/h).

The following year a Continental GT driven by four times World Rally Champion Juha Kankkunen accomplished something astonishing and unusual. At the wheel of a near-standard Continental GT prepared by Mäkelä Auto-Tuning, Kankkunen set a world record speed for driving on ice. He achieved a two-way average of 321.65km/h (199.86mph) on a 12km (7.5-mile) section of frozen sea, 50km (30 miles) north of Oulu in Western Finland. This comfortably beat the existing record of 296.34km/h (184.14mph) set by a Bugatti EB 110 Super Sport at the same location.

A rollcage was fitted to the car, which ran on studded Nokian ice tyres. Aerodynamic tweaks included a deeper front spoiler, blanked-off grille and lights, and low-drag wheel discs. The engine was standard, though its management system was remapped for the non-standard fuel needed to cope with the extreme cold. Temperatures as low as minus 30 degrees Celcius were experienced, and the cold ambient air reaching the intake and intercoolers helped to enhance the Continental GT's performance. The Bentley took 5km (3.1 miles) to reach its top speed on the 70cm- (28in-) thick ice, and was then timed over a measured kilometre. After a brief check, it was turned around and made to run in the opposite direction, peaking at 206mph (332km/h). Kankkunen reported that the car was very stable at high speed despite the rough track surface, and could be stopped from 200mph (322km/h) in around 500 metres (547yds).

Crewe had also been working on making the Continental go faster, and the result was a new high-performance model, the Continental GT Speed, which was announced alongside a set of revisions common to all the Continentals. There was a revised power steering system, and a new front end with a more upright grille. All the W12 engines got a new crankcase, more efficient catalytic converters, a lighter single-chain camshaft drive, a faster-response cam sensor and a new engine management system. The Speed engine also benefitted from lighter connecting rods, new pistons and a recalibrated engine management system. Power was up to 600bhp, raising the top speed to 202mph (325km/h). The Speed rode 10mm (0.4in) lower at the front and 15mm (0.6in) lower at the rear than the standard Continental, and had new springs, dampers and anti-roll bars, together with 20-inch wheels and wider Pirelli P Zero tyres.

If that wasn't exclusive enough, you could send your new Continental GT Speed to the Milanese coachbuilder Zagato along with a cheque for something in excess of £500,000, and if you were one of the first nine to do so they would turn it into a Continental GTZ. The idea for the Zagato Continental came in 2006 when Andrea Zagato met Bentley chief executive Dr Franz-Josef Paefgen at the Pebble Beach Concours d'Elegance, and pointed out that there had been Zagato Aston Martins, Ferraris, Maseratis and even once a Rolls-Royce, but never a Zagato Bentley.

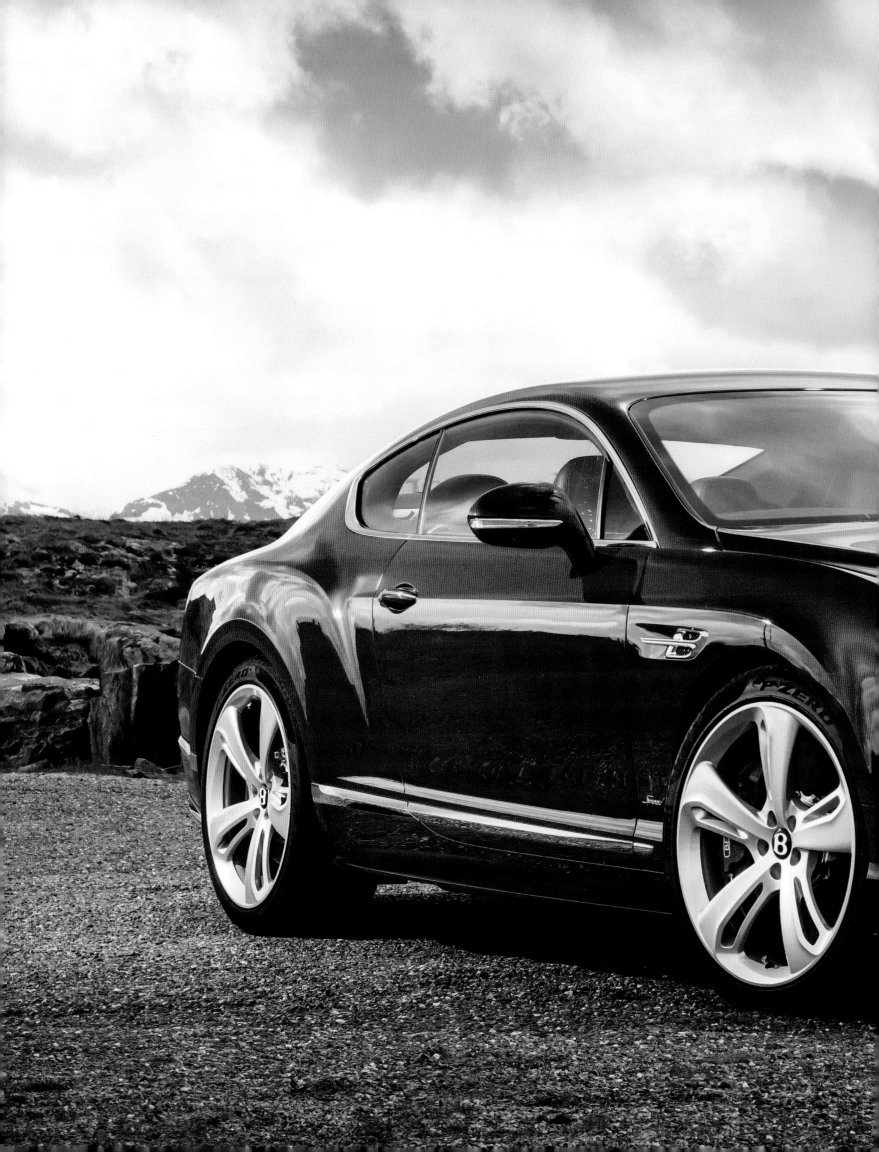

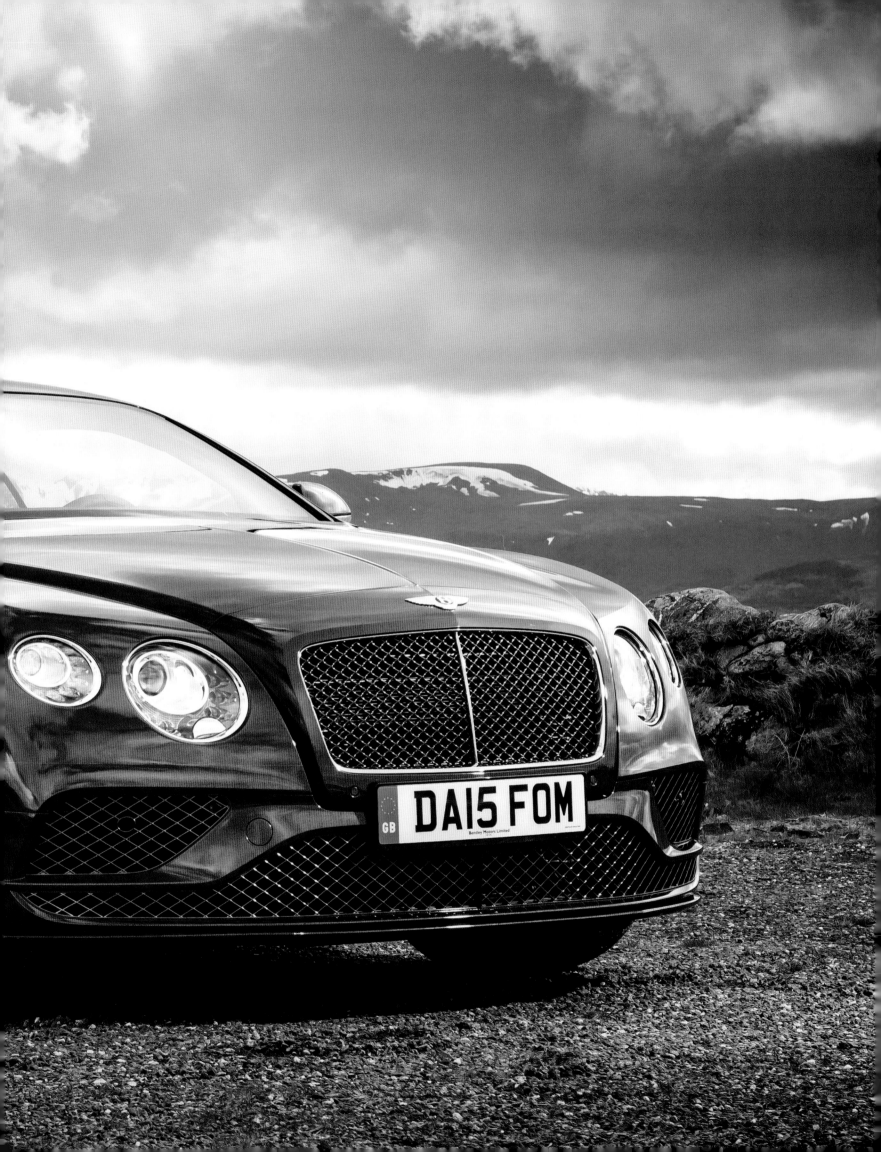

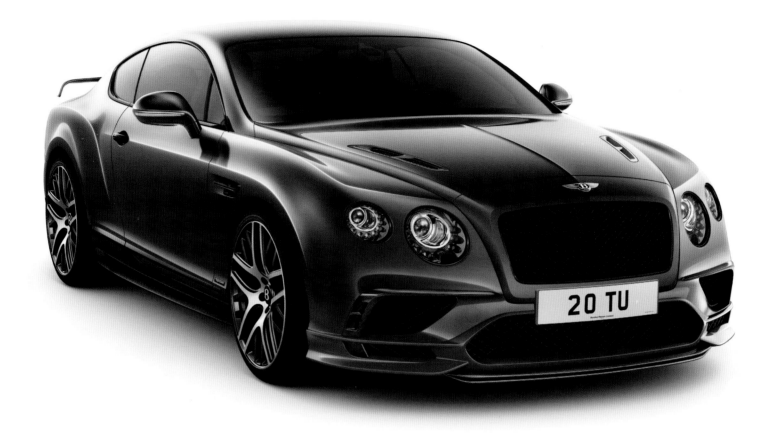

The body shape Zagato created had echoes of the original Continental GT, but more aggression, and familiar Zagato features like the 'double bubble' roof. With a 100kg (220lb) weight advantage over the standard car, it would have been a little quicker, too.

An even faster Continental began as a series of experiments with weight reduction. The Continental Supersports production car of 2009 was 110kg lighter than the GT Speed, due to the adoption of carbon ceramic brakes and carbon composite sports seats, and the deletion of the rear seat. The Supersports had more power, too, thanks to increased turbo boost, with the W12 engine now generating 621bhp at 6,000rpm and 800Nm of torque from 1,700rpm. The engine could also run on bioethanol, an alternative to petrol which could be made sustainably.

Big intakes in the front bumper fed more air to the intercoolers, and there were twin bonnet vents to release hot air from the engine bay. The transmission was a new version of the familiar six-speed ZF automatic dubbed Quickshift, which could change gear twice as fast as before. The four-wheel drive system was retuned to give a 40/60 split biased towards the rear for better handling, and there was lightweight suspension with stiffer bushes to improve agility. Larger-offset wheels increased the rear track by 50mm (2in), improving stability.

A GTC Supersports followed in 2010 and the following year Juha Kankkunen used one in an attempt to break the record speed for driving on ice that he had set in 2007. The car was again prepared by Mäkelä Auto-Tuning. Most of the modifications made to the car were similar to the previous record attempt's – roll cage, blanked-off grille and lights, wheel discs and so on – but now the car was running on standard Pirelli studded winter tyres and a

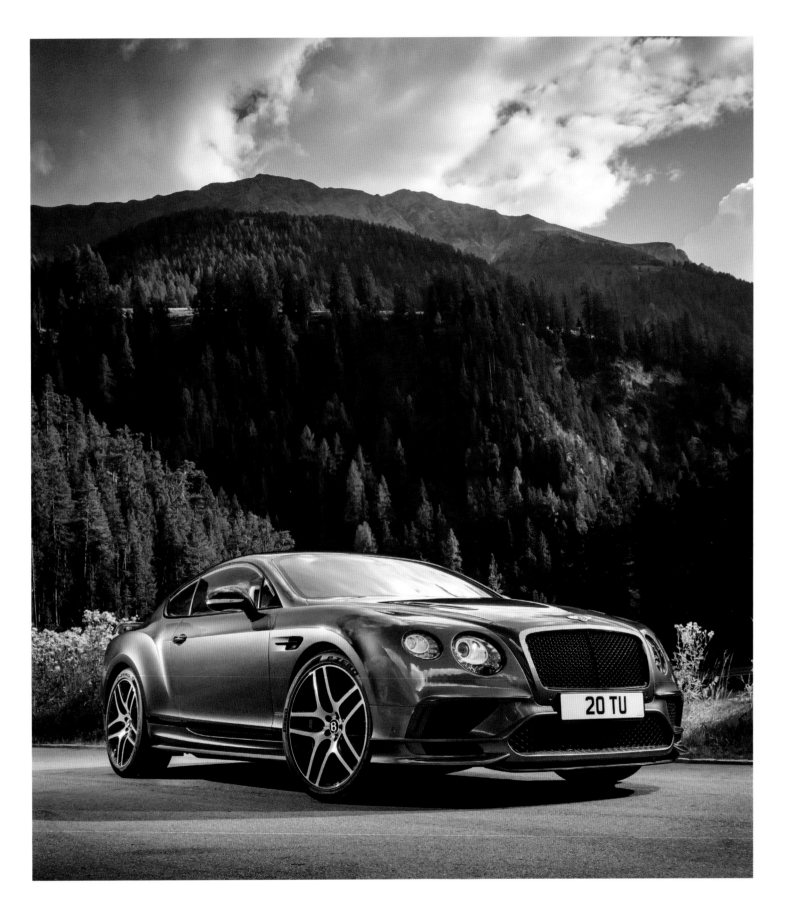

Above: Bentley's publicity for the Continental Supersports extolled the car's 'agile handling, blistering acceleration and awe-inspiring top speed'.

large aluminium alloy duck-tail spoiler had been added to the boot lid. A parachute was also fitted at the rear for high-speed stopping power. Breitling supported the record attempt and Derek Bell was on hand to see if Kankkunen could raise the record to more than 200mph (322km/h).

Using the extra power of the Supersports, Kankkunen achieved a two-way average of 330.70km/h (205.49mph). A Guinness World Records official was present and confirmed the new record. A few weeks later Nokian ran their own attempt with an Audi and beat Kankkunen's speed by less than 1km/h, but as the test was private – when the GWR rules state it must be public – the Bentley team was adamant that their record still stood. To celebrate the achievement Crewe built 100 special edition Continental Supersports Convertible ISR (Ice Speed Record) cars with new intake and exhaust systems to liberate 631bhp.

Later in 2011 a second-generation Continental went on sale. Launched the previous September at the Paris show, the new car offered incremental changes over the original Continental. The exterior had crisper lines with tighter-radius curves, and the revised four-headlamp front end now incorporated LED daylight running lamps. The tracks were wider front and rear, but extensive work on the underside had dropped the coefficient of drag to 0.33 and lift at high speed was also reduced. Inside there was a new infotainment system with a touchscreen and an 11-speaker Naim sound system which audio experts rated the best of any production car. New front seats were both more comfortable and more supportive, and they could be specified with ventilation and massage systems. Scalloped backs to the seats improved rear legroom.

The 6.0-litre W12 engine continued in a revised form. Lower friction, lighter-weight internals and low-inertia turbochargers contributed to a small increase in power, now 567bhp. Coupled with a 65kg (143lb) reduction in weight the new Continental GT could complete the 0–60mph (97km/h) dash in just 4.4 seconds, with a top speed still just under the 200mph (322km/h) mark. Performance was as easy to extract as ever, thanks to the six-speed ZF automatic transmission which was now in the Quickshift specification first seen on the Supersports; the GT also adopted the Supersports' 40/60 rear-biased torque split.

Early in 2012 a second engine was added to the Continental range, a 4.0-litre twin-turbo V8 co-developed with Audi which produced 500bhp at 6,000rpm and 660Nm of torque from 1,700rpm to 5,000rpm. It was coupled to a new ZF eight-speed automatic transmission and could deliver a 0–60mph (97km/h) sprint time of 4.6 seconds, and a 188mph (303km/h) top speed. Ultimately the W12 models were faster and more refined, but the new V8 models were more than enough for most people – and they were more fuel-efficient than the W12s, thanks to the smaller capacity and a sophisticated engine management system which deactivated cylinders when full power was not required. The V8 was initially available in the GT and GTC, but it later spread to other Bentley models.

The first signs of a revival in Bentley's motorsport ambitions came at the Paris show in 2012, where Crewe unveiled the Continental GT3 Concept Racer and announced plans for a racing comeback in 2013. Bentley chief executive Wolfgang Schreiber said customers wanted Bentley to have a presence in motorsport; but rather than

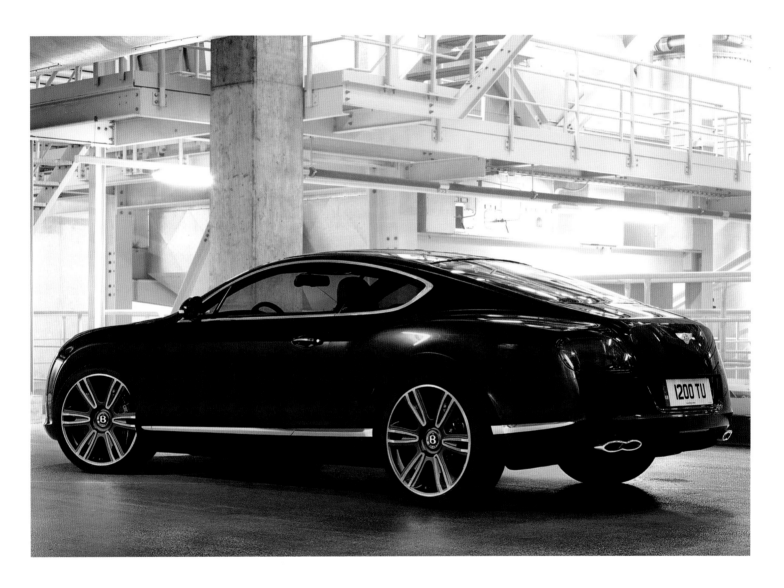

Above: The Continental GT was offered with a twin-turbo V8 engine
from 2012. Performance of the revised model almost matched that
of the W12 cars, and fuel economy was considerably improved.

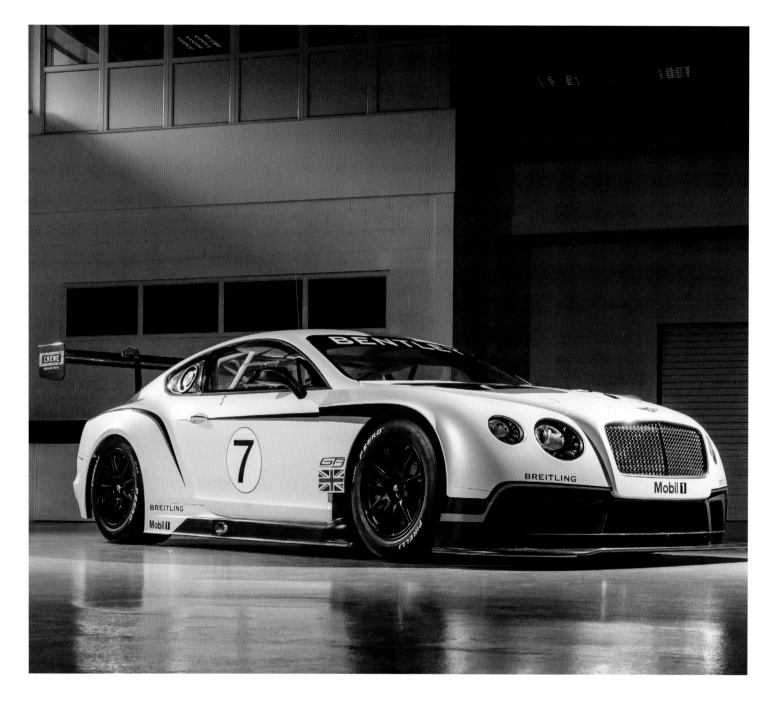

Above: The second-generation Continental GT3 was designed to build
on the fine results achieved by its predecessor in sports car racing.

develop a full-blown LMP1 sports prototype, Bentley decided to produce a racing version of the Continental GT, which it based on the Speed model. For Bentley there was a clear advantage in racing a car based on its road-going models, demonstrating the capability of the engineering in cars customers could buy. Another benefit was that the race cars were developed by factory engineers, exposing them to new ways of operating which could feed back usefully to their non-racing work. Former rally driver Malcolm Wilson's M-Sport operation provided technical support.

The definitive GT3 racer was seen in public for the first time at the Goodwood Festival of Speed in July 2013, where it was driven up the hill by Guy Smith, one of the drivers of the 2003 Le Mans-winning Bentley Speed 8. Though the fastest Continental road cars were still powered by W12 engines, the GT3 racer was fitted with a race-prepared, dry-sump version of the 4.0-litre twin-turbo V8 engine which produced 600bhp. The transmission was very different to the road cars': the engine drove the rear wheels only, through a carbon propshaft and a rear-mounted Xtrac six-speed sequential gearbox with a pneumatic paddle shift. Deleting the drive to the front wheels meant the engine could be positioned much further back in the engine bay, behind the front wheel centreline, for improved handling. There was double-wishbone suspension with conventional coil springs instead of the air springs of the road cars, and Öhlins adjustable dampers front and rear. Vast Brembo slotted steel discs, clamped by six-pot calipers at the front and four-pot calipers at the back, took on the tricky task of stopping the 1.3-tonne machine from race speeds. The system had adjustable front/rear bias, and anti-lock.

The steel monocoque structure was retained but the bonnet, boot lid, doors and extended wings were now carbon composite panels. A front splitter, rear diffuser and enormous rear wing provided up to 800kg (1764lb) of downforce. The GT3 racer was more than 1,000kg (2,205lb) lighter than the road car, in large part because the interior was stripped of its complex dashboard and console, wood trim, leather upholstery, masses of sound and heat insulation and the big, comfortable road car seats. A single carbon-fibre bucket seat was fitted, along with a six-point racing harness, and there was a full steel roll cage and a fire extinguisher. Despite the ruthless campaign of ejecting luxury items to save weight, the air conditioning was retained to ensure cockpit temperatures remained below the FIA-mandated limit.

M-Sport entered a pair of Continental GT3s for the 2014 Blancpain Endurance Series, using the same race numbers – 7 and 8 – as the Speed 8s had done eleven years earlier. Number 7 had an all-British crew of Guy Smith, the 2003 Le Mans winner, with Andy Meyrick and Steven Kane. Number 8 was driven by former F1 driver Jérôme D'Ambrosio, Duncan Tappy and Antoine Leclerc. The season commenced at Monza in April where the white and green cars made a promising start, finishing seventh and eighth. Better was to come: Kane, Meyrick and Smith won the second round at Silverstone, the first British race for 84 years for a Bentley works team. The number 7 car triumphed again in round three of the Blancpain Endurance Series, at Paul Ricard in France. But at the Spa 24 Hours both cars sustained damage through no fault of their own, and could do no better than score a few championship points.

The number 7 Bentley finished the final round of the season, the gruelling Nürburgring 1000km, in a fine second place and that was enough to secure second place in the Teams' Championship for Bentley M-Sport. It was an excellent result for the team's debut year and one that gave plenty of encouragement for the future.

To link the race cars even more obviously with the road-going Continentals, Bentley introduced a Continental GT3-R in 2014. All 300 cars were finished in Glacier White with two-tone green stripes – this was reminiscent of the works racing cars, but the GT3-R was a very different machine which had far more in common with the regular road cars. Weight was saved by fitting carbon-fibre door cars and a titanium exhaust, and by leaving out the rear seats, but this car still had a full complement of interior luxuries, together with air suspension and four-wheel drive, which featured torque vectoring for the first time. As Autocar remarked, it weighed more than a Mercedes S-Class, and yet, with its 4.0-litre V8 tuned to produce 572bhp, it could sprint to 52mph (84km/h) from rest in just 3.7 seconds, making it the fastest-accelerating Bentley production car ever.

M-Sport's racing line-up for 2015 had the same three drivers in car number 7 but a new crew for car 8: Maximilian Buhk, Andy Soucek and Maxime Soulet. Again the number 7 car led the way: there were no wins, but a second place at Paul Ricard and another at the Nürburgring gave them second place in the Drivers' Championship and second for Bentley M-Sport in the Teams' Championship for the second year running.

For 2016 there were changes to the driver line-ups on both cars. Vincent Abril replaced Andy Meyrick in the number 7 car, while Wolfgang Reip took the place of Maximilian Buhk in the number 8. In addition to the factory entries there were two customer cars run by Team Parker Racing. Consistent scoring, including bonus points for leading at the half-way mark in the Spa 24 Hours, saw the number 8 crew finish third in the Drivers' Championship, and Bentley M-Sport drop the third in the Teams' Championship.

The 2017 was the last for the original Continental GT3. By now customer cars were racing in China, Australasia, Europe, the US and Japan. In the works M-Sport team Vincent Abril joined Soucek and Soulet in the number 8 car, and Oliver Jarvis came in to drive the number 7 car alongside regulars Kane and Smith. The car went out on a high note with a win in France and second place at the Spa 24 Hours to win the Endurance Cup Teams' Championship. Team Parker Racing won the British GT Championship, and by the end of the season the Continental GT3 had competed in 528 races in 20 countries, achieving 120 podium finishes and 45 wins.

A new Continental GT3 racer was ready to take over for 2018, following a new-generation Continental GT road car that aimed to build on the success of the original, which had sold more than 50,000 examples since 2003. Crewe was also about to unveil two new models to run alongside the third-generation Continental: a new flagship car in the grand Bentley tradition, and a brand-new road car which would forever change what a Bentley was expected to be.

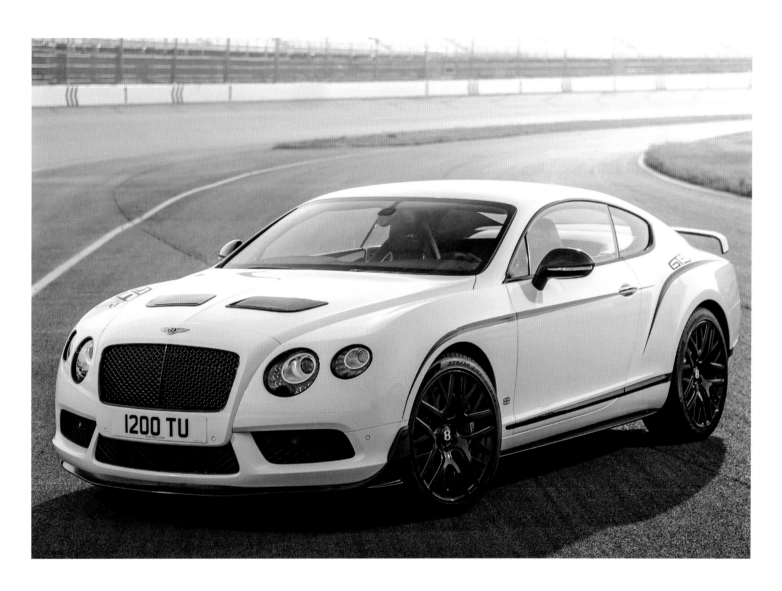

Above: The 2014 GT3-R was a road car with a flavour of the GT3
racer. Just 300 were built, all featuring this white and green livery.

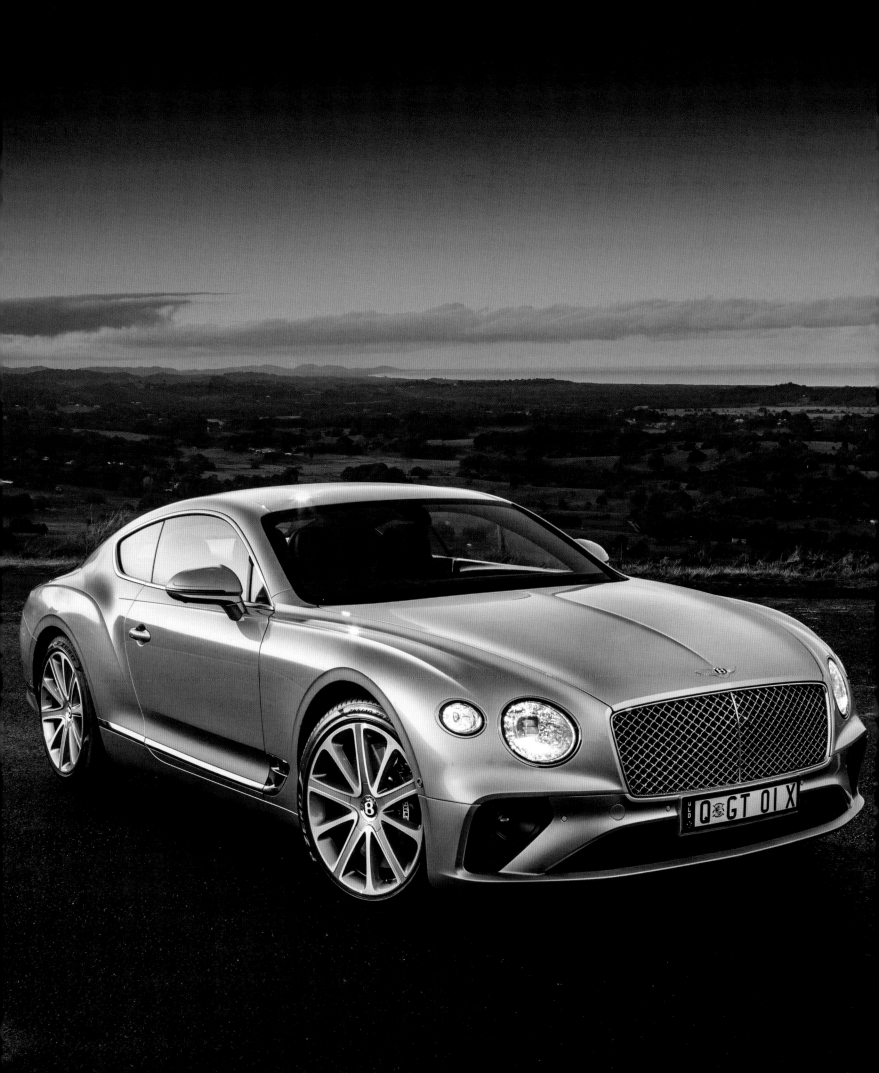

Chapter 10

ONWARDS AND UPWARDS

The Pebble Beach Concours d'Elegance is one of the most prestigious automotive events in the calendar and attracts dozens of the world's finest vintage and classic cars, not to mention thousands of visitors, every year. It was at Pebble Beach, in 2009, that Bentley unveiled its latest flagship – a full-size Bentley saloon in the grandest style to replace the Arnage.

The new car saw a return to an old name, Mulsanne, and a reaffirmation of the Bentley marque's most traditional values alongside the best of new technology. It was based around a comprehensively reworked version of the venerable 6.75-litre V8 engine, which Crewe said had more than 300 new or significantly re-engineered components. The new version featured variable cam phasing and cylinder deactivation to improve efficiency.

The body was all new, and built in a recently constructed body production facility at Crewe where modern production technology such as superforming for the aluminium alloy front wings sat alongside traditional crafts like hand brazing of steel joints. With more leather and wood than any other modern Bentley – including a novel 'ring of wood' circling the cabin at shoulder height – the Mulsanne was crammed full of craftsmanship. Each one took nine weeks to build. Personalisation options were almost endless, with a palette of 114 standard paint colours and the offer to match any colour the customer wanted, provided it was technically feasible.

A Mulliner Driving Specification for the Mulsanne was added in 2012, featuring unique two-piece, 21-inch alloy wheels, 'flying B' wing vents and quilted leather trim, plus sport-tuned suspension and steering. Crewe also announced two new Mulsanne options – a large tinted-glass sunroof and an electrically operated bottle cooler complete with lead crystal champagne flutes.

If the Mulsanne's remarkable craftsmanship represented the modern embodiment of Bentley's traditions, the Bentayga opened up a whole new era for the marque. The first signs that a Bentley SUV was on the way came at the Geneva show in March 2012, where Crewe showed off a concept called EXP 9F. Some of the design cues, like the matrix grille and four round headlamps, were shared with other Bentleys. It was the form of the body that was unusual for the marque – if not entirely unprecedented, as estate cars were built in the heyday of the 'Blackpool projects' era of the 1990s, and there was even a handful of 4x4s, apparently based on Range Rovers. The EXP 9F's tall body offered plenty of space, a commanding driving position and an imposing demeanour. Crewe said customer reaction would shape any plans for production, though even at the EXP 9F's launch there was talk of 'refining the concept further'.

Crewe claimed the Bentayga production car unveiled in September 2015 was the fastest, most powerful, most luxurious and most exclusive SUV in the world. It was one of the first vehicles to be based on the updated version of Volkswagen's MLB platform, a modular system which allowed key components to be shared across different models while still permitting flexibility in the size of each vehicle and the powertrain that drove it. The Audi Q7 was founded on the same platform, as were several subsequent Audi models, plus the 2018 Lamborghini Urus, 2018 Volkswagen Touareg, and 2019 Porsche Cayenne. The

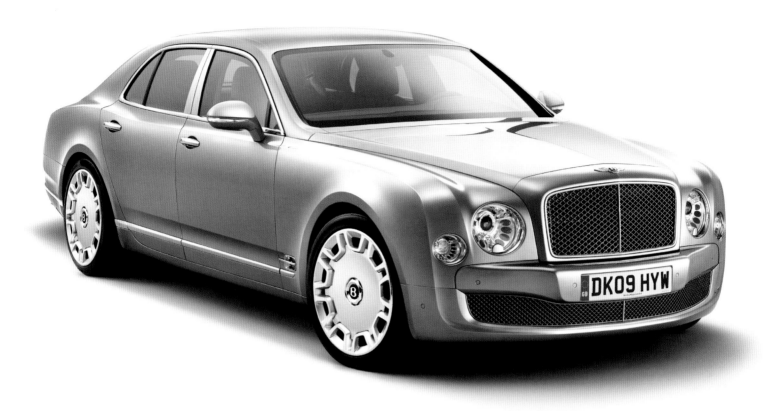

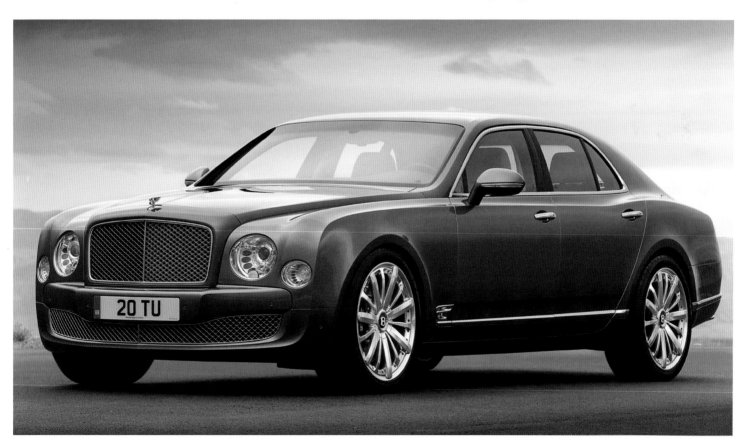

Top: The Mulsanne was an effective blend of traditional craftsmanship, ingenious design and modern technology.

Above: The Mulsanne Mulliner Driving Specification, introduced in 2012, could achieve a remarkable 184mph (296km/h).

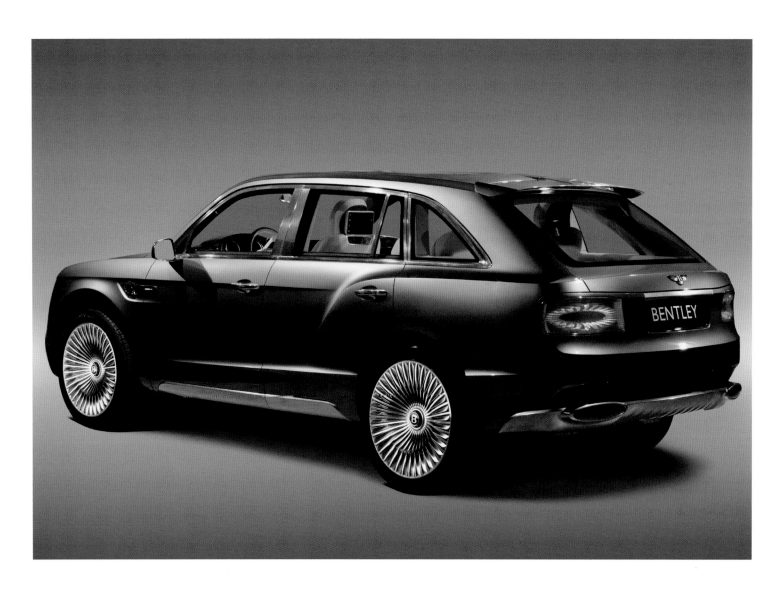

Above: Bentley's EXP 9F concept car received a mixed reception when it was unveiled at Geneva in March 2012 – but luxury SUVs were an obvious new market for the company.

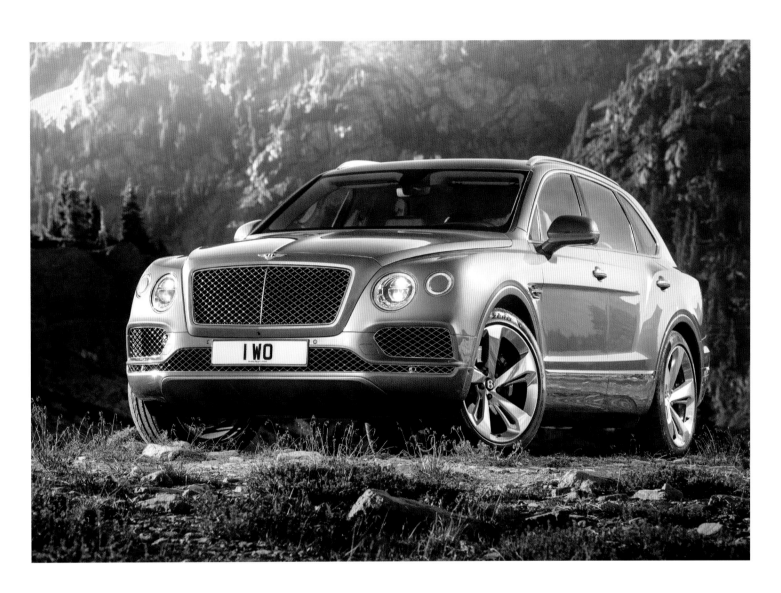

Above: The production SUV was called the Bentayga. The name and
the looks were controversial, but there was no doubting the car's
extraordinary capabilities, especially for off-road use.

Bentayga's bodyshell was built at the Volkswagen plant in Bratislava alongside the bodies for the Urus, Touareg, Q7 and Cayenne. The shells were then shipped to Crewe for trimming and finishing alongside other Bentley models.

Bentley said the unusual name was derived from Taiga, the world's largest transcontinental snow forest, and the Roque Bentayga mountain in the Canary Islands. As it can hardly have come simultaneously from both that sounded rather dubious, but whatever its source the name was one which split opinions: some thought it was awful, others said it did not matter much what the name was as long as the vehicle was good. The styling was controversial too: the EXP 9F had been a like-it-or-loathe it car, and the Bentayga's odd proportions put it into the same category.

There was no doubting the Bentayga's capabilities, however. It had been developed to offer plenty of off-road ability, and prototypes had proved their worth on the dirt and gravel of South Africa, the sand dunes of Dubai and – no doubt the toughest of all – the muddy fields of Cheshire. A hill descent control was provided to make slippery downhill grades less nerve-wracking, and there was a multi-mode air suspension system which could be raised up to increase ground clearance for off-roading or lowered to assist in hitching a trailer or loading the boot. On the road, where virtually all of them would spend the majority of their time, the Bentaygas had plenty to offer. Prototypes lapped the Nürburgring Nordschleife circuit more than 400 times while their suspension and stability control systems were fine-tuned. A key new feature was Dynamic Ride, a 48-volt electric active roll control system which varied roll resistance depending on the car's motion,

and gave good control without affecting the ride quality the way conventional stiff anti-roll bars could. The Bentayga had variable ratio steering with electric power assist.

A heavily revised W12 engine provided 600bhp and used both direct and indirect fuel injection, switching seamlessly between the two systems to maximise power and minimise particulate emissions. Like the Mulsanne's V8 it was capable of shutting down cylinders when full power was not needed, running as a six-cylinder engine to improve part-load efficiency. Further gains were made by adding start-stop technology, and introducing a coast mode for high-speed cruising. There was an eight-speed ZF automatic gearbox, and the four-wheel drive system was like the Continental's in having a Torsen centre differential and a 40/60 rear-biased torque split.

The Bentayga's European debut came at the Geneva show in March 2016, and it shared the Bentley stand with a new concept car called EXP 10 Speed 6. Crewe said this curvy two-seater sports car – which was lower and obviously lighter than the Continental GT – was one option for a future Bentley model line. The muscular exterior shape was said to have been inspired by the aerodynamic forms of aircraft wings and fuselages, yet still incorporated classic Bentley features like the four round headlamps and the matrix grille, which was now a 3D metal-printed

Opposite: The Bentayga displays the same outstanding craftsmanship and attention to detail as Bentley's saloons and sports cars.

Following pages: The superb EXP10 Speed 6 concept made its debut at the 2016 Geneva Motor Show.

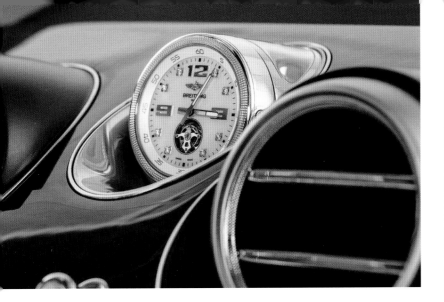
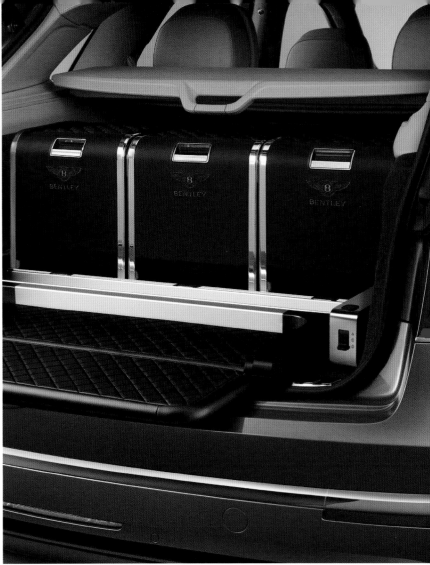
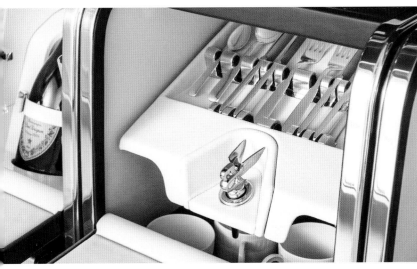
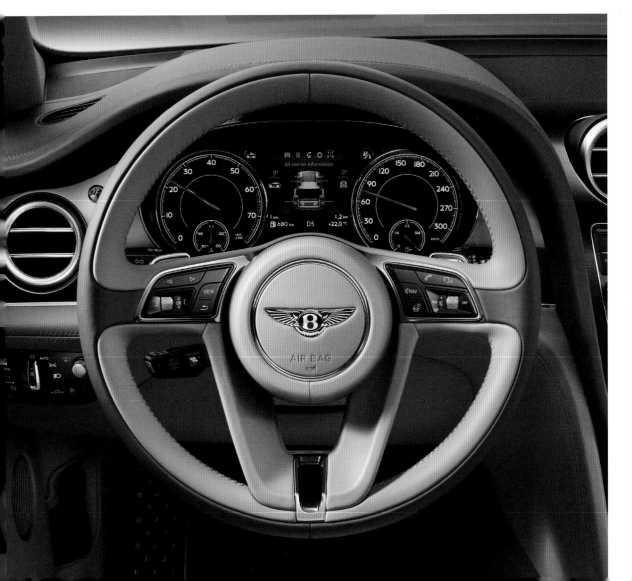
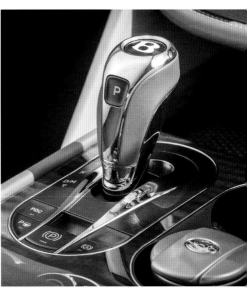
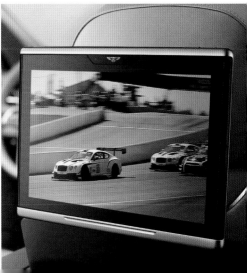

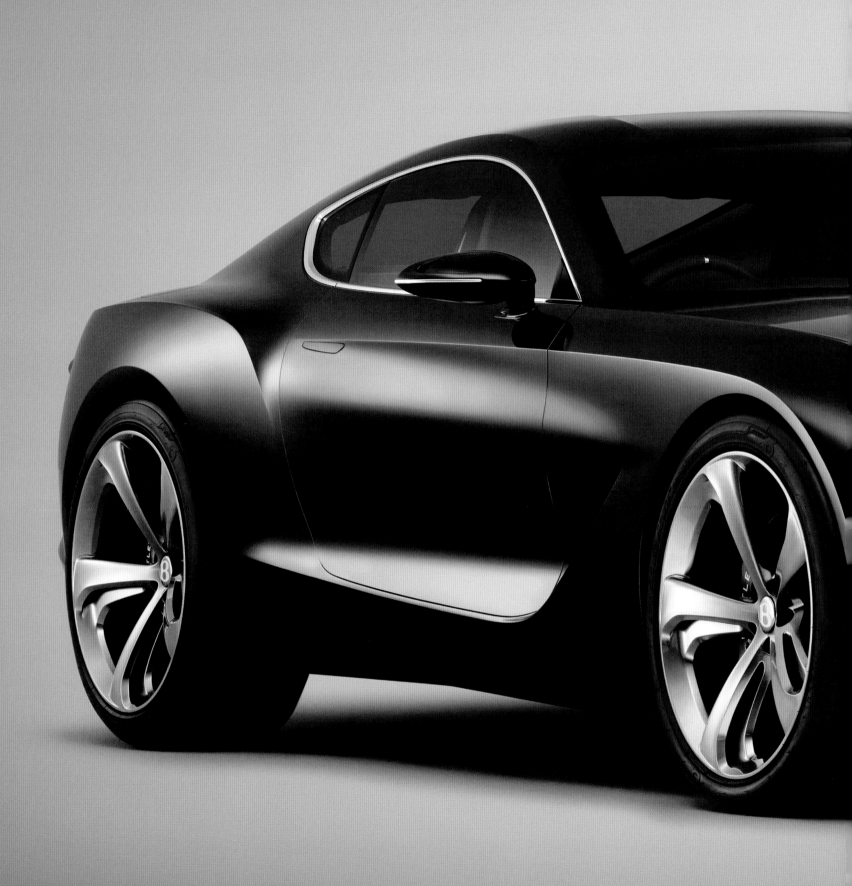

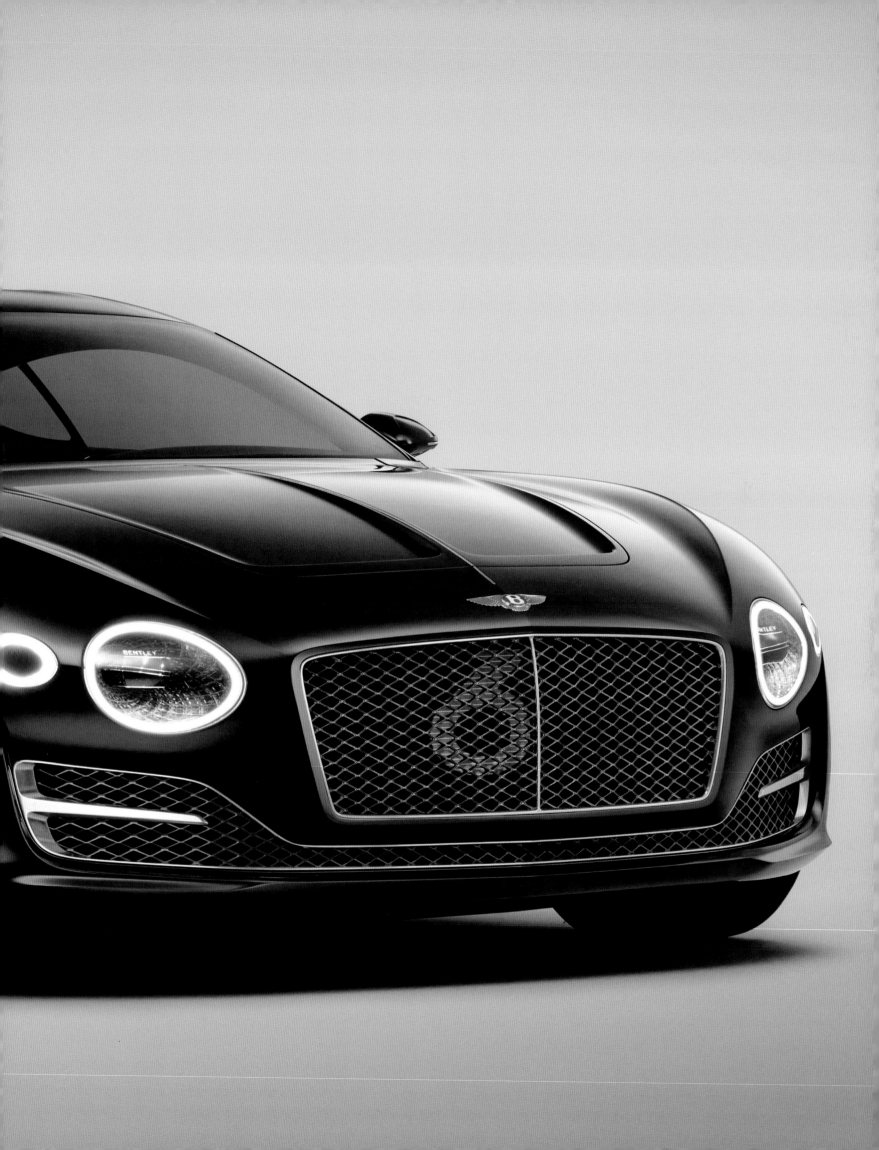

component with a three-dimensional structure only visible when viewed from the correct angle. The short front overhang, long bonnet and shallow glasshouse gave the EXP 10 a more overtly dynamic shape than any recent Bentley design: while opinion was split on the Bentayga, nobody had anything but praise for the shape of the sports car.

The interior was just as impressive. A continuous line ran around the cabin through the narrow centre console, either side of which sat two sports seats trimmed in quilted Poltrona Frau leather. Controls were made using steel and copper, and wood door trims in straight-grain cherry were inset with diamond-shaped copper panels. The instruments rose into view when the car was started, using a button floating in the top of the gear selector.

The next major news from Crewe was an update for the Mulsanne, with a revised front end using adaptive LED headlamps and a wider grille with stainless steel vertical vanes. There was now a three-model range: the standard Mulsanne saloon; an Extended Wheelbase car which was 250mm (10in) longer to provide generous rear seat space; and a Mulsanne Speed focused on driver satisfaction. The Speed model's V8 was still 6.75 litres but power was up from the 505bhp of the standard car to 530bhp, and the eight-speed ZF automatic gearbox was recalibrated to make the most of the extra power. The 0–60mph (97km/h) time was reduced from 5.1 seconds to 4.8, and the top speed raised from 184mph (296km/h) to 190mph (306km/h). But Crewe seemed to have given up on the idea of full-size coupé and convertible cars: since the demise of the Arnage-based Azure convertible in 2009 and Brooklands coupé in 2011 buyers had been forced to look to the Continental

range if they wanted fewer than four doors, and there were no signs that Mulsanne-based coupés or convertibles were on the horizon.

In 2017 the EXP 10 Speed 6 concept was back, but in a new and radical form. The two-seat coupé had now been turned into a stylish roadster, but that in itself was an evolution rather than a revolution. What made the new EXP 12 Speed 6e special was that it had a full electric drivetrain. Bentley released little detail about the car, but suggested an electric Bentley should be able to drive from London to Paris or Milan to Monaco on a single charge – requiring a range of at least 280 miles (451km) – and would boast contactless inductive charging as an alternative to fiddling with cables. The concept's interior featured copper highlights, using the colour of a metal known for its electrical conductivity to underline the 6e's new powertrain. Buttons on the steering wheel provided a performance boost and a speed limiter.

The third generation of the Continental GT was announced late in 2017, adopting some of the technology pioneered on the Bentayga – and introducing a new transmission. The eight-speed automatic gearbox was replaced by an eight-speed dual clutch transmission, which offered greater overall efficiency and faster gearchanges. Sport mode provided the fastest shifts, but there was also a Comfort mode which was slightly less rapid but swapped gears almost imperceptibly. Maximum speed was achieved in sixth gear, with seventh and eighth offering relaxed cruising. The four-wheel drive system now used rear-wheel drive as much as possible for optimum handling and better fuel efficiency, delivering power to the front wheels only when necessary.

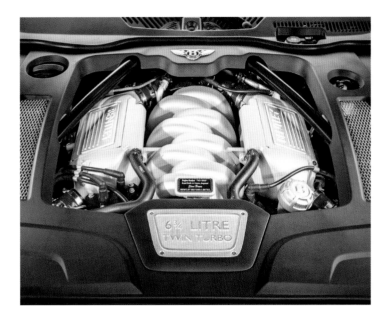

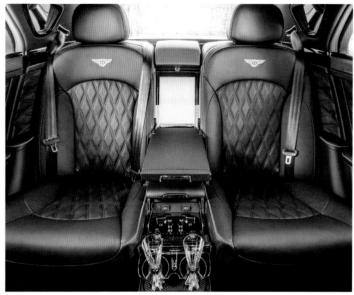

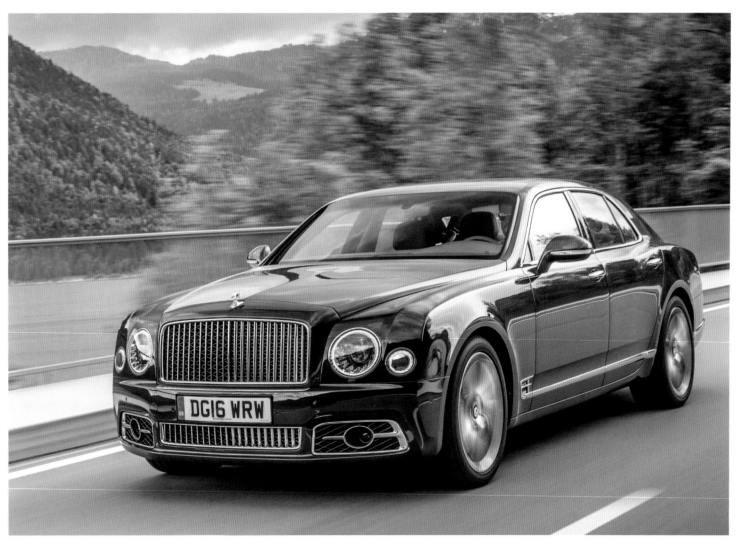

Top and above: The Mulsanne Speed had 530bhp from its hand-built

6.75-litre V8 engine – whose lineage could be traced back to 1959.

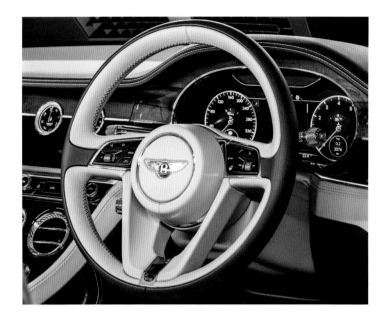

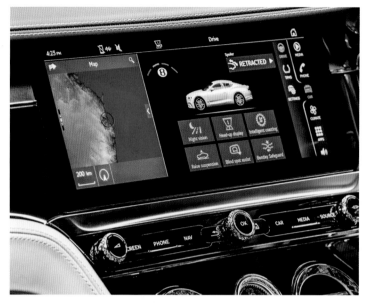

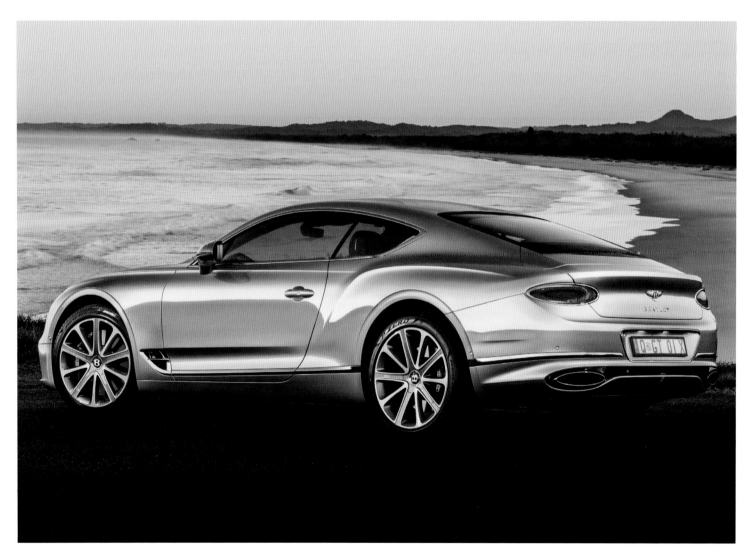

Top and above: The third-generation Continental GT shared a platform
with the Porsche Panamera and was substantially lighter than before.

Since 2014 Crewe had been the Volkswagen group's centre of excellence for W12 engines, leading their design and development and manufacturing them for other brands that used them (Audi and Volkswagen). The W12 engine that went into the Continental was a further fettled 626bhp version of the TSI engine from the Bentayga, fitted with a more powerful engine management system capable of 300 million software calculations per second. The Conti GT could now sprint from rest to 60mph (97km/h) in 3.6 seconds – courtesy of a new Sport Launch mode – and topped out at 207mph (333km/h).

The Continental also adopted the 48-volt electrical system first seen on the SUV, together with its Dynamic Ride active anti-roll system. The air suspension used three-chamber air springs with 60 per cent more volume than in the previous model, giving more scope for the suspension engineers to improve the ride, and there was a new version of the Continuous Damping Control system. The Continental now rode on 21-inch wheels as standard, with a choice of two styles, and a 22-inch lightweight, forged wheel was offered as an alternative together with a hand-finishing option that gave a 'twisted' polished finish. The adoption of electric power assistance for the steering meant the Continental could also be equipped with modern driver assistance features such as active lane assist, traffic jam assist and park assist.

The Continental was based on the Volkswagen MSB platform that was common with the Porsche Panamera. The new body, though slightly longer, was 80kg (176lb) lighter than before, and was the first production shell to have the entire body side made in superformed aluminium. The front wheels were pushed forward by 135mm (5in) and the engine was now positioned behind the front axle instead of in front, improving the weight distribution and giving the new Continental more agile handling. The headlamp design, inspired by cut crystal glasses, had transparent internal surfaces with sharply defined edges which caught the light, making them look like glowing gemstones. The elliptical tail lights were designed in a similar way.

The interior, as always, was a blend of fine leather, wood and metal. The instruments looked like analogue gauges but were fully digital and configurable, and the display could also show data from the infotainment system. The dashboard now incorporated a novel rotating display panel which had three faces. One was veneered to match the dashboard, the second had a 12.3-inch (312mm) touchscreen for the navigation system, and the third had three analogue dials – a clock, a compass and an outside temperature thermometer. The Continental was offered with a new Koa veneer, and there were dual veneer options for the first time. Crewe said the Continental cabin had ten square metres (108sq ft) of wood panelling which took nine hours to create. The centre console could be specified with a finish known as Côtes de Genève (known in the US as damaskeening) where a pattern of stripes is machined onto 0.6mm aluminium alloy panels. The new 20-way adjustable seats were available with a 'diamond in diamond' quilted pattern made using both stitching and embroidery – a process which took eighteen months to develop. Three audio systems were offered: the standard system with 10 speakers and 650 watts of amplification; a 1,500-watt, 16-speaker Bang & Olufsen system; and a superb 2,200-watt

18-speaker Naim set-up which incorporated transducers in the seats to ensure the occupants felt bass sounds as much as they heard them.

Though the W12 was the only engine available in the new Continental at launch it would only be a matter of time before the appearance of a V8 version and a plug-in hybrid. The first of the new generation of Continentals with V8 power turned out not to be a road car: instead it was EXP 11, otherwise known as the new GT3 racer, which appeared for the 2018 season. The new car aimed to fix the old one's biggest problem, which was its nose-heavy weight distribution. The driver was seated 300mm (12in) further back, and the transmission was now behind the rear axle, using a new bespoke Ricardo gearbox instead of the previous Xtrac item. The new transmission allowed the clutch to be changed in just three minutes, and contributed to rebalancing the car as it meant the fuel tank and oil tank could be mounted lower and further back. The result was weight distribution close to the ideal 50:50 balance, and a lower centre of gravity – both of which contributed to better handling. Work at Porsche's Weissach wind tunnel focused on increasing downforce at the front of the car to kill understeer. Another innovation on the new-generation GT3 was a removable front end assembly which made mid-race accident repairs quicker and easier.

The works team was again run by M-Sport, with regular drivers Guy Smith and Steven Kane joined by Frenchman Jules Gounon in the number 7 car and the number 8 driven by Vincent Abril, Andy Soucek and Maxime Soulet. The new cars recorded a second place finish at the Paul Ricard 1,000km, and were running strongly in the Spa 24 Hours until both were forced to retire. Team Bentley finished fifth in the Blancpain Endurance Cup.

The first-generation GT3 continued to race in private hands, notably in the US where K-PAX Racing entered a pair of cars in the Pirelli World Challenge (which despite the title took place entirely in North America). The team's regular drivers were Rodrigo Baptista and Alvaro Parente, supplemented by works drivers Soucek and Soulet at races requiring two drivers. The team won its first race at Virginia International Raceway in April, where Baptista and Soulet teamed up to take the victory. After strong results throughout the season Baptista won the final two rounds at Watkins Glen in September to give K-PAX the teams' title in the Pirelli World Challenge.

Back at Crewe the Bentayga's appeal was widened by the introduction of alternative engines. A diesel model – Bentley's first – debuted in 2017 using a 4.0-litre, 429bhp V8, and Crewe claimed it was the world's fastest diesel SUV, with a 0–62mph (100km/h) time of 4.8 seconds and a top speed of 168mph (270km/h). It also had a range on a tank of fuel of up to 621 miles (1,000km). The engine, co-developed with Audi, used a pair of twin-scroll turbochargers supplemented by an electric supercharger which could provide boost at low revs even when the turbos were not up to speed. As a result the diesel engine's maximum torque was reached at just 1,000rpm. But the backlash against diesel engines came at just the wrong time for the Bentayga diesel, and it was dropped in Europe in 2018.

A V8 petrol engine was added to the range the same year, using the 4.0-litre unit from the Continental GT, then in June the Bentayga was back in the news when Rhys

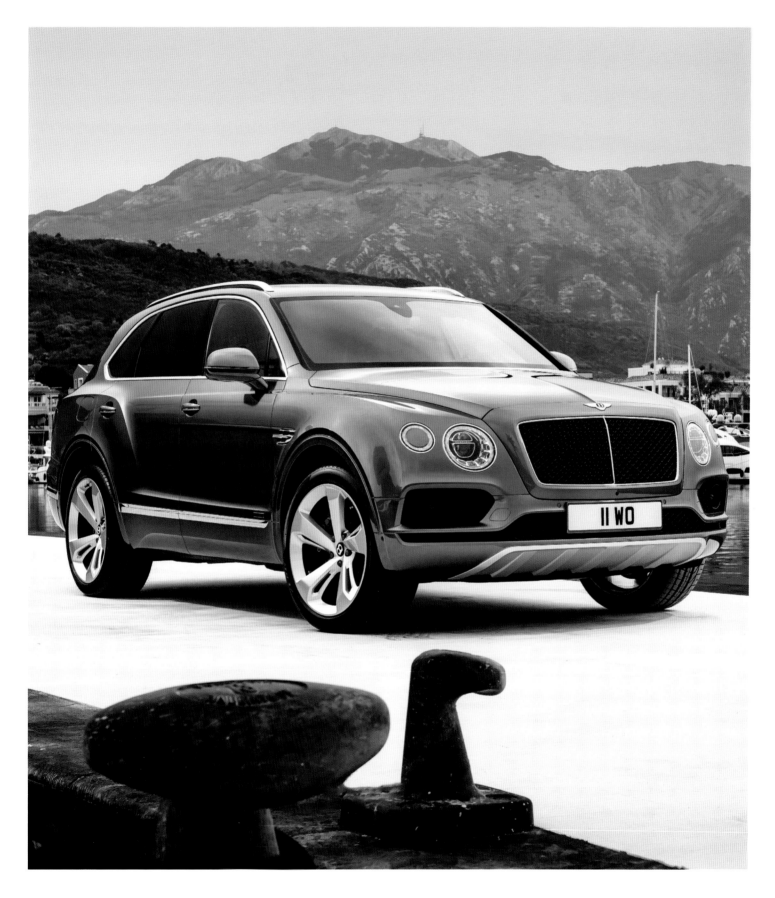

Above: Bentley's first-ever diesel engine, a 4.0-litre turbo V8, was offered in the Bentayga in 2017. A V8 petrol engine followed later that year.

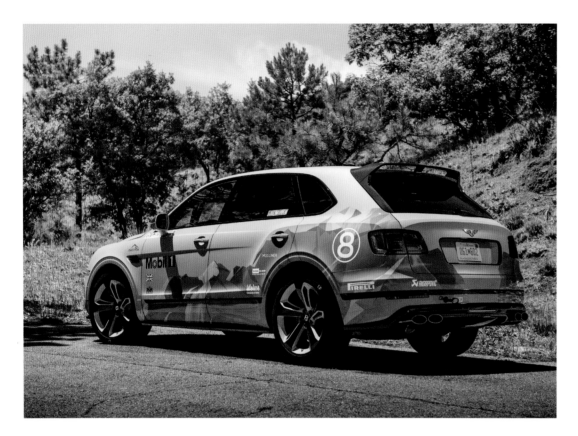

Left: Rhys Millen cut nearly two minutes off the Pikes Peak hillclimb SUV record in this Bentayga in 2017.

Below: The Bentayga now has W12, V8 and hybrid options.

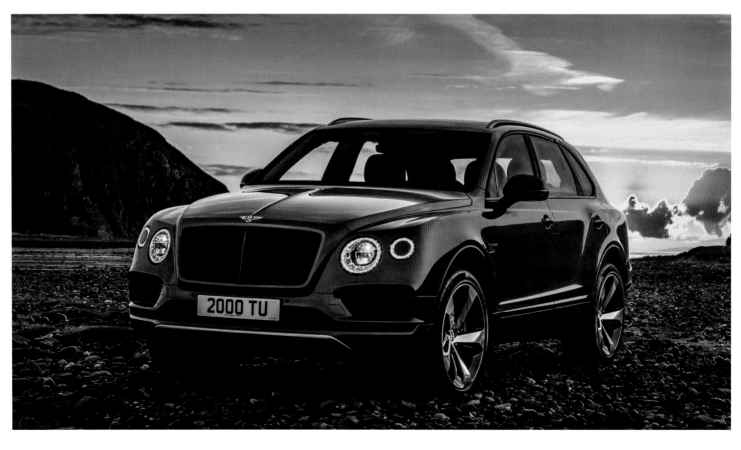

Millen attempted to break the record for a production SUV at the Pikes Peak hillclimb in Colorado. The Bentayga was fitted with a roll cage, a fire extinguisher and an Akrapovič sports exhaust, and had a carbon-fibre front splitter, side skirts, diffuser and rear spoiler which were Bentley options. Around 300kg (660lb) was saved by removing unnecessary interior trim, but otherwise the Bentayga was in standard specification. Millen completed the Pikes Peak hillclimb – a 5,000ft ascent with 156 corners – in 10 minutes 49.9 seconds, cutting nearly two minutes off the previous record.

To take the place of the diesel, Bentley offered a Bentayga Hybrid production car. A hybrid Mulsanne concept had been unveiled in 2014, but where that car combined electric power with the existing 6.75-litre V8 engine, for the hybrid Bentayga there was a 3.0-litre V6 engine. A similar powertrain was seen in the Porsche Cayenne E-Hybrid. The hybrid was said to be capable of up to 31 miles (50km) on electric power only, and could recharge from a domestic socket in 7.5 hours, or – using a heavy-duty electrical supply – in just 2.5 hours. Bentley offered a Philippe Starck-designed home charging unit.

The hybrid Bentayga was the first step towards the electrification of Bentley models. Crewe said all its cars would be available with electric assistance, at least, by 2025 – but it's also likely that a Bentley with a full electric powertrain will be launched in the next few years. Crewe can look to the developments being made elsewhere in the Volkswagen group, particularly with Porsche's Taycan electric vehicle due late in 2019. It's likely that technology from this car will be used to underpin Bentley's first electric vehicles, which could be on sale from 2021. In 2018 new design director Stefan Sielaff said the first Bentley EV would probably be a four-door saloon rather than a sports car like the EXP 12 Speed 6e, though it might have some visual similarity to the concept. It's possible that the successor to the Mulsanne, due in the early 2020s, will be a full EV.

Not that Crewe has lost sight of Bentley's long and illustrious heritage. The Mulsanne W.O. Edition announced in 2018, a special 100-off limited edition to celebrate Bentley's centenary, featured trim in 'Heritage Hide' which had the patina of a vintage leather interior. The car also featured a cocktail cabinet which was adorned with a slice from the original crankshaft of W.O.'s own 8 Litre car, which was replaced many years ago.

The challenge for Crewe – led since the start of 2018 by new chief executive Adrian Hallmark, and new engineering director Dr Werner Tietz – will be to make the transition to electric power without losing the connection to this heritage and the unique feel of the Bentley brand. Their job will be easier than for many top-end brands because the way an electric vehicle performs – with silence and smoothness, and a lot of torque available from low speeds – is very much in line with the kind of performance Bentley buyers expect. But it will be fascinating to see how the design opportunities presented by new electric powertrains will be exploited, and how Crewe will reinvent the Bentley brand as it powers into its second century.

Following pages: Bentley marked a centenary of outstanding car design and production with the 100-off Mulsanne W.O. Edition.

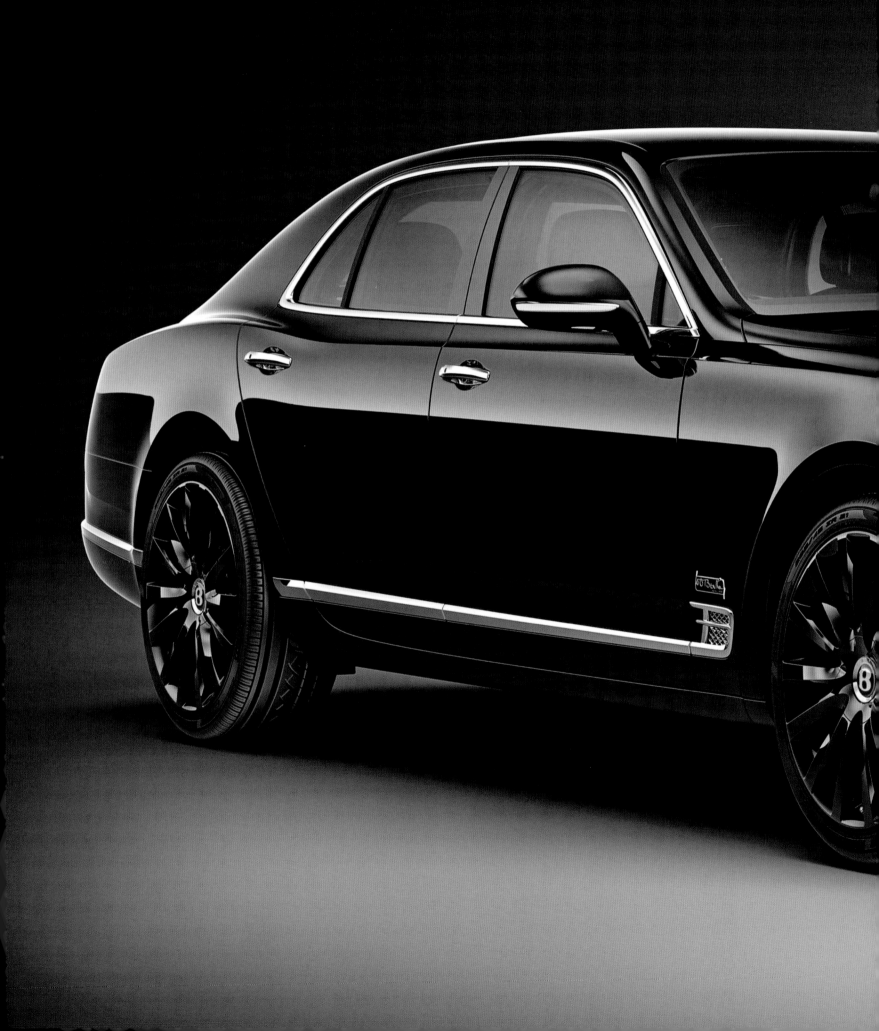

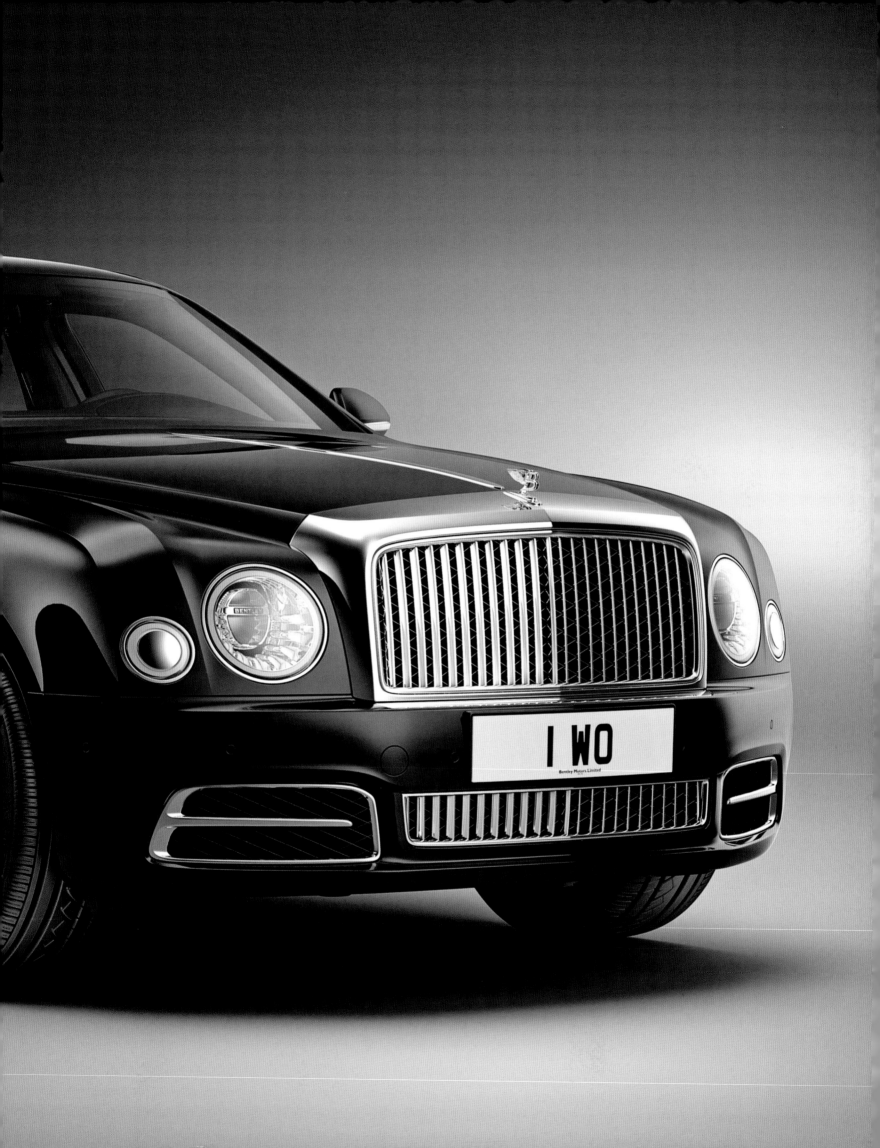

SPECIFICATIONS

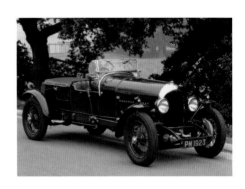

3 LITRE

Construction	Ladder chassis with separate body
Engine	2,996cc in-line four-cylinder, overhead cam, 16 valves
Transmission	Four-speed manual, rear-wheel drive
Suspension	Front: beam axle, semi-elliptic leaf springs
	Rear: live axle, semi-elliptic leaf springs
Brakes	Mechanical, rear drums (drums all round from 1924)
Power	80bhp
Top speed	80mph (129km/h) approx.
Acceleration	N/A

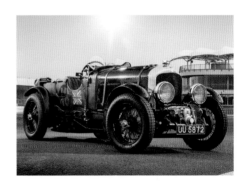

4½ LITRE 'BLOWER'

Construction	Ladder chassis with separate body
Engine	4,398cc in-line four-cylinder, overhead cam, 16 valves, Amherst-Villiers supercharger
Transmission	Four-speed manual, rear-wheel drive
Suspension	Front: beam axle, semi-elliptic leaf springs
	Rear: live axle, semi-elliptic leaf springs
Brakes	Mechanical, drums all round
Power	182bhp @ 3,900rpm
Top speed	100mph (161km/h) approx.
Acceleration	N/A

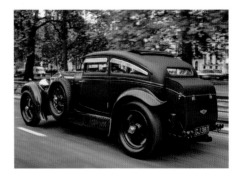

SPEED 6

Construction	Ladder chassis with separate body
Engine	6,597cc in-line six-cylinder, overhead cam, 24 valves
Transmission	Four-speed manual, rear-wheel drive
Suspension	Front: beam axle, semi-elliptic leaf springs
	Rear: live axle, semi-elliptic leaf springs
Brakes	Mechanical, rear drums, servo assisted
Power	180bhp
Top speed	Over 90mph (145km/h)
Acceleration	N/A

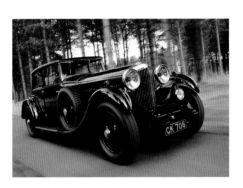

8 LITRE

Construction	Ladder chassis with separate body
Engine	7,983cc in-line six-cylinder, overhead cam, 24 valves
Transmission	Four-speed manual, rear-wheel drive
Suspension	Front: beam axle, semi-elliptic leaf springs
	Rear: live axle, semi-elliptic leaf springs
Brakes	Mechanical, drums all round, servo assistance
Power	225bhp
Top speed	Over 100mph (161km/h)
Acceleration	N/A

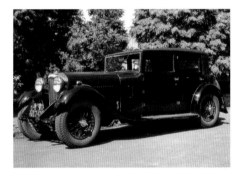

4 LITRE

Construction	Ladder chassis with separate body
Engine	3,915cc in-line six-cylinder, inlet over exhaust, 12 valves
Transmission	Four-speed manual, rear-wheel drive
Suspension	Front: beam axle, semi-elliptic leaf springs
	Rear: live axle, semi-elliptic leaf springs
Brakes	Mechanical, drums all round
Power	120bhp @ 4,000rpm
Top speed	85mph (137km/h) approx.
Acceleration	N/A

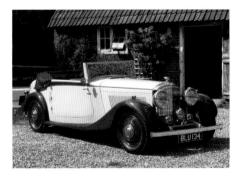

3½ LITRE

Construction	Ladder chassis with separate body
Engine	3,669cc in-line six-cylinder, pushrods, 12 valves
Transmission	Four-speed manual, rear-wheel drive
Suspension	Front: beam axle, semi-elliptic leaf springs
	Rear: live axle, semi-elliptic leaf springs
Brakes	Mechanical, drums all round
Power	105bhp approx.
Top speed	90mph (145km/h) approx.
Acceleration	0–60mph (97km/h): 20sec approx.

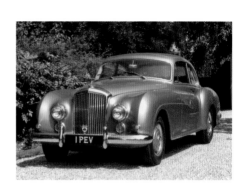

R-TYPE CONTINENTAL

Construction	Cruciform chassis with separate body
Engine	4,566cc (later 4,887cc) in-line six-cylinder, pushrods, 12 valves
Transmission	Four-speed manual, rear-wheel drive
Suspension	Front: coil springs, double wishbones, anti-roll bar
	Rear: live axle, leaf springs
Brakes	Mechanical/hydraulic, drums all round, servo assistance
Power	153bhp
Top speed	120mph (193km/h) approx.
Acceleration	0–60mph (97km/h) in 13.5sec approx.

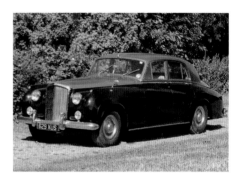

S2

Construction	Ladder chassis with separate body
Engine	6,230cc V8, pushrods, 16 valves
Transmission	Four-speed manual, rear-wheel drive
Suspension	Front: coil springs, double wishbones, anti-roll bar
	Rear: live axle, leaf springs, anti-roll Z-bar
Brakes	Mechanical/hydraulic, drums all round, servo assistance
Power	200bhp approx.
Top speed	113mph (182km/h) approx.
Acceleration	0–60mph (97km/h) in 13.5sec approx.

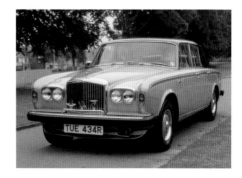

T-SERIES

Construction	Unitary body
Engine	6,750cc V8, pushrods, 16 valves
Transmission	Three-speed automatic, rear-wheel drive
Suspension	Front: independent, double wishbones, coil springs
	Rear: semi-trailing arms, coil springs, anti-roll bar, hydraulic self-levelling
Brakes	Discs all round, power assisted
Power	200bhp approx. @ 4,000rpm
Top speed	120mph (193km/h)
Acceleration	0–60mph (97km/h) in 9.4sec

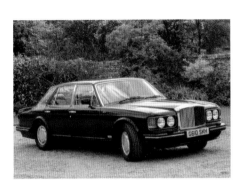

TURBO R

Construction	Unitary body
Engine	6,750cc V8, pushrods, 16 valves, turbocharger
Transmission	Three-speed (later four-speed) automatic, rear-wheel drive
Suspension	Front: independent, double wishbones, coil springs, anti-roll bar
	Rear: semi-trailing arms, coil springs, anti-roll bar, hydraulic self-levelling
Brakes	Discs all round, anti-lock
Power	320bhp approx. @ 4,200rpm
Top speed	137mph (220km/h)
Acceleration	0–60mph (97km/h): 6.7sec

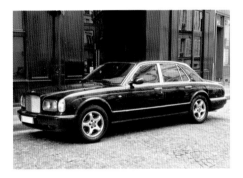

ARNAGE GREEN LABEL

Construction	Unitary body
Engine	4,398cc BMW V8, double overhead cams per bank, 32 valves
Transmission	Five-speed automatic, rear-wheel drive
Suspension	Front: independent, double wishbones, coil springs
	Rear: semi-trailing arms, coil springs, anti-roll bar, hydraulic self-levelling
Brakes	Discs all round, anti-lock
Power	350bhp @ 5,500rpm
Top speed	149mph (240km/h)
Acceleration	0–60mph (97km/h): 6.5sec

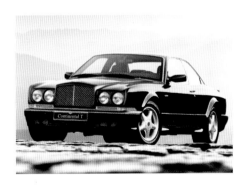

CONTINENTAL T

Construction	Unitary body
Engine	6,750cc V8, pushrods, 16 valves, turbocharger
Transmission	Four-speed automatic, rear-wheel drive
Suspension	Front: independent, double wishbones, coil springs, anti-roll bar
	Rear: semi-trailing arms, coil springs, anti-roll bar, hydraulic self-levelling
Brakes	Discs all round, anti-lock
Power	420bhp @ 4,000rpm
Top speed	168mph (270km/h)
Acceleration	0–60mph (97km/h): 5.8sec

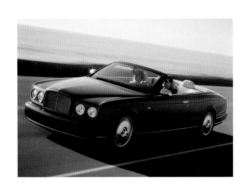

AZURE

Construction	Unitary body
Engine	6,750cc V8, pushrods, 16 valves, turbocharger
Transmission	Four-speed automatic, rear-wheel drive
Suspension	Front: independent, double wishbones, coil springs, anti-roll bar
	Rear: semi-trailing arms, coil springs, anti-roll bar, hydraulic self-levelling
Brakes	Discs all round, anti-lock
Power	400bhp @ 4,100rpm
Top speed	155mph (249km/h)
Acceleration	0–60mph (97km/h): 6.3sec

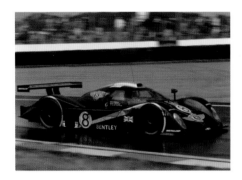

EXP SPEED 8

Construction	Composite monocoque
Engine	3,600cc V8, double overhead cam per bank, 32 valves
Transmission	Six-speed Xtrac sequential
Suspension	Front: double wishbones, torsion bars, anti-roll bar
	Rear: double wishbones, coil springs, anti-roll bar
Brakes	Discs all round
Power	600bhp approx.
Top speed	207mph (333km/h)
Acceleration	N/A

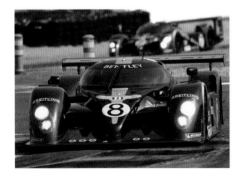

SPEED 8

Construction	Composite monocoque
Engine	4,000cc V8, double overhead cam per bank, 32 valves
Transmission	Six-speed Xtrac sequential
Suspension	Front: double wishbones, torsion bars, anti-roll bar
	Rear: double wishbones, torsion bars, anti-roll bar
Brakes	Discs all round
Power	615bhp approx.
Top speed	202mph (325km/h)
Acceleration	N/A

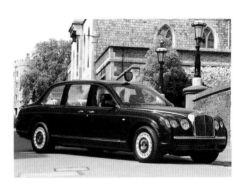

STATE LIMOUSINE

Construction	Ladder chassis with separate body
Engine	6,750cc V8, pushrods, 16 valves
Transmission	Four-speed automatic, rear-wheel drive
Suspension	Front: independent, double wishbones, coil springs, anti-roll bar
	Rear: independent, double wishbones, coil springs, anti-roll bar
Brakes	Discs all round, anti-lock
Power	420bhp @ 4,000rpm
Top speed	130mph (209km/h)
Acceleration	N/A

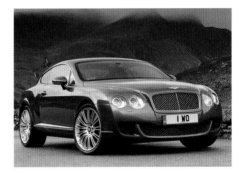

CONTINENTAL GT

Construction	Unitary body
Engine	5,998cc W12, double overhead camshaft per bank, 48 valves
Transmission	Six-speed automatic, four-wheel drive
Suspension	Front: independent, double wishbones, air springs
	Rear: independent, multi-link, air springs
Brakes	Discs all round, anti-lock
Power	552bhp @ 6,100rpm
Top speed	198mph (319km/h)
Acceleration	0–60mph (97km/h): 4.7sec

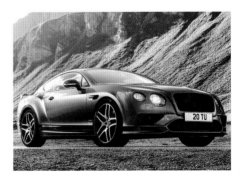

CONTINENTAL SUPERSPORTS

Construction	Unitary body
Engine	5,998cc W12, double overhead camshaft per bank, 48 valves
Transmission	Six-speed automatic, four-wheel drive
Suspension	Front: independent, double wishbones, air springs
	Rear: independent, multi-link, air springs
Brakes	Discs all round, anti-lock
Power	621bhp @ 6,000rpm
Top speed	204mph (328km/h)
Acceleration	0–60mph (97km/h): 3.7sec

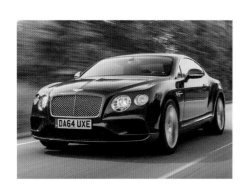

CONTINENTAL GT V8

Construction	Unitary body
Engine	3,993cc V8, double overhead camshaft per bank, 32 valves
Transmission	Six-speed automatic, four-wheel drive
Suspension	Front: independent, double wishbones, air springs
	Rear: independent, multi-link, air springs
Brakes	Discs all round, anti-lock
Power	500bhp @ 6,000rpm
Top speed	188mph (303km/h)
Acceleration	0–60mph (97km/h): 4.6sec

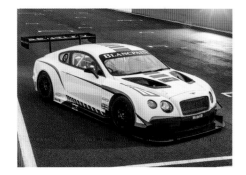

CONTINENTAL GT3

Construction	Unitary body
Engine	3,993cc V8, double overhead camshaft per bank, 32 valves
Transmission	Six-speed Xtrac sequential, rear-wheel drive
Suspension	Front: independent, double wishbones, coil springs
	Rear: independent, double wishbones, coil springs
Brakes	Discs all round, anti-lock
Power	600bhp approx.
Top speed	166mph (267km/h) approx.
Acceleration	0–60mph (97km/h): 4.7sec

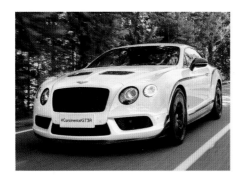

CONTINENTAL GT3-R

Construction	Unitary body
Engine	3,993cc V8, double overhead camshaft per bank, 32 valves
Transmission	Eight-speed automatic, four-wheel drive
Suspension	Front: independent, double wishbones, air springs
	Rear: independent, multi-link, air springs
Brakes	Discs all round, anti-lock
Power	572bhp @ 6,100rpm
Top speed	170mph (274km/h)
Acceleration	0–60mph (97km/h): 3.6sec

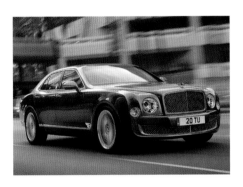

MULSANNE

Construction	Unitary body
Engine	6,750cc V8, pushrods, 16 valves
Transmission	Eight-speed automatic, four-wheel drive
Suspension	Front: independent, double wishbones, air springs
	Rear: independent, multi-link, air springs
Brakes	Discs all round, anti-lock
Power	505bhp @ 4,200rpm
Top speed	184mph (296km/h)
Acceleration	0–60mph (97km/h): 5.1sec

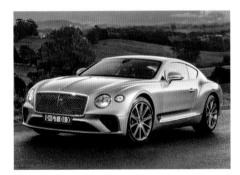

CONTINENTAL GT

Construction	Unitary body
Engine	5,950cc W12, double overhead camshaft per bank, 48 valves
Transmission	Eight-speed automatic, four-wheel drive
Suspension	Front: independent, double wishbones, air springs
	Rear: independent, multi-link, air springs
Brakes	Discs all round, anti-lock
Power	626bhp @ 6,000rpm
Top speed	207mph (333km/h)
Acceleration	0–60mph (97km/h): 3.6sec

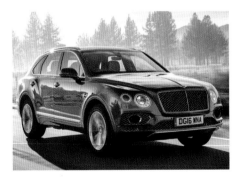

BENTAYGA HYBRID

Construction	Unitary body
Engine	2,995cc V6, double overhead camshaft per bank, 48 valves, supercharger
Transmission	Eight-speed automatic, four-wheel drive
Suspension	Front: independent, double wishbones, air springs
	Rear: independent, multi-link, air springs
Brakes	Discs all round, anti-lock
Power	335bhp engine plus 126bhp electric motor
Top speed	158mph (254km/h)
Acceleration	0–60mph (97km/h): 5.2sec

INDEX

PICTURE CREDITS

© Bentley Drivers Club: 8, 10, 12, 15, 17, 21, 22, 23, 25, 26, 27, 28, 30, 31, 35, 36, 37, 39, 43, 44, 45, 50, 51, 52, 53, 54, 55, 56, 57, 60, 62, 63, 74, 75, 84–85, 99, 105, 117, 118, 123, 127, 161.

© Getty Images: 18 Heritage Images, 46 MacGregor/Stringer, 87 Heritage Images, 93 Heritage Images, 96 Print Collector, 172 (above) Tim Graham, 172 (below) Tim Graham, 172–173 Max Mumby/Indigo, 179 Mark Thompson/Allsport, 180 Adrian Dennis/AFP, 182 Mark Thompson/Allsport, 183 Mark Thompson/Allsport, 186 Bryn Lennon, 187 Andre Durand/AFP.

Neill Bruce/© Reg Coote Collection: 32, 40, 41, 47, 49, 58, 59, 64, 67 (montage), 70, 73, 76, 78, 79, 83, 88, 90, 91, 94, 95, 97 (montage), 100, 101, 111, 113 (montage), 114, 119, 120, 130–131, 133, 134, 136, 145, 146, 147, 150–151, 153 (montage), 193 (montage), 230 (above), 231 (centre), 231 (below), 232 (above), 232 (below), 233 (above).

Newspress/© Bentley Media: 1, 3, 4, 11, 42, 61, 65, 66, 68–69, 80–81, 98, 102, 106–107, 108, 125, 129, 135 (above), 149 (below), 154, 155, 156, 157, 158, 164, 166, 167, 168, 169, 171 (montage), 144–175, 176, 184, 185, 189 (montage), 190, 194–195, 197, 198, 200–201, 202, 203, 205, 206, 209, 210, 213, 214, 215, 217 (montage), 218–219, 221, 222, 225, 226, 228–229, 230 (centre), 230 (below), 231 (above), 232 (centre), 233 (below), 234, 235, 236, 237.

Magic Car Pics/ © Bentley: 135 (below), 139, 140, 143, 149 (above), 163.

Creative Commons License: 233 (centre) Vetatur Fumare.

While every effort has been made to credit contributors and copyright holders, the publishers would like to apologise should there have been any omissions or errors and would be pleased to make the appropriate correction to future editions of the book.